PRAISE FOR GRIDIRON GOSPEL

The NFL San Francisco 49ers were named after the California gold-rush of the mid 1800s. The cry heard then was, "There's gold in those hills!" And that's what's in this book. Pure gold. Gold that Len and Chris have mined and refined as rugged, motivational wisdom for a victorious life. Not just one good season, but back-to-back-to-back championship seasons are the result. With the brilliant Playbook guide and page-turning content Sweet and Eriksen have drawn up the plays that will score every time. This is coaching at its best, in your face and to the heart.

    PAUL LOUIS COLE
    President, Christian Men's Network

In *Gridiron Gospel*, Len and Chris go deep into fields of faith and football to give a fresh and fun revelation of the Good News Gospel of Jesus. In a world of spectators, we are challenged to suit up to discover our divine destiny. We were created to be in the Gospel game of moving chains. This book is a deep dive into both faith and football history. It is a framework of beliefs affecting behavior. It's Scripture and story, with a wealth of wisdom and wit. It's a coaching gem to help the Church recover the fumbles that have let cultural substitutes become places of misplaced worship.

The Huddle Guide at the end is a full playbook of helpful devotional practices that will transform locker rooms, conference rooms, or family dining rooms.

Thank you, Len and Chris, for running with this to the end. It's a game-winning drive at a critical time. I'm encouraged to break the huddle, line up with my team, and play my position to move some chains. I've got my touchdown celebration dance ready as we recover who God created us to be.

    JASON BOLLINGER
    Lead Pastor, Grace Houston, Houston, Texas

Jesus was the master of metaphor, the genius of parable, and the ultimate teacher of context. As the Word made flesh, he skillfully communicated profound theology and difficult truths by connecting with both the hearts and minds of his audience. He used everyday, relatable illustrations that brought the Gospel to life. Similarly, Leonard Sweet and Christopher Eriksen achieve this with *Gridiron Gospel*. The book bridges timeless truths with modern culture, much like Jesus' parables of the lost coin or the Good Samaritan resonated in his day. Through wit, compelling stories from the world of football, and the eternal truths of the Gospel, the authors offer a playbook rich in insight and inspiration, urging readers to step off the sidelines and into the game of faith.

    SCOTT R. JONES
    DMin. Lead pastor, professor, and arm-chair quarterback

Gridiron Gospel: Faith That Moves Chains, by Leonard Sweet and Christopher Eriksen, is an engaging call to discipleship in The Church through the metaphor of football, and the narratives that are a part of what has been called simply, The Game. As someone who played football at the collegiate level, I found their book as interesting as it was both compelling and challenging. Once again Dr. Sweet has coined a word for disciple to move us forward, to advance—"gospeller"—a word that encapsulates both evangelism and the discipline of discipleship. The authors share stirring exhortations to … Follow well. Listen. Pay attention. The Coach is calling us to "get in the game." "For God has not given us a spirit of timidity, but of power and love and discipline" 2 Timothy 1:7 (NASB).

    REV. DR. ROBERT CASTRO
    D. Min., preacher, former football, rugby player and onetime competitive body-builder

The revelations in *Gridiron Gospel* will captivate any football fan, from the surprising fact that actual gameplay amounts to just eleven minutes, to the powerful ways athletes transform their stadium into a spiritual stage. While many Christians quietly practice their faith within church walls, these gridiron gladiators boldly proclaim their relationship with Christ, turning the field into their pulpit. This compelling and convicting book showcases how some professional athletes fearlessly weave their spiritual convictions into America's most popular sport.

    MIKE PARNELL
    CEO Oakley, founder director NDIF.ORG kidney foundation, owner Billings Outlaws, professional Indoor Football team

Len Sweet's vast knowledge of multiple subjects is amazing to me. He can address complex issues in the world of technology, then take a popular thing like sports and from it draw great life lessons. After reading Len Sweet's and Chris Eriksen's marvelous book, *Gridiron Gospel: Faith That Moves Chains*, I believe that either of them could have been an NFL coach! Their grasp of the intricacies of football and their ability to apply that to life is an immeasurable gift. Their football terminology, coupled with Biblical faith language, makes a great book for people who are looking for ways to live out their faith and have an interest in football. Len and Chris introduce you to so many new concepts in the language of football as it is applicable to faith. You will know a lot more about football when you read this book, but you will know even more about how your life can be more productive and victorious. Get ready to serve and win as you read this book.

> JOHN ED MATHISON
> Accomplished athlete, author, award-winning speaker, and founder of John Ed Mathison Leadership Ministries after serving thirty-six years as senior minister of Frazer Memorial in Montgomery, AL

If you love Jesus (or are just curious), and you enjoy football, you'll savor *Gridiron Gospel*! Filled with compelling quotes, insights and anecdotes from pro football, Sweet and Eriksen masterfully apply these to the game of life and to the life of faith in a way that will challenge and inspire you.

> ADAM HAMILTON
> Pastor, Chiefs' fan, and author of The Message of Jesus.

Imagery. *Gridiron Gospel* is a book about imagery. A definition suggests "the use of pictures or words to create images, esp. to create an impression or mood." This book uses powerful imagery from the popular sport of football to connect people with the truths of the Kingdom. When understood, it reframes your convictions and belief systems, building a firm biblical foundation for troubled times. Imagery was the Gospel strategy of the Master and it altered the world's trajectory. I highly recommend *Gridiron Gospel* by Leonard Sweet and Christopher Eriksen. It will reframe your faith for these critical days.

>GLENN BURRIS
>Author, pastor, international preacher, and former President of The Foursquare Church

In 1951, a Baptist pastor's son named Jarrell McCracken got a request: would he consider speaking to a Baptist youth on the subject of Christianity and football? In response, he created "The Game of Life," an imaginary play-by-play recording using football as a metaphor for the Christian life. His recording delighted Christians around the country, and led to the creation of Word Records. Now, in 2025, comes Leonard Sweet and Christopher Eriksen's exploration of the Christian faith through football. *Gridiron Gospel* is a clever collection of reflections sure to delight those looking for divine life lessons—on and off the field.

>LEAH PAYNE
>Associate Professor at Portland Seminary and winner of the 2024 "Book of the Year Award in History and Biography" for God Gave Rock & Roll to You: A History of Contemporary Christian Music (Oxford University Press)

Every sports fan should read *Gridiron Gospel*. The book is clever, insightful, challenging, and downright fun to read. Paraphrasing the advertisement for "The Master's Golf Tournament," *Gridiron Gospel* is "a book like none other." For those of us who have been NFL and college football followers most of our lives, *Gridiron Gospel* takes us down memory lane reliving many of the great moments of the sport and remembering the great players of the game. At times I thought I was reading an encyclopedia of football lore. Games, players, coaches, specific plays, game-time moments, memorable experiences, football terms, and game strategies all are remembered, described, and interpreted with application for our spiritual formation and corporate expression.

The book is not about football but about living our faith and how the people of God have expressed themselves in their collective gatherings. *Gridiron Gospel* is about living life with a kingdom mindset, infusing the temporal with the values of the eternal while investing in the temporal for eternal rewards. The reader is admonished, challenged, and instructed in their spiritual pilgrimage using the sights, sounds, and experiences of the game of football.

When most books begin losing their appeal by halftime, *Gridiron Gospel* just gets better climaxing in the "Fourth Quarter" section, just like the game itself. And like the game, the book has an "extra point" for pastors. If you have the responsibility to preach weekly, there are over a dozen sermon outlines buried throughout the book waiting to be expanded and preached during the football playoffs. By my calculation, this gives you three years of sermon series for January during the NFL Playoffs.

ESPN's Sports Center commentators would highlight two quotes as summaries of the experience of reading the book:

> ... football isn't just a game. It's a lens through which we can better understand our walk with God, our relationships with each other, and the peculiar way that grace plays out in the end zones of our lives.

> Here in a nutshell is the theme of the book: What if we treated our faith lives with such passion? What if we celebrated conversions like touchdowns, treated every baptism like a Super Bowl victory, approached worship with the enthusiasm of a fourth-quarter drive? Jesus, after all, is the ultimate quarterback, calling audibles in our lives, reading the defense of our doubts, threading the needle of grace through the tightest coverage of our sin.

JULES GLANZER
Avid sports fan, Tabor College President Emeritus, Senior Consultant The Timothy Group

Gridiron GOSPEL

Faith That Moves Chains

**LEONARD SWEET
CHRIS ERIKSEN**

The Salish Sea Press
Orcas Island
Washington

DEDICATION I–LEN

To Leonora Grace,

Born beneath March skies as the Ides drew near in 2024,
who already knows how to furrow her brow
like her grandfather.

My dearest namesake,
They say football is a game of inches,
but legacies are measured in generations.

As you inherit the Sweet's trademark expressions—
that thoughtful scowl, that hearty laugh—
I dream of Sundays yet to come:
You and me, cheering our Bills and Seahawks,
debating play calls, sharing Granna's
Buffalo chicken dip and sliders,
our matching furrowed brows softening into smiles.

May this book be your playbook for life,
teaching you that faith, like football,
is about getting back up after every fall,
moving chains one yard at a time,
and believing in fourth-quarter miracles.

While Caesar feared his Ides of March,
you bravely came as spring's sweetest blessing,
a gift more precious than all Rome's glory.
With a love as fierce as our gameday faces.

Proudly,

Grandsire ("Ancestor") Leonard

Dedication II—Chris

I met my beloved spouse Jean in 2008 at Drew University in one of Len's United Methodist evangelism courses. Since our 2009 marriage, we have experienced the joy of the birth of Thea Jennifer in 2017, and twins Alexandra Jean and Christian Joseph in 2019.

Love and family are God's gifts of incalculable price.

I dedicate this book to my beloved family:

Jean Arlea
Thea Jennifer
Alexandra Jean and Christian Joseph

They have been deep and abiding blessings in my life. I could not imagine life and happiness without them.

Gridiron Gospel: Faith That Moves Chains

ISBN softcover edition: 978-1-63613-036-1

Published by The Salish Sea Press. Box 1492, Absecon, NJ 08201.
https://salishsea.press
https://www.facebook.com/thesalishseapress/

The Salish Sea Press is a program of SpiritVenture Ministries.
https://leonardsweet.com/

Copyright © 2025 by Leonard Sweet and Chris Eriksen. All rights reserved.

Interior designed by Carmen Barber | keepingyouwriting@gmail.com
Cover designed by by Anthony Gorrity, Johnnyo Design | johnnyodesign.com

Unless otherwise indicated, Scripture quotations are the author's own paraphrase. If the notation LIS is used, this also indicates the author's own paraphrase. Other versions are noted in the back matter.

The Salish Sea Press

Contents

Game I
First Down, First Love
TOUCHDOWNS IN THE KINGDOM... 17

Game II
The Divine Handoff
WHEN GOD CALLS THE PLAY... 29

First Quarter
FAITH TAKES THE FIELD.. 39

Game III
From the Sidelines to the Stars
REDISCOVERING FAITH IN A FAITHLESS GAME................... 43

Game IV
Two Minute Warning
DIVINE TIMING... 85

Second Quarter
TACKLING LIFE'S CHALLENGES... 99

Game V
Breaking Huddle
STEPS OF FAITH... 103

Game VI
Resilient Roots
THE ENDURING TRIUMPH OF FAITH AND FOOTBALL.......... 119

Game VII
Heaven's Scoreboard
MEASURING WHAT MATTERS.. 167

Halftime
THE SECOND WIND.. 183

Game VIII
The Lombardi Legacy
DISCIPLINE AS DEVOTION... 185

Game IX
The Belichick Blueprint
Strategy and Spirit.. 205

Third Quarter
Game On: The Field Not the Sidelines..................... 229

Game X
Crossing the Goal Line
Where Heaven Meets Earth... 231

Game XI
Red Zone Redemption
From Fumbles to Faith.. 255

Game XII
Playing Injured
Grace Under Pressure.. 273

Game XIII
The Ultimate Championship
Building God's Team.. 287

Fourth Quarter
Touchdowns in Eternity... 301

Game XIV
When Tailgates Become Talegate Testaments
Fellowship in the Parking Lot................................... 305

Game XV
More Than Games
From Arena to Altar... 317

Game XVI
Beyond the Goalposts
From Kickoff to Kingdom Come................................ 331

Game XVII
Laterals of Love
Passing Faith Through Life's Chaos........................... 345

THE FINAL DRIVE
FOURTH DOWN FAITH AND HAIL MARY LIVING 355

VICTORY CELEBRATION
THE CHAMPIONSHIP MINDSET 365

ACKNOWLEDGMENTS 371

ABOUT THE AUTHORS
FROM SIDELINE TO SCRIMMAGE 375

GAMEDAY HUDDLE GUIDE 383

BIBLIOGRAPHY 479

SCRIPTURE VERSIONS 487

NOTES 489

Game 1

First Down, First Love

Touchdowns in the Kingdom

> What I know most surely about morality and the duty of man I owe to sport.
>
> RUGBY PLAYER AND PHILOSOPHER
> ALBERT CAMUS (1913-60)

In every corner of America, from sunbaked southern stadiums to frozen northern fields, football transcends mere sport to become something sacred—a weekly ritual that reveals our deepest longings for belonging, meaning, and redemption. Like ancient liturgy, it shapes our calendar, commands our attention, and binds communities together in shared devotion.

Before we dive deeper into this *Gridiron Gospel*, let me tell you about Richard and Jane Jameson, whose marriage proves that sometimes the greatest tests of faith come not from theological differences, but from the divided loyalties between Tennessee orange and Crimson Tide. Their story, like so many in these pages, reminds us that football isn't just a game. It's a lens through which we can better understand our walk with God, our relationships with each other, and the peculiar way that grace plays out in the end zones of our lives.

Richard and Jane Jameson, two of the Lord's finest servants, found each other at Kinfolk Camp Meeting in Brownsville, Tennessee, the oldest continuous camp-meeting in US history and one of Len's favorite places to preach—so much so that three of his kids were baptized there. Apparently, the Holy Spirit was working overtime at camp-meetings to help Richard and Jane overlook their "unequally yoked" collegiate differences. Jane teaches math at the junior high, Richard farms the land, and they've raised wonderful children together. They're what we call in this book "gospellers"—folks who live and breathe their faith.

But every fall, their household becomes a house divided, with Richard bleeding Tennessee orange and Jane rolling with the Crimson Tide. They've learned that watching games together is about as peaceful as mixing oil and holy water. Their solution? The season's victor claims the living room throne (aka the big screen TV), while the vanquished retreats to bedroom exile with the portable set.

Jane's mother, bless her diplomatic heart, gifted them a Christmas ornament that would make Solomon proud: a two-sided pillow featuring "Go Vols" in orange and white on one side and "Roll Tide" in crimson and white on the other. The winning team's colors get to shine directly under the Star of Bethlehem—a yearly battle for celestial real estate that would make Jacob and Esau proud.

The true test of their divided house came late one night when their security system went haywire as Richard returned home. When the monitoring service asked for the password, Richard called out to Jane for help. With a mischievous glint in her eye that would rival any serpent in Eden, she sweetly replied, "Roll Tide." Richard, faced with this ultimate test of loyalty, declared he'd rather stand guard all night than let those words pass his lips—proving that some commitments run deeper than marriage vows, though perhaps not quite as deep as the gospel truth.

As we kick off this gospeller exploration of the game of football, and what it might mean for living the Christian life, we carry with us the wisdom of Bruce Mayer, one of Chris's former high school football coaches, who wrote in Chris's high school yearbook that "In football, as in life, your first step is the most important." So, dear reader, strap on your helmet and join us on this spiritual scrimmage. We may not have Super Bowl rings, but we've got a playbook filled with life lessons, gospel faith, and a deep love for the game that transcends the end zone.

Welcome to *Gridiron Gospel*—where dirty pigskin meets divine providence, and every down is a chance for a touchdown in eternity. Plus, grab your gameplan with the *Gameday Huddle Guide* appended at the end of this book—your playbook for breaking through life's defense and scoring big in your faith journey. Gather some friends to watch a game with you, and see how this little resource can help turn your life's fourth downs into divine first downs. If you would like a more in-depth playbook for solo or group study, there is a companion volume *Playbook for Gridiron Gospel: Faith That Moves Chains* (2025, Salish Sea Press) available separately. Though the huddle book and playbook were designed with men in mind, the authors joyfully acknowledge that many women share a love for the game and will be cherished voices in the group experience.

> The NFL owns a day of the week. The same day the church used to own. Now it's theirs.
>
> DR. CYRIL WECHT (ALBERT BROOKS) TO DR. BENNETT OMALU (WILL SMITH) IN THE MOVIE CONCUSSION (2015)

WHAT'S THIS BOOK ABOUT?

This book is very simply about the gridiron grace where faith meets football.

The legendary Vince Lombardi—the man whose name now graces football's ultimate prize—knelt in a quiet church each morning before heading to the frozen tundra of Lambeau Field. This titan of football, who could make grown men tremble with a single glare, started every day in humble prayer. Jerry Kramer, who battled in the trenches for Lombardi's Packers, loves to tell how the Coach would transform biblical figures into football players with his passionate storytelling. There was Lombardi, eyes blazing with intensity, bringing the Apostle Paul's words to life: "Run to win!" (1 Corinthians 9:24–27). In Lombardi's vibrant imagination, you could almost see Saint Paul calling plays at the line of scrimmage.

Now, we can hear the skeptics clearing their throats. "Football? Really? You're going to draw spiritual lessons from a game where grown men chase a leather egg across a painted field?" These critics might roll their eyes so hard they risk a sprain of spirit. Perhaps they're missing something profound in their rush to dismiss the gridiron's gospel.

On any given Sunday, football demands a dedication to holiness that would make the ancient prophets nod in approval. Every play is a test of commitment, every game a crucible of character. Miss a block, lose focus for one second, show up unprepared—and suddenly you're trending on X (and not in a good way). The game tolerates no half-measures, no lukewarm efforts. Sound familiar? There's a certain book that has strong opinions about being lukewarm or milquetoast.

During their heyday in the 1970s and early 1980s, the fearsome Oakland Raiders didn't just talk about "commitment to excellence"—they lived it, breathed it, and wore it like armor. Al Davis made it more than a motto; he made it a mission. Which brings us to an uncomfortable question: When was the last time your church service burned with that kind of intensity? While NFL players study playbooks like scripture and treat practice like prayer, how many Christians approach their faith with the same fierce dedication? Super Bowl winning John Harbaugh, Head Coach of the Baltimore Ravens for seventeen years, challenged his team to bring the four E words to every game in 2024: Energy, Enthusiasm, Execution, Excellence. What if gospellers brought the four E-words to every mission and meeting?

Don't get us wrong—we're not suggesting turning Sunday service into Super Bowl Sunday. But maybe, just maybe, those "stupid game" critics might want to take a second look. Because when twenty-two men line up on a football field, pursuing perfection with every fiber of their being, they're demonstrating something that goes beyond sport—they're showing us what wholehearted commitment looks like in action. And isn't that exactly what our faith calls us to do?

> It's Superbowl Sunday. If you care as much for the church as for football, when your pastor finishes the sermon, pour Gatorade on his/her head.
>
> INTERNET MEME

In the grand stadium of life, this book emerges as a Hail Mary pass—a spiraling confluence of passion for the eternal playbook and the gridiron chronicle. It is also a closure of our joint complaint that the rise of professional sports, one of the great consumer revolutions of the nineteenth and twentieth centuries, has failed to attract the attention it deserves in theological circles.

We, your humble authors, write this sports book in the hopes that you'll be a good sport about the fact that we have no sporting credentials. We come to you as pilgrims in the cathedral of athletics who, aside from our wild youthful daydreams, never had the faintest chance or serious aspiration of playing professional sports. Yet perhaps it's precisely our status as outsiders—observers who never quite made it past the sidelines—that gives us a unique vantage point for this theological exploration of sport.

Like devoted fans in the nosebleed section, we may lack the insider's view, but our passion for the game runs just as deep. Consider us your fellow travelers: not the decorated athletes whose jerseys hang in halls of fame, but the everyday faithful who find something sacred in the sweat and struggle of competition.

In fact, it was the "amateurs"—those unbound by the chains of conventional wisdom—who orchestrated the symphony of scientific and technological progress until the mid-nineteenth century. Think of Charles Darwin, nature's curious spectator, or Galileo and Newton, mathematical maestros who dared to rewrite the cosmic score. Perhaps it takes those unfettered by the locker room of academia to spot the game-changing plays that seasoned scholars, ensconced in their ivory towers, have long since overlooked.

Indeed, our eyes must remain wide open, for we stand witness to a seismic shift in the cultural landscape. The cathedral of Global Christendom is being rapidly outpaced by the coliseum of Global Fandom. Philosopher Simon Critchley positions football fandom as "a viable polytheistic religion, given that it allows the worship of multiple gods (teams), accepts that everyone thinks theirs is the best, that they all rally around a common history and set of values, and that it teaches fans how to accept failure and disappointment."

In our intensifying fragmented world, fandom has emerged as a powerful new architecture of belonging. It provides an instant source of social legitimacy and collective meaning, offering participants a way to plug into shared narratives that are unscripted, thrilling to watch, and—perhaps most significantly—convenient.

This "fan mindset" has become so deeply embedded in contemporary culture that we now transform virtually every human endeavor into a sport-like spectacle, from singing and dancing to cooking and courtship. Even politics has not escaped this transformation, as complex civic discourse increasingly adopts the language and dynamics of team rivalry. Sports now reign supreme as the world's preeminent sacred ritual, with fan culture transforming every facet of life into a high-stakes sports contest:

- Culinary clashes on the Food Network
- Romantic rivalries from *The Dating Game* to *The Bachelor*
- Vocal victories on *American Idol* and *The Voice*
- Choreographic competitions on *Dancing with the Stars*
- Political playoffs that reduce governance to a spectator sport

What makes this shift particularly noteworthy is how fandom offers a more passive and accessible path to belonging than traditional community structures. Unlike the demanding work of building and maintaining conventional social bonds, fandom provides ready-made communities, complete with established narratives, clear roles, and instant cultural touchstones. This democratization of belonging through fandom has become a defining feature of our time, unifying disparate aspects of culture under a common framework of spectatorship and participation. Yet this very convenience raises questions about the depth and sustainability of such connections, even as it reshapes how we relate to each other and the world around us.

Where Christendom once offered a path of belonging anchored in a shared narrative, Fandom now steps in to fill the void. Yet, this new faith trades active participation for passive spectatorship, replacing the thrill of divine service with the vicarious rush of watching from the sidelines. In the United States, the tally of Super Bowl viewers rivals that of presidential election voters—a sobering testament to our shifting allegiances. And this doesn't even account for the virtual arenas of fantasy football or the high-wire act of sports betting, both online and in the flesh.

In the game of life, we're all called to be more than just fans. As we lace up our cleats and prepare to kick off this theological exploration, let us remember: We're players

FIRST DOWN, FIRST LOVE

in a cosmic contest, where the ultimate victory has already been won, but every day offers a new chance to score points for the kingdom. In God's championship game, Christ has already secured the ultimate victory in overtime. Yet we're still on the field playing every down with eternal stakes. While the final score is written in the heavens, we're called to keep driving toward the end zone, living in that sacred space of in-betweenness—between the game-winning play and the final whistle, and already and the not yet.

> My chains fell off, my heart was free.
> CHARLES WESLEY, "AND CAN IT BE" (1738)

We are gospellers on kingdom's gridiron, players moving chains toward an eternal goal line. We embrace that Old English word "gospeller" not as mere decoration, but as our team identity. A gospeller is one who doesn't just clutch truth like an unused playbook, but takes it to the field. With each down and distance, through victory and defeat, we live out the gospel's power. Like athletes who measure their progress chain by hard-fought chain, we mark our journey not by passive profession, but by the ground we gain living out God's beauty, truth, and goodness on life's unforgiving turf.

GAME II

THE DIVINE HANDOFF
WHEN GOD CALLS THE PLAY

> In the East Coast, football is a cultural experience. In the Midwest, it's a form of cannibalism. On the West Coast, it's a tourist attraction. And in the South, football is a religion, and Saturday is the holy day.
>
> LEGENDARY COLLEGE FOOTBALL COACH
> MARINO CASEM[1]

The stadium lights pierce the gathering darkness like search beams, turning the field below into a stage where our deepest stories play out in cleats and shoulder pads. Watch closely now—there's more happening here than just a game.

See that rookie, crossing himself before taking the field?

He's enacting an ancient ritual of dedication, marking this ground as sacred space. The arena becomes cathedral; the grass, consecrated ground.

Look at the quarterback, head bowed in the huddle. To some, he's calling plays; to those with eyes to see, he's leading a congregation in their moment of shared purpose. The signals he barks aren't just plays—they're liturgy, a shared language binding individuals into one body.

And there—the running back who just scored, kneeling in the end zone. The crowd roars, but he's found a pocket of silence. Six points on the scoreboard, but he's counting different math: grace upon grace.

This is where sport becomes sacramental:

- In every comeback, we see resurrection's promise;
- In every team, we glimpse the body of Christ;
- In every fall, we feel the weight of Eden;
- In every redemption, we taste amazing grace.

A defensive player makes a game-saving tackle and points skyward. The crowd sees celebration; we see confession. "Not me," his finger says, "Something greater."

The losing team's coach meets his counterpart at midfield. Their embrace is brief but real—a moment of shared understanding that transcends victory and defeat. This is

THE DIVINE HANDOFF

where competition bows to communion, where the game submits to grace.

In the locker room after the game, a veteran player leads both teams in prayer. Winners and losers kneel together on the same floor. The uniforms that divided them now soaked with the same sweat. This is church, raw and real, where the ground is level at the foot of the cross.

This is what Rome never understood. The reigning Emperor's bread and circuses could fill a stomach, occupy a mind, even pacify a population. But they couldn't feed a soul. They couldn't create true community. They couldn't offer grace.

But here, in these temples of sport, we have a choice. We can settle for spectacle, or we can seek the sacred. We can be mere fans, or we can be fellow pilgrims. We can chase victory, or we can pursue something victory can never give us—the grace that makes both winning and losing bearable, the love that makes both success and failure navigable, the truth that makes both glory and shame redeemable.

The lights are bright, but it's in the shadows where the real game is played. Not on the scoreboard but in the soul. Not on the stat sheet but in the spirit. Not in the win-loss column but in the moment-by-moment choice to see beyond bread and circuses to the bread of life, beyond spectacle to sacrament, beyond competition to communion.

The game clock runs down to zero, but the other clock—the one that measures moments of grace, opportunities for redemption, chances to see the sacred in the ordinary—that one keeps running. In the end, that's the only score that matters.

Jesus doesn't offer us bread and circuses. He offers us bread and wine, body and blood, death and resurrection. He doesn't ask us to be heroes. He asks us to be human. Not humanoids. Humans.[2] And in that humanity, whether we're Malcolm Butler making the play or Pete Carroll missing the call, we find the grace that Rome never could.

The Divine Handoff: How Football Intercepted USAmerica's Soul

Imagine, for a moment, two titanic forces locked in an epic struggle for the heart of a nation. In one corner, wearing robes of tradition and wielding the power of faith, stands the Church. In the other, donning helmets and shoulder pads, armed with pigskin and playbooks, crouches the NFL—the golden goose of sports.[3] The prize? Your Sunday. This isn't just any matchup. It's the grudge match of the century.

The date is 28 December 1958. As the Baltimore Colts and New York Giants clash in what would be dubbed "The Greatest Game Ever Played," something far more

THE DIVINE HANDOFF

profound than a mere championship is at stake. Unbeknownst to the sweat-drenched gladiators on the field or the millions glued to their newfangled television sets, this game marks the opening drive in football's audacious campaign to steal Sunday from the sanctuary.

Fast forward to 2025. The scorecard tells a tale that would've seemed blasphemous just decades ago:

- Churches: Closing faster than a defensive line on a rookie quarterback.
- NFL: Expanding with the relentless ambition of manifest destiny, conquering new territories from global fanbases to female viewership.

How did we end up here? When did "Sunday best" go from pressed suits in pews to team jerseys on couches?

ANY GIVEN SUNDAY

This seismic shift didn't happen overnight. It was a slow burn, a gradual usurpation so subtle that by the time anyone noticed, football had already planted its flag deep in the cultural endzone. Pete Rozelle, the NFL's mastermind commissioner, didn't just read the room—he rewrote the playbook of USAmerican leisure, turning Sunday into a holy day of a different sort. Football stole Sunday from the church not as a thief-in-the night, but in plain sight, albeit sometimes in relative slow motion over a period of years, and with meek and ineffectual objections at most.

But here's the million-dollar question, the game-changing play of cultural introspection: From Labor Day to Super Bowl Sunday, what truly captures the USAmerican soul? Is it the whispered prayers echoing in increasingly empty churches? Or the roar of the crowd as a last-second touchdown unfolds in high-definition glory?

> As we gather for Super Bowl Sundays and celebrate our sports GOATS (Greatest Of All Time), let us not forget those Jesus also called us to serve: the SHEEP (Smallest, Hurting, Excluded, Endmost, and Poorest) in our communities. Our true measure lies not in how we honor champions, but in how we lift up the least among us.
>
> LEONARD SWEET
> FACEBOOK POST 07 FEBRUARY 2025

Let's be brutally honest. For many, "What's the score?" has replaced "What was the sermon about?" as the quintessential Sunday inquiry. Potlucks in fellowship halls have been replaced by football food in parking lots to the point where tailgating has become the new communion. Fantasy leagues have usurped Bible study groups. And the passion once reserved for hymns and robed choirs now erupts in face-painted, team-colored, foam-finger-waving fervor.

Sports have become the dominant force in global culture. Wherever you go in the world, a sports star is more than just a sports star. But this book isn't just about sports' rise; it's a stark referendum on the church's fall from cultural prominence and its own culture of denial. In the span of sixty years—a mere blink in the grand scheme of human history—we've witnessed an ecclesial fumble of epic proportions.

So, dear reader, strap on your chin strap. We're about to embark on a no-holds-barred exploration of how Christianity got where it is today, why it matters we're not where we should be, and what lessons both followers of Jesus and the church might glean from its surprising Sunday rival. This isn't just a book—it's a two-minute drill for the soul of USAmerica's weekend.

Are you ready for some football? More importantly, are you ready for some two-a-days soul-searching?

Gridiron Gospel is your all-access pass to this sacred intersection of faith in the Almighty and devotion to the gridiron. Whether you are:

- **A Seeker of Sacred Parallels:** For those who've felt their heart pound during both altar calls and fourth-quarter drives, who know in their bones that the roar of the stadium and the hush of the sanctuary spring from the same deep well of human devotion.

- **A Cultural Archaeologist or Semiotician:** For those wrestling to understand how a single game has become America's modern religion, where Sunday worship splits between pews and fifty-yard lines, and where ritual and devotion take on new meaning under stadium lights.

- **A Gridiron Pilgrim:** For those who've sensed something deeper in the clash of titans on the field, who feel the weight of ancient warrior-poet traditions living on in modern gladiators, and who hunger to understand the sacred choreography hidden in every snap.

- **A Witness to Convergence:** For those compelled to trace how two of humanity's oldest impulses—the drive to compete and the need to believe—have fused into something uniquely USAmerican, creating stories almost as epic as any biblical narrative.

- **A Spiritual Explorer:** For those drawn to the edges where faith and culture collide, who sense that in the intersection of stadium and sanctuary lies a truth about what moves the nation's soul, and who dare to ask what higher power draws

100,000 people to kneel together in a secular cathedral.

... this book is your ticket to the big game.

We're not just saying you'll enjoy this book—we're guaranteeing you'll be moved by it. *Gridiron Gospel* isn't just a read; it's a revelation, a touchdown pass that connects the end zone with the eternal. It's where heaven touches down ... and scores touchdowns in your life. So slip on your game face, adjust your halo, and get ready for kickoff.

The whistle's about to blow on a journey that'll change how you see Sundays—both on and off the field.

The start is what stops most people.

MIAMI DOLPHINS ICONIC HEAD COACH DON SHULA
RECORD HOLDER FOR MOST CAREER WINS IN THE NFL

THE JESUS PLAYBOOK: LAUGHTER, LIGHT, AND LEGACY

Forget the stereotype of the sour-spirited, dour-faced Christian. In *Gridiron Gospel*, we're running a different play.

Jesus is the Ultimate Coach, not just calling for dedication and discipline, but also signaling for a holy huddle of humor. We believe the Almighty has a playbook filled with joy, and laughter is the divine audible.

This book may tackle serious subjects, but we've thrown in enough wit and wag to keep you on your toes. Think of humor as the Holy Spirit's Gatorade—refreshing, reviving, and ready to fuel your faith's workout.

Gridiron Gospel isn't destined to warm the bench of your bookshelf, collecting dust like unused equipment. It's a high-energy training session for your mind and soul, designed to keep you flipping pages faster than a quarterback's snap count.

As you journey through these chapters, may the Holy Spirit be your personal trainer, helping you flex your faith muscles and sprint towards your own spiritual end zone. Our goal? To see you score touchdowns in eternity, leaving a legacy that echoes long after the final whistle.

So, reader, are you ready to suit up? The game of a lifetime is about to begin, and you're our MVP—Most Valuable Pilgrim. Let's make every down count, blitz the devil, and secure your and others' spot on heaven's roster.

First Quarter
FAITH TAKES THE FIELD

It's not the will to win that matters—everyone has that. It's the will to prepare to win that matters.

COACH PAUL "BEAR" BRYANT
(SIX NATIONAL CHAMPIONSHIPS)

Sacred Focus: What Athletes Can Learn from a Century of Praying Nuns

In 1986, Dr. David Snowdon began what would become one of science's most fascinating investigations into the human mind. His subjects? Six hundred and seventy-eight School Sisters of Notre Dame, whose lifelong dedication to prayer would unexpectedly illuminate the powerful connection between focused practice and peak performance.

The "Nun Study," as it became known, initially sought to understand aging and Alzheimer's disease. Instead, it revealed something extraordinary: these sisters, who spent hours each day in contemplative prayer, demonstrated remarkable cognitive resilience well into their ninth and tenth decades. Some maintained razor-sharp mental acuity past age one hundred—an achievement that puzzled researchers until they recognized a striking parallel in an entirely different domain.

Elite athletes, like these remarkable nuns, cultivate excellence through dedicated daily practice. The sisters' meditation cushions and rosary beads might seem worlds apart from an athlete's pre-game routine, yet both practices forge the same neural pathways to excellence.

At Hall of Fame middle linebacker Mike Singletary's last home game before his retirement, his '85 teammate, also a Hall of Famer, Dan Hampton, gave a "eulogy" during half time. He said that everyone wants to succeed. What set Mike Singletary apart was his commitment to excellence and his willingness to architecture his life to scaffold and structure excellence.[1]

The Architecture of Excellence

- **Sustained Focus:** Where the sisters maintained hours

of unbroken contemplative practice, successful athletes cultivate laser-like concentration through methodical preparation routines. Both groups train their minds to remain steady under pressure, whether facing life's ultimate questions or crucial game moments.

- **Ritualized Practice:** The sisters' daily prayers—practiced at specific times with unwavering dedication—mirror the carefully choreographed pre-game routines of elite athletes. These aren't mere habits but powerful cognitive frameworks that enable peak performance.

- **Transcendent Mission:** The nuns approached prayer as a pathway to something greater than themselves. Similarly, athletes who connect their preparation to a deeper purpose—whether team success or personal excellence—consistently outperform those focused solely on immediate outcomes.

The Nun Study reveals that cognitive excellence, like athletic achievement, isn't merely gifted—it's cultivated through intentional, focused practice. Whether in a chapel or on a playing field, the path to extraordinary performance is paved with dedicated preparation and unwavering commitment to the process of prayer.

As one centenarian sister remarked, "Prayer feeds us." So too does steadfast preparation fuel the athlete's pursuit of greatness.

GAME III

FROM THE SIDELINES TO THE STARS

REDISCOVERING FAITH IN A FAITHLESS GAME

We are the only civilization in human history living in the ruins of our own creation.

PULITZER-PRIZE WINNING SCIENTIST/HISTORIAN
JARED DIAMOND[1]

What's the scouting report on the strength of Personal Faith and Team Christianity? Brace yourselves—it ain't pretty.

Christianity finds itself in prevent defense, and not just on home turf. In the spiritual Super Bowl of society, our team's looking more like the '76 Bucs than the '72 Dolphins. Especially in the authors' home stadiums—

the Northeast and Pacific Northwest—admitting you're a Christian is about as popular as wearing the visiting team's jersey to a Raiders game.

The Scorecard: A Hard Look from the Press Box

From our perch in the spiritual press box, we're watching a game that's turning brutal. Christianity, once the driving force in Western civilization, is playing like a team that's lost its playbook. We're not just talking about a few bad quarters—this is a fundamental breakdown that would make Vince Lombardi weep.

Take Len's home territory in the Pacific Northwest, where the fastest-growing spiritual demographic is the "none of the above" crowd. Here in Seattle, telling someone you're a Christian at a dinner party creates the same awkward silence as admitting you still think the Seahawks shouldn't have passed on that final play in Super Bowl XLIX. The Northeast isn't any kinder. Try being a vocal believer in Boston, and you'll feel about as welcome as a Yankees cap at Fenway Park.

The stats tell a story that's harder to swallow than a linebacker's mouthguard. A recent Pew Research study shows church attendance dropping faster than a quarterback's approval rating after a four-interception game. Major networks portray Christians with all the nuance of a blind-side hit, casting believers as either dim-witted receivers who can't catch a logical pass, or zealous defenders stuck playing by an outdated rulebook.

And if you think that's rough, try adding "evangelical" to your spiritual jersey. That label now carries more baggage than a team equipment truck. In Hollywood, Silicon Valley, and university campuses, identifying as an evangelical Christian is like showing up to a black-tie gala in AstroTurf cleats. The cultural commentators have thrown more flags on evangelical beliefs than a rookie ref in his first playoff game.

This isn't just about losing home-field advantage. We're talking about a fundamental shift in the cultural league standings. A society that once gathered around church potlucks now congregates around smartphone screens, where faith gets treated like a medieval playbook in a world of spread offenses. We've gone from "Amazing Grace" to amazing odds on DraftKings, from Sunday worship to Sunday NFL RedZone.

In the neighborhood where Len has taught for twenty-three years (Portland, Oregon), where church steeples once dominated the skyline like goalposts, three historic churches have been converted: one into a microbrewery, another into luxury condos, and the third—in what feels like cosmic irony—into a sports bar where parishioners once prayed for the Trailblazers.

In this game, saying "I am a Christian" isn't just a statement. It's a penalty flag, drawing unsportsmanlike conduct calls from a culture that's traded its Bible for a betting app.

Christians no longer own the home court-advantage, but are only playing away games with the crowds cheering for the other team(s) to win.[2]

BLIND TO THE LIGHT: THE MEDIA'S JESUS ILLITERACY

In the halls of elite media, a startling blindness festers—a profound ignorance of the Jesus story and its vibrant and breathtaking significance. Even the doors of the ivory towers are closed. This arrant and arrogant illiteracy goes unchecked, a blight on those who shape our cultural narrative.

Christianity isn't merely a belief system; it's the bedrock of Western civilization, a cornerstone of the culture of the West, shaping its political, cultural, social, legal, philosophical, artistic, educational, and healthcare systems. Without Jesus, our world would likely be unrecognizable, lacking democratic values, compassion for the powerless, forgiveness, freedom, intellectual inquiry, human rights, universal healthcare, and literacy. An historical revolution took place when the early church upended Graeco-Roman concepts of male power and domination, finding strength and power in the lowest and weakest members of society.[3]

FROM THE SIDELINES TO THE STARS

For two millennia, Jesus' life has been the fulcrum upon which the Western world turns, the pivot point of human history, sending ripple effects that have reached every corner of existence. Even truth-seeking skeptics—atheists and agnostics alike—must consider the overwhelming evidence. Jesus' influence is indelibly etched into every aspect of our existence. Evading this reality is a futile quest—a clinging to shadows, and denying the radiant presence that casts them. This endeavor is doomed, for Jesus' impact is not only profound but also inescapable.

Understanding Jesus is not optional; it's foundational. Deny this, and you construct a worldview on shifting sands, doomed to crumble in confusion and disarray. And when you take God out of the picture, the picture falls down. Cut God from the scene, lose the whole screen. No God, no frame.

You see this in the personality cults of atheistic dictators who slaughtered millions in pursuit of utopian ideals. Joseph Stalin, Mao Zedong, and Pol Pot—architects of regimes responsible for over one hundred million deaths—exemplify this darkest aspect of human nature. Their regimes' characteristics—totalitarian control, forced labor, and state-sponsored terror—starkly reveal the horrors that unfold when absolute power converges with godless ideology.

> No need to fear when you have faith.
> PHILADELPHIA EAGLES PLAYER SAQUON BARKLEY[4]

THE SILENT FAITH: RETHINKING EVANGELISM

There's an ancient whisper in the book of Jeremiah that echoes hauntingly through history: "Truth has perished; it has vanished from their lips" (Jeremiah 7:28 NIV). In the original Hebrew, these words carry an even starker warning: "Faith ceased; it was cut out of their mouths." Strip away the poetry, and we're left with a devastating truth: Faith dies in silence.

This book, in its heart, is a covert reconnaissance mission—a gentle conspiracy to resurrect evangelism from the grave of four-letter words where our culture has buried it. Even within church walls, we've grown hesitant to speak its name, as if sharing faith has become more scandalous than faith itself.[5]

We live in an age where our educational institutions perform elaborate intellectual gymnastics, contorting themselves to equate any expression of faith with colonial aggression. "Jesus talk" has been exiled even from private conversations, branded as an invasion of personal space—a violation of the unwritten commandment of our times:

"Thou shalt not impose thy beliefs." The result? Faith has become a timid ghost of itself, so thoroughly sanitized of any "excluding" elements that it resembles more a diplomatic communiqué than a transfigurative truth.

The NFL stands as a remarkable exception to USAmerica's usual reticence about religious expression. Unlike most professional spheres where faith remains private, football has become a unique platform where players openly celebrate their religious beliefs. From post-touchdown prayers to scripture-inspired tattoos to eye black crosses to Bible verses on helmets, expressions of faith are woven into the fabric of the game.

My faith is No. 1. That will never change, no matter what, good or bad.

NEW ORLEANS SAINTS QB DEREK CARR[6]

Ten years ago (2015) a study of starting quarterbacks in the NFL revealed that 75 percent were evangelical Christians (this does not include "professing Christians").[7] Today's (as of this writing) NFL quarterbacks who lead this spiritual chorus are stars like Derek Carr, Russell Wilson, Kirk Cousins, C. J. Stroud, Dak Prescott, Geno Smith, Tua Tagovailoa, Jameis Winston, Patrick Mahomes, Brock Purdy, Andy Dalton, Nick Foles, Lamar Jackson, Jordan Love, and Jalen Hurts. All of them regularly weave references to God and Jesus into their interviews and social media posts.

"God is good" and "I want to thank God" have become familiar refrains in post-game conversations. C. J. Stroud famously says "First and foremost I've got to thank my Lord Savior Jesus Christ" during interviews. Patrick Mahomes confesses, "Faith is huge for me … Before every game, I walk the field and I do a prayer at the goalpost."[8] After the Bills' first game since safety Damar Hamlin collapsed on the field, quarterback Josh Allen (raised a Methodist) described the day as "spiritual" and in his postgame press conference confessed: "I was just going around to my teammates saying, 'God's real.' You can't draw that one up, write that one up any better."[9] When Jacksonville Jaguars defensive end Arik Armstead received his award as the 2024 Walter Payton NFL Man of the Year, he described faith as "foundational" to his identity and integrity.

> The horse is preparing for battle, but victory comes from the Lord. So I'm depending on the Lord.
>
> JAMEIS WINSTON TO AMAZON PRIME THURSDAY NIGHT FOOTBALL REPORTER KAYLEE HARTUNG IN PREGAME INTERVIEW[10]

This faith extends beyond words to visible expressions. Players point skyward after touchdowns, kneel in prayer on the sidelines, and carry their beliefs on their skin—literally. Many athletes showcase their faith through biblical tattoos: DeVonta Smith bears Psalm 23 on his right arm, Christian McCaffrey displays Philippians 4:13 on his left forearm, and Alvin Kamara wears Psalm 27:1. Stars like Odell Beckham Jr. and Ezekiel Elliott have chosen to ink crosses on their bodies. Saquon Barkley has body art that includes religious imagery and quotes, such as crosses and Bible verses.

Eye black tells stories. For some athletes, it speaks of earthly coordinates—like Reggie Bush's painted homage to San Diego's area code, a GPS pin dropped in gridiron culture. But for Tim Tebow, his eye black pointed to different coordinates altogether: John 3:16. While Bush marked his physical address, Tebow was marking his spiritual one. Both were saying the same thing: "This is where I'm from. This is what shaped me."

But God wasn't done writing this story in eye black. God had a bigger canvas in mind. On 08 January 2009, in the swirling lights of the BCS National Championship, Tebow's eye black became a digital beacon. Those four characters—"3:16"—sent millions on a spiritual scavenger hunt, with 94 million Google searches trying to decode this cryptic message about a God who loved so much that He gave everything.

Three years later, to the day, the Divine Playwright penned what sports writers would call "The 3:16 Game." In a playoff duel between Tebow's Broncos and the Pittsburgh Steelers, heaven's mathematics began to play out in stunning synchronicity: 316 yards through the mile-high air, 31.6 yards per completion, Nielsen ratings peaking at 31.6, the Steelers holding the ball for 31:06, and—in a touch that seems almost playfully divine—an interception thrown on 3rd and 16.

One NFL executive, confronted with this string of holy happenstances, could only shake his head and declare, "I'm converting." But Tebow, the man at the center of this numerical sermon, simply pointed upward. He knew what any good quarterback knows: sometimes you're just the vessel for someone else's gameplay.

In these moments, sports became more than a game—it became a parable. While some saw coincidence, others saw coordination. While some saw statistics, others saw sermon. And in the space between eye black and end zones, God was still doing what God's always done: using the earthly to tell eternity stories.

The tradition of faith in football runs deep, exemplified by influential figures like Tony Dungy and Reggie White—the latter so committed to both his faith and his defensive prowess that he earned the nickname "Minister of Defense." Their legacy, along with today's players, cements the NFL's position as a rare space where religious expression flourishes openly in USAmerican professional life.

FROM THE SIDELINES TO THE STARS

While NFL players boldly display their faith under stadium lights and national scrutiny, many of our churches huddle in the shadows of cultural accommodation. These athletes demonstrate that authentic faith naturally overflows into public life—not through manufactured programs or sanitized presentations, but through genuine expressions that flow from deep conviction. Their example challenges our churches, which too often trade the power of authentic testimony for PowerPoint presentations, and substitute real relationship-building for rigid talk-and-stalk recruitment strategies.

> I'm a man of God. Waking up every morning and having a routine where I can gain some wisdom, learn His Word, and just walk by the Spirit, I strive to do that daily. And I challenge myself to spread that Word organically.
>
> JALEN HURTS, QB FOR THE PHILADELPHIA EAGLES AND 2025 SUPER BOWL MVP[11]

If you think we're being too harsh on the church, here are a few defining fumbles, starting with COVID. When COVID hit like an all-out blitz, many churches retreated to the locker room entirely. While grocery clerks, delivery drivers, massage therapists, liquor store employees, construction workers, and medical staff suited up daily for the front lines, numerous churches didn't just move online. They went dormant. The contrast was stark: Walmart stayed open as an essential service, but many houses of worship didn't fight for the same designation. Some even surrendered this status voluntarily, despite constitutional protection. In Los Angeles, Grace Community Church stood out precisely because its resistance to closure was so rare.

- When major corporations adopted controversial social positions, many megachurches responded with studied silence rather than clear biblical teaching.

- The rise of self-censorship in youth ministries, where tough biblical topics are often sidelined to avoid parental pushback.

- The growing trend of dropping words like "sin" and "repentance" and "blood" from church websites and marketing materials to appear more "seeker-friendly."

- Churches rebranding themselves with vague names like "The Journey" or "Life Community" rather than owning their denominational heritage and Jesus identity.

Contrast this with the sports world, where:

- NFL players like Justin Fields and Jalen Hurts

openly pray on the field despite social media mockery

- Teams like the Buffalo Bills publicly prayed on national television during Damar Hamlin's cardiac arrest
- College football programs like Liberty University and Baylor maintain their religious identity despite media criticism.

A 2020 Barna study showed that 32 percent of practicing Christians stopped attending church (even virtually) during the pandemic. Mainline Protestant churches have seen a 50 percent decline in membership since the 1960s. The average sermon length has decreased from forty-five minutes to twenty minutes over the past three decades, suggesting less appetite for deep theological engagement.

What makes this especially pointed is that historically, churches led during crises:

- During the 1918 Spanish Flu, many churches converted to hospitals
- In the Civil Rights era, churches were often headquarters for activism
- Throughout history, churches have been front-line responders during natural disasters

Today's timidity isn't just about COVID. It's about a broader pattern of choosing institutional survival over prophetic witness. While NFL players ink Bible verses on their eye black and kneel in prayer after touchdowns, many churches are running a prevent defense against cultural criticism, hoping to avoid controversy by running out the clock.

This contrast becomes even sharper when we consider how sports figures handle adversity. When Kansas City Chiefs' Harrison Butker was mocked for wearing ashes on his forehead during Ash Wednesday, he didn't apologize or remove them. He explained their significance. Meanwhile, many churches have removed crosses from their exterior walls to appear more "welcoming."

Want an even more tangible example? Look at the difference in boldness between a Tim Tebow taking a knee in prayer despite ridicule, and the average church's carefully worded, focus-grouped mission statement that could easily be mistaken for a corporate wellness program.

> I've found that prayers work best when you have big players.[12]
>
> KNUTE ROCKNE, THE LEGENDARY FOOTBALL COACH OF NOTRE DAME, AFTER BEING ASKED IF PRAYER WAS THE SECRET OF HIS SUCCESS

The NFL's faithful remind us that true evangelism happens not through carefully crafted programs but through lives lived openly in grace—whether on a football field, at a neighborhood cookout, or across a coffee table. Like these athletes who seamlessly integrate their faith into their professional calling, we're invited to let our faith shape every aspect of our lives, creating natural opportunities for sacred conversations in unexpected places.

TAKE A KNEE

A person, a church, on its knees seems weak, maligned, overcome. But in this posture of seeming defeat lies our greatest strength. For the church has a glorious future precisely because it stays on its knees—not in surrender to the world, but in surrender to God.

- On its knees in repentance, acknowledging its brokenness.
- On its knees in prayer, seeking wisdom and revival.
- On its knees in humility, serving others as Christ served.

And when we stumble, as we inevitably will, we know the way back: return to those knees, again and again, to reclaim our strength in weakness and find healing in brokenness. For it's in this paradoxical posture that we discover our true power: Churches that kneel are churches that rise. Christians grow tall on their knees. A church or a person shrinks and shrivels when they stand on their own two feet.

There's a profound irony in the human condition: we all possess knowledge deeper than our knowing. Hidden in the folds of our consciousness lies a truth we don't know we know until someone dares to speak it: Jesus is Lord. It awaits only the courage of a voice to call it forth.[13]

Try as you might, you won't find a version of The Great Commission that reads: "Go into all the world and keep your mouth shut, your head down, your guard up, your nose clean, your fingers crossed." Yet this seems to be the translation many of us are living by—a gospel of silence in an age desperate for song.

This crisis of evangelical muteness isn't merely about lost opportunities; it's about lost essence. When we cease to speak of faith, we don't just fail to spread it—we begin to lose it ourselves. Like a language unused, it atrophies in our mouths until we forget we ever knew its words.

Austrian neurologist and founder of psychoanalysis Sigmund Freud relates a dialogue between a child and his aunt. "Auntie, speak to me! I'm frightened because it's so dark."

His aunt answered her: "What good would that do? You can't see me."

"That doesn't matter", replied the child, "if you speak, it gets light."[14]

Evangelists speak the sacred semiotics of Jesus, and it

gets light.[15]

Our call, then, is deeper than to rethink evangelism but to rediscover it—to unearth it from beneath layers of cultural anxiety and institutional hesitation. Sharing faith isn't an act of aggression but an offering of love, not an imposition but an invitation to see the world through eyes of wonder and love.

For in the end, faith isn't meant to be a carefully guarded secret but a story burning to be told, a song yearning to be sung, a light refusing to be hidden under the bushel of our current discomfort. Perhaps it's time we stopped apologizing for having something to say about the divine adventure that has captured our hearts.

Faith, then family, then football.
MANTRA OF DEVOUT CATHOLICS JOHN AND JIM HARBAUGH[16]

When Faith Touched the Stars

It's Christmas Eve, 1968. The vast emptiness of space stretches before three men hurtling through the dark, their spacecraft a tiny island of warmth and life against the infinite void. They are among the rarest of humans—only 628 souls have ever crossed the Kármán line, that invisible boundary 100 kilometers above Earth where atmosphere gives way to the cosmos.

It began with Yuri Gagarin in 1961, when his Vostok 1 spacecraft first breached that barrier, making him the pioneer of human spaceflight. Alan Shepard followed mere weeks later, carrying USAmerica's hopes into the heavens. But it was William Anders,[17] the twenty-fourth human to cross that threshold, who would capture an image that would forever change humanity's perspective of itself.

That Christmas Eve, aboard Apollo 8, Anders took the photograph that would become known as "Earthrise"—our blue marble suspended in the black velvet of space, the stark lunar surface a silent witness in the foreground. The image struck a chord deep in our collective consciousness: here was our entire world, every mountain and ocean, every triumph and tragedy, every soul who had ever lived, contained in one fragile sphere.

As their voices crackled across the void, Anders and his fellow astronauts—Jim Lovell and Frank Borman—took turns reading from Genesis. Their words, ancient and profound, bridged the gap between the infinite and the intimate, between human achievement and divine mystery:

> "In the beginning, God created the heaven and the earth ..."

A few months later, another celestial pilgrim would carry his faith to an even more distant shore. Buzz Aldrin, the nineteenth human to cross the Kármán line, brought a communion kit to the moon itself. After the Eagle landed, before the historic first steps, Aldrin paused for a moment of sacred reflection. As he took communion himself, his words echoed across a quarter-million miles of space: "I'd like to take a few moments of silence … to ask for the blessings of the Almighty on our endeavors."[18]

In the lunar dust, Aldrin read from John 15:5, partaking in humanity's first extraterrestrial communion: "I am the vine, you are the branches. Whoever remains in me, and I in him, will bear much fruit; for you can do nothing without me."[19]

Today, such expressions of faith from the final frontier seem almost unimaginable. Our "modern" space program, though technically more advanced, navigates a different kind of space—one bounded by institutional caution and cultural sensitivities. Where once we united in collective wonder at both scientific achievement and spiritual mystery, we now often find ourselves a house divided, our sense of shared transcendence fractured by the very technologies that connect us.

As we reach ever farther into the cosmos, these early space missions remind us of a time when human achievement and spiritual wonder weren't seen as contradictions but as complementary expressions of our deepest aspirations. They challenge us to consider whether, in our relentless march forward, we might have left something essential behind—the ability to stand together in awe of mysteries both scientific and divine.

From Stardust to Sterility: The Fading Light of Faith in Science Fiction: The longstanding and longitudinal trend of atrophied public expressions of faith is evident even in popular science fiction, which is a partial reflection of the underlying culture. The cultural phenomenon of *Star Trek* provides an illustrative case.

Imagine a cultural time machine, whisking us from the bold frontiers of the 1960s to the sanitized space of today. Our vehicle? The evolution of *Star Trek*, a mirror reflecting the changing face of faith in USAmerican culture.

In the original Enterprise, Jewish actors William Shatner and Leonard Nimoy brought life to Kirk and Spock. Despite their personal backgrounds, they sailed a ship where Christianity could still ignite wonder. Who can forget Kirk's impassioned monologue in "Bread and Circuses," his voice thrumming with excitement at the thought of witnessing the birth of a faith? "Caesar and Christ. They had them both," he marvels, eyes alight with possibility. "Wouldn't it be something to watch, to be a part of it?"[20]

Now, fast-forward a mere two decades. The sleek lines of

the Enterprise-D slice through a vastly different cultural space. Here, in *The Next Generation*, faith has become a relic, a quaint artifact to be studied rather than embraced. Captain Picard, brilliant and cultured as he is, views religion through the cold lens of anthropology. Christianity? Never mentioned. Instead, we get fleeting nods to Hinduism ("Festival of Lights"[21]) or ancient Mesopotamian myths—safer territory, perhaps, in an increasingly post-Christian world. When Captain Picard had a golden opportunity to mention the far more famous story from the Book of Genesis, Picard instead regaled a dying alien ship captain with a summary of the *Epic of Gilgamesh*, which also had an ancient flood story.[22] Humanity was much larger and God was much smaller in the distorting funhouse mirror of humanity's soul adrift in space.

This new Enterprise sails not by starlight, but by the dim glow of "stardates," scrubbing even our calendar of its Christian roots. The ship's corridors, once perhaps echoing with quiet prayer or philosophical debate, now hum only with the certainty of scientific materialism. Picard's god is "truth," but it's a truth as sterile as a laboratory, devoid of the mystery that once made space the "final frontier."

The transformation reaches its nadir in the episode "The Chase."[23] Here, the very origins of life are reduced to an alien science experiment, a cosmic accident stripped of any divine spark. Picard's delight at this revelation is a funeral dirge for wonder, a celebration of a universe robbed of meaning beyond the material.

This shift in *Star Trek* mirrors a broader cultural erosion. We've traded the awe-inspiring for the explainable, the transcendent for the tangible. In our rush to map the cosmos, have we lost our ability to marvel at it? As our ships probe further into the void, are we leaving behind the very thing that made that journey worthwhile—our capacity for faith, wonder, and the recognition of something greater than ourselves?

The contrast between Kirk's evangelical fervor and Picard's cool rationalism isn't just about changing television tastes. It's a cautionary tale about a culture slowly draining itself of spiritual vitality, replacing the infinite possibilities of faith with the finite certainties of science. As we reach for the stars, we must ask ourselves: in this vast, mysterious universe, are we truly better off alone?

Star Trek boldly goes where many skeptics have gone before—straight into the heart of religious origin stories. In "Who Watches the Watchers"[24] we witness a cosmic parable that feels ripped from both ancient scrolls and modern headlines. The stage? Mintaka III, a Bronze Age world where Clarke's Third Law ("Any sufficiently advanced technology is indistinguishable from magic") is about to collide with raw human spirituality. When

Enterprise medicine saves a life, something extraordinary happens: a new religion is born. "The Picard" becomes their god, their miracle-worker, their resurrection story.

Here's where it gets juicy. Picard, our enlightened twenty-fourth-century captain, recoils from his unexpected deification. Like a secular missionary, he's determined to pull back the curtain and show the great and powerful Oz is just a man behind a control panel. The message couldn't be clearer if it was written in antimatter: sophisticated societies don't need deities; they need understanding.

The episode dangles a provocative question before us: if advanced technology could spawn a religion in a pre-industrial society, what does that suggest about our own sacred narratives? The parallel to Christianity's central miracle—resurrection—isn't just coincidental; it's a SETI-sized signal pointing to broader skepticism about religious faith.

In this cosmic drama, Picard becomes both unwitting messiah and determined iconoclast, desperate to prevent his "miracles" from fossilizing into faith. It's a story that asks us to consider where divine intervention ends and misunderstood technology begins—all while surfing the edge of *Star Trek's* prime directive.

FROM JINGLES TO HUSH-UPS: VANISHING ACT OF FAITH IN ADVERTISING

A family car zips down a Sunday morning street, the radio

buzzing with a catchy McDonald's jingle. "We'll have breakfast at McDonald's, and still get to church on time!" It's more than a commercial; it's a time capsule, a glimpse into an era when faith was as much a part of the cultural fabric as fast food and catchy tunes.

Now, fast-forward to today. Imagine that same jingle playing on current airwaves. The mere thought feels almost jarring, doesn't it? It's as if we've entered a parallel universe where such open references to religion have become taboo in the world of big business.

This shift isn't just about changing tastes. It's a seismic cultural transfiguration, reflecting a corporate world now walking on eggshells, terrified of offending anyone. The fear isn't just about alienating those of different faiths—it's about the growing voice of those who eschew faith altogether.

Remember Michael Jordan's famous quip, "Republicans buy sneakers too"? Today's equivalent might be a McDonald's executive nervously whispering, "Atheists buy Big Macs too." It's a stark reminder of how the pursuit of profit has reshaped our public discourse, scrubbing it clean of anything that might ruffle feathers or, heaven forbid, acknowledge the existence of Sunday services.

But what are we losing in this sad, sanitized landscape? Those old jingles weren't just about selling burgers. They were cultural touchstones, reflecting and reinforcing a shared experience. They acknowledged that for many, a quick breakfast and a church service were both part of a typical Sunday morning.

These expressions of faith are not unique to these players but are representative of a broader trend in the culture. Former world judo champion Nemanja Majdov was banned from competing for five months for making the Sign of the Cross at the 2024 Paris Olympics.[25] In our rush to be inclusive, have we inadvertently excluded a fundamental aspect of many people's lives? Has our fear of offending the few led to a bland, flavorless public square that truly satisfies no one?

This isn't just about nostalgia for old commercials. It's about the gradual erosion of our ability to acknowledge faith in public life. As we've expanded our cultural menu to include more voices (a worthy goal), we've somehow decided that faith must be pushed off the table entirely.

The irony is palpable. In trying to make everyone feel welcome, we've created a world where a significant part of many people's identities must be checked at the door. It's as if we're saying, "Come as you are ... except for that part of you."

As we navigate this unbrave new world of hyper-cautious corporate messaging, we must ask ourselves: In our quest for inoffensive universality, are we losing something essential—the particularity and rootedness of identity? Are we trading the rich, complex warp and woof of a diverse society for a bland, beige backdrop where nothing of substance can be said at all?

> I may win and I may lose, but I will never be defeated.
>
> DALLAS COWBOYS RUNNING BACK EMMITT SMITH AND LEAGUE'S ALL-TIME LEADING RUSHER (18,355 YARDS)

Perhaps it's time to find a new recipe—one that allows for the acknowledgment of faith without exclusion, that celebrates our differences instead of pretending they don't exist.

And how are we pretending? We pretend in multiple ways that strike at the heart of authentic faith:

We pretend ecumenism means avoiding hard conversations. Rather than engaging in robust theological dialogue about real differences between denominations or faith traditions, we often resort to vague platitudes like "we all worship the same God" without wrestling with genuine theological distinctions. This isn't true unity. It's conflict avoidance dressed up as inclusion.

We pretend by sanitizing our language. Churches increasingly adopt corporate-speak and self-help vocabulary instead of biblical terminology. We talk about "life change"

FROM THE SIDELINES TO THE STARS

instead of repentance, "personal growth" instead of sanctification or holiness, and "finding your best life" instead of dying to self. This isn't contextualization. It is capitulation.

We pretend by downplaying distinctives. Many churches minimize or entirely avoid discussing historic Christian positions on gender, the particularity of Christ, or the reality of hell—not because their theology has changed, but because they fear cultural backlash. This isn't wisdom. It's cowardice wearing a diplomatic mask. And unacknowledged and unresolved conflict typically leads to toxic resentment.

We pretend in our worship. Many services are carefully curated performances that leave no room for lament, doubt, or the messiness of real faith. We pretend everyone is "fine" when many are struggling with deep questions or pain. This isn't celebration. It's spiritual theater.

We pretend about our differences with other faiths. Rather than acknowledging and respectfully discussing genuine theological disagreements with other religions, we often reduce faith to its lowest common denominator of generic spirituality. This isn't respect. It's relativism masquerading as tolerance.

True celebration of differences requires first acknowledging they exist and matter. Real unity isn't pretending we're all the same. It's loving each other despite our differences and engaging in honest, respectful dialogue about them. The Holy Spirit's work isn't uniform; it's unified in purpose but diverse in expression. We need the courage to be honest about who we are and what we believe while remaining humble enough to learn from those who see things differently. The Holy Spirit works in many different ways. After all, in a world as diverse as ours, shouldn't our public discourse be just as colorful and varied as the people it aims to reach?

> We don't' walk down the same street as the person walking beside us.
> NOVELIST ANNE ENRIGHT, *THE WREN, THE WREN* (2024)

THE COSMIC GAME

If football serves as a parable for the cosmic struggle between good and evil, we're already deep in trouble before the game's really started—or to put it in football-ese, we find ourselves in the first quarter in what appears to be a fourth-quarter deficit.

The forces of evil seem to have seized momentum—their offense running wild with technological terrors, cultural decay, religious persecution, and existential threats to humanity itself. Evil has always been with us. What is alarming is evil's increasing social acceptance and even celebration across a wide spectrum of society.

- When Sam Altman was briefly ousted from OpenAI in late 2023, a significant portion of social media celebrated the potential disruption to AI's development, even if it meant potential economic devastation. The hashtag #TechCollapse trended with people actively hoping for technological and economic breakdown.

- The rise of "doxxing" and cyber harassment is now being reframed as "accountability." A 2023 Pew study showed 28 percent of young adults view doxxing as "sometimes justified" when targeting people they disagree with politically.

- There is a dramatic increase in "swatting" incidents (false emergency calls meant to trigger SWAT team responses) against public figures, with perpetrators often livestreaming these potentially lethal pranks for entertainment. In 2023, there were over two hundred swatting incidents targeting officials and public figures.

- The rise of "financial terrorism" where individuals deliberately attempt to crash companies or markets. The "meme stock" movement has evolved from seeking profit to explicitly aiming to destroy targeted companies, with online communities celebrating when businesses fail and workers lose jobs.

- Social media platforms' algorithms increasingly favor conflict and outrage, with studies showing that posts celebrating violence or schadenfreude receive significantly higher engagement. A 2023 MIT study found that posts expressing joy at others' suffering received 67 percent more engagement than neutral or positive content.

According to recent social media sentiment and polls, approximately 41 percent of USAmericans aged 18–29 (Gen Z) believe the actions of Luigi Mangione in shooting the CEO of UnitedHealthcare in cold blood were either "completely" or "somewhat acceptable."[26]

From Europe's emptying cathedrals to the violent persecution of Christians across continents, from the rise of AIs to the decline of authentic faith, evil appears to be calling many of the plays, controlling the tempo, and even trash-talking from the sidelines.

Yet this cosmic game is far from over. Just as football teams must adapt or perish, the gospellers today face a critical choice: retreat into a defensive shell, or mount a bold counteroffensive through creative, Spirit-driven discipleship. The future of this cosmic contest doesn't hinge on playing it safe—it demands the courage to form an unstoppable "flying wedge"[27] of faith, powered by the synergy of love, conviction, and holy imagination. After all, history's greatest comebacks begin when things look bleakest.

FROM THE SIDELINES TO THE STARS

My identity is in Jesus Christ. I love playing football, but football is just a game. I identify as a Christian before I identify as a football player.

SAN FRANCISCO 49ERS QB BROCK PURDY[28]
KNOWN FOR BEING THE LAST PICK IN THE 2022 NFL
DRAFT, DUBBED "MR. IRRELEVANT"

Jesus stands as a towering figure of transfigurative power, calling His followers not to passive acceptance but to vibrant, dynamic faith. This call beckons us toward what might be termed a "muscular Christianity"—though not in the narrow confines of physical strength. Can you envision a ninety-five-year-old woman, her prayer life so potent it radiates spiritual strength more commanding than any athlete's physique? Yet this strength must find expression beyond whispered prayers; we are summoned to be both contemplatives and competitors on life's great field of purpose. The game isn't coming—it's already here.

Saints are those who love the most. You are called to be a saint. We are all called to live a saintly life. But sainthood is a process, not a prerequisite for powerful faith. Paul, Christianity's most prolific evangelist, carried within himself deep personal struggles yet changed the world. Look to the twelve disciples, whose moments of doubt and misstep fill the gospel narratives. Yet after witnessing the risen Christ, eleven of these ordinary men became extraordinary channels of God's power, carrying His message to the furthest reaches of their known world. These were not marble saints, but flesh-and-blood humans who stumbled, questioned, and sometimes failed—just as we do.

Their stories offer twin gifts: their human frailties give us permission to acknowledge our own imperfections, while their Spirit-empowered achievements illuminate the astounding possibilities that await when ordinary people surrender to extraordinary purpose. In their weaknesses made strong, we glimpse our own potential for transfiguration.

THE PERFECT IMPERFECTION

They say there's a right way to do everything. Stand like this. Hold your arms just so. Plant your feet exactly here. But Tom Dempsey never got that memo, and thank God for that.

Born with half a right foot and a deformed right arm, Dempsey should never have been a football player at all, let alone an NFL placekicker. After all, kicking is an art of precision, of perfect form learned through thousands of identical repetitions.

But Dempsey had something better than perfect form. He had coaches who saw past what wasn't there to what could be. Through San Dieguito High School in Encinitas, California, and Palomar College in San Diego County, these mentors did something extraordinary. Instead of forcing him into the "right" way, they helped him find his way.

Most NFL teams looked at Dempsey and saw where he came from and what was missing. The New Orleans Saints looked at him, where he was now, and saw what was possible.

That possibility crystallized on one fateful Sunday afternoon in a game against the Detroit Lions. With two seconds left on the clock and the Saints trailing 17–16, Dempsey trotted onto the field to attempt what seemed impossible: a 63-yard field goal.

The longest successful field goal in NFL history was 57 yards. But Dempsey wasn't thinking about history or limitations. He was thinking about all those coaches who had helped him remember how he did things right, rather than telling him how he did things wrong.

The ball sailed through the uprights, and history was made. But the real miracle wasn't in the distance of the kick. It was in what came after, when a reporter asked him how he'd done it. Dempsey's answer revealed the profound truth that had shaped his entire journey: "All of my life, I've had wonderful coaches. All the way through high school and college and now in the pros, they've spent so much time encouraging me that they simply forgot to tell me what I couldn't do!"

This truth echoes the wisdom of legendary coach Bear Bryant, who, when asked about his method for training kickers, replied, "I don't have any. I just watch carefully to see when they do it well, and then try to help them remember how they did it right."

Bryant understood what Dempsey's coaches had discovered: that greatness doesn't come from forcing everyone into the same mold, but from helping each person perfect their own unique way.

We are all, in our own ways, differently abled. Each of us carries our own limitations, our own wounds, our own half-feet. But perhaps these aren't limitations at all—perhaps they're invitations. Invitations to find our own way, to discover the strength that comes not from being perfect, but from being perfectly ourselves as God made us.

Tom Dempsey's story isn't just about a record-breaking kick. It's about the beauty of finding your own way, about the miracle of coaches who forget to tell you what you can't do, and about the grace that turns our supposed limitations into our greatest strengths. Despite a culture that might have overlooked his voice or dismissed his abilities, Dempsey taught us that true greatness comes when we refuse to conform and instead speak with the voice only we can offer. For in our brokenness, in our uniqueness, in our different ways of doing things—that's where the real miracles happen.

FROM THE SIDELINES TO THE STARS

This is a team sport.
You're not going to win anything by yourself.

PEYTON MANNING
(EPISCOPALIAN WHEN IN DENVER,
PRESBYTERIAN WHEN IN NASHVILLE)

THE HOLY SPIRIT: THE ULTIMATE TEAM PLAYER

The gospel understanding of community is not an individualism or a collectivism but a koinonia, a term that means the most intimate human relationships possible where the uniqueness of each person is preserved. In koinonia each unique person is willing to sacrifice, even lay down their lives, for the other. But in koinonia the best gift you can give a community is not your conformity, but your unique way of being and seeing.

This is the miracle of grace: not that it makes us whole in the way others define wholeness, but that it helps us discover the wholeness that was already within us, waiting to be recognized. Just as a brown guy named Jesus came not to make us all the same, but to invite each of us to become fully who we were created to be, which can only take place in the context of a team where everyone is not playing their own game. Everyone is building the same play, the same mission, together.

Football is called a "team sport" for a reason. Tom Osborne's approach to Cornhusker football during his tenure as head coach at the University of Nebraska (1973–1997) was based on a gridiron version of koinonia. Osborne taught a "Move the Line Forward, Not the Ball" philosophy where the success of the team came above individual accolades. Teamwork was everything. In Osborne's offensive strategy, particularly his reliance on the I-formation running game, the offensive line's ability to consistently "move forward" dictated the success of the team in gaining yards and wearing down opponents. The team superseded the stars. While Osborne coached many outstanding athletes, he emphasized team cohesion and a "no-star" mentality. Players were expected to focus on their roles and contribution to the team without prioritizing personal achievements. Osborne's Nebraska teams were built around a culture of unselfishness, valuing players who were willing to sacrifice individual glory for team spirit and success. The game is a constant procession on and off the field of different players with different strengths and skill sets depending on field conditions.

THE ENDURING MAGIC OF PROFESSIONAL FOOTBALL

Life unfolds in a kaleidoscope of moments—our highest

triumphs and quietest struggles, the steadfast embrace of family and friends, the relentless rhythm of change that shapes our days. Yet amid this ever-shifting landscape, there remains one constant source of joy that transcends generations and teleports joy. A wellspring of memories that unfailingly brings us back to moments of pure excitement, community, and shared passion.

That source is professional football.

The NFL stands today as more than just a sports league; it's a living monument to the visionaries who built it from the ground up. Practicing Christians like George Halas (Catholic) and Paul Brown (Protestant)—imperfect giants whose shadows still stretch across today's gridirons. Though their footsteps no longer echo on the sidelines, their legacy resonates in every snap, every touchdown, every moment of gridiron glory.

Unlike European team sports, where the winner-takes-all mentality dominates and championships are open to even the newest teams, the NFL's sporting socialism (salary cap, team parity, concentrated closed markets of thirty-two teams) makes up for in funds what it lacks in fans *vis-à-vis* Europe. In 2022, the NFL raked in a staggering $19 billion, nearly triple the revenue of the English Premier League, a league which "boasts more fans worldwide than all the American sports put together."[29]

> The biggest sport in the world has this crazy glitch in it—that the best team on the day won't necessarily win. Yes, over a season, the league table tells no lies, but game by game Lady Luck is always roaming the pitch, with so much cruelty.
>
> BRITISH WRITER AND TV PERSONALITY ADRIAN CHILES[30]

Europeans tend to embrace football (soccer) because it reflects a harsh truth about life: sometimes the better team loses, and the lesser team wins. Life is unfair, but a fairy-tale ending is always possible. USAmericans often dislike this aspect—the idea that superior effort doesn't always guarantee victory.[31] This innate disrespect for discipline and tradition may also have been one of the reasons why Margaret Thatcher, former Prime Minister of the UK, loathed soccer so much. Ironically, European football embraces a capitalist model of participation, while the NFL prioritizes profits within a socialist framework. From 2012 to 2022, the average NFL team's value soared over 300 percent, outpacing the stock market's 170 percent growth.[32]

While we may be too young to have witnessed Vince Lombardi's legendary Packers firsthand, the immortal voice of John Facenda still sends shivers down our spines:

FROM THE SIDELINES TO THE STARS

"Lombardi—a certain magic still lingers in that name. It speaks of duels in the snow and the cold November mud." These words paint pictures of an era when legends were forged in frozen fields and autumn storms.

Through the decades, we've witnessed a parade of greatness that reads like football's sacred scripture:

- The Steel Curtain of Pittsburgh—Chuck Noll's devastating defense led by Mean Joe Greene, coupled with Terry Bradshaw's cannon arm and Franco Harris's "Immaculate Reception," forging four Super Bowl crowns in six remarkable years.

- The Dallas Cowboys transforming into "America's Team" under Tom Landry's stoic leadership, his fedora as unchanging as his principles, while Roger "Captain America" Staubach led charges down the field between glimpses of those iconic cheerleaders.

> I was ten years old when my parents took me to my first Dallas Cowboys game. When we arrived at Texas Stadium, I asked my mom: "Why is there a hole in the roof?" She said: "So God can watch His favorite team play on Sunday."
>
> PLANO, TEXAS, PASTOR KORY KNOTT

- Don Shula's Miami Dolphins achieving perfection—their undefeated season sandwiched between three straight Super Bowl appearances—before later reinventing themselves around Dan Marino's golden arm.

- The Oakland Raiders, professional football's beloved rebels, with Al Davis and John Madden unleashing Ken "The Snake" Stabler's maverick spirit on the league.

- The San Francisco dynasty of Bill Walsh, Jerry Rice, and Joe Montana—four Super Bowl victories without a single interception, painting masterpieces on the field with their West Coast precision.

- The 1985 Chicago Bears, reincarnating the "Monsters of the Midway" with equal parts ferocity and flair, their "Super Bowl Shuffle" capturing both their dominance and their joy.

- Bill Parcells and Bill Belichick molding the Giants into champions, with Lawrence Taylor redefining defensive dominance en route to two Super Bowl triumphs.

- Joe Gibbs's Washington teams, powered by the legendary "Hogs," muscling their way to three Super Bowl victories with three different quarterbacks.

- The 1990s Cowboys' resurrection under Jimmy

FROM THE SIDELINES TO THE STARS

Johnson, with the unstoppable trinity of Troy Aikman, Emmitt Smith, and Michael Irvin claiming three Super Bowl titles in four years.

- The Manning brothers writing their own chapters in NFL history—Peyton, the field general whose mind matched his arm, leading both Indianapolis and Denver to glory; and Eli, the giant-killer who twice outdueled the seemingly invincible Patriots, including the shocking toppling of their perfect season.

- The Patriots dynasty of Belichick and Brady was without precedent or parallel, setting standards of sustained excellence that seemed impossible to match.

- And now, Patrick Mahomes, Andy Reid and their Kansas City Chiefs, reinventing the game before our eyes, their creative brilliance and adaptability ushering in football's next golden age.

> A coach is someone who tells you what you don't want to hear, who has you see what you don't want to see, so you can be who you have always known you could be.

TWENTY-NINE-YEAR DALLAS COWBOYS HEAD COACH TOM LANDRY, PRO FOOTBALL HALL OF FAMER

These stories, these teams, these moments—they're more than just sports history. They're parables of excellence, testament to human potential, and proof that even in our flawed pursuits of greatness, we can achieve something transcendent. In the end, professional football teaches us that while perfection may be unattainable, the pursuit of it creates legends that inspire generations.

The pantheon of NFL legends stretches far beyond these tales, each fan harboring their own sacred memories, their personal heroes who defined autumn Sundays. Yet these giants of the gridiron—brilliant but flawed, triumphant yet human—offer us something far more profound than mere athletic spectacle. Behind the stratospheric achievements and crushing defeats, beyond the highlight reels and statistics, lies a masterclass in human potential and perseverance that transcends the game itself. The lessons hidden in these moments of gridiron glory? They're about to change how you see not just football, but the very nature of life and faith itself.

GAME IV

TWO MINUTE WARNING
DIVINE TIMING

> Entire subway car mesmerized by
> small gizmo clutched in hand. Some
> sort of worship?
>
> JOYCE CAROL OATES IN 2019,
> ALONGSIDE A PHOTO OF RIDERS HOLDING
> MOBILE PHONES, AS IF IN PRAYER

Saint Augustine of Hippo, the brilliant fourth-century African theologian, had remarkable insights about the nature of time. He understood time not as a rigid, linear construct but as something more fluid—an idea that would find surprising validation centuries later in Einstein's Theory of Relativity.

Using Augustine's concept of traveling in "our mind's eye," let us transport ourselves back to 28 December 1958—a pivotal moment when USAmerica stood on the cusp of profound cultural change. At this time our "national pastime," and most popular sport, is professional baseball. Professional football during most of the 1950s was less popular in the United States than baseball, college football, horse racing and even professional boxing. On Sunday mornings like this one in 1958, church pews across the nation were typically filled with worshipers. Professional football was about to challenge this sacred tradition.

THE GREATEST GAME EVER PLAYED

The NFL of the 1950s was widely viewed as crude and uncouth, a veritable "wild west" of USAmerican sport. But on this winter Sunday, the sport was poised for its defining moment. The championship game between the New York Giants and Baltimore Colts would become more than just a contest—it would mark the moment when television transformed professional football into a cultural phenomenon.

In the fading light of that December afternoon, a revolution was brewing. Nearly every USAmerican home with a television set—forty-five million viewers strong—was about to witness a game that would reshape the nation's cultural landscape forever.

On one side stood the New York Giants, their offensive

hopes pinned to the versatile Frank Gifford, a halfback who could run like a stallion and throw like a quarterback. Behind him prowled two titans-in-waiting on the sidelines: Vince Lombardi orchestrating the offense and Tom Landry marshaling the defense—two future legends who would soon forge their own dynasties in Green Bay and Dallas.

Facing them were the Baltimore Colts, led by the indomitable Johnny Unitas, a blue-collar gladiator in cleats whose very name would become synonymous with quarterbacking greatness. The stage was set for what would become known simply as "The Greatest Game Ever Played."

For nearly sixty minutes, these titans clashed in a contest so gripping that USAmericans couldn't tear themselves away from their television sets. Then came the unprecedented: sudden death overtime. The nation held its breath as Unitas engineered a masterful 80-yard drive, culminating in Alan Ameche's one-yard plunge into football immortality. Colts 23, Giants 17. Roughly one quarter of the United States' population at that time (45 million) watched the game, and the whole nation went from spellbound to smitten.

The real victory that day belonged to neither team. As Tom Landry would later reflect, this was "the time, the game, and the place where pro football really caught on."[1] The NFL had found its moment, and USAmerica had found its new Sunday ritual. Within a few short years, what was once merely a game would become a cultural juggernaut. By 2014, even the NFL draft—a mere off-season ceremony—would command more viewers than the championship games of baseball, basketball, and hockey combined.

Yet as professional football ascended to its Sunday throne, another cultural shift was quietly unfolding. Like a glacier reshaping a landscape, the role of traditional Sunday worship began to erode. The church pews that had once been the center of USAmerican Sunday life were gradually emptying, as a new cathedral—one built of television screens and roaring stadiums—rose to take their place.

> We don't have million-dollar contracts. None of us will retire off the money we're making in the CFL, but that's not the point. It's really for the love of playing.
>
> CALGARY STAMPEDERS ALL-STAR LINEBACKER
> MICAH AWE

To restate one of our initial theses, the NFL today isn't just a sport—it's a year-round religion. Where players once clocked out after the Super Bowl to work everyday jobs, now the game never truly sleeps. The sacred calendar of this new faith runs ceaselessly: combines, drafts, minicamps, training camps, preseason, regular season, playoffs, free agency—each with its own rituals and devoted followers.

In the cathedral of professional football, coaches have become high priests, living monastic lives hunched over film rooms and playbooks. Yet unlike traditional faiths, that have focused on the presentational and representational, the NFL has mastered what artist and designer Edwin Schlossberg calls "interactive excellence"—where greatness lies less in performance than in participation. Through fantasy leagues, social media, merchandise, and interactive platforms, fans aren't mere spectators or consumers of a story; they're active participants in an unfolding drama. They draft their own teams, analyze statistics, debate strategies, and forge communities both online and off. The NFL has intuited what digital culture demands: an EPIC experience that's Experiential, Participatory, Image-rich, and Connective.[2]

The Power of Participation: From Observants to Participants

Nowhere is the shift from passive observation to active participation more evident than in the storied tradition of the "12th Man."[3]

During your authors' youth, crowd interference was strictly prohibited. Referees would halt play if the quarterback's calls were inaudible due to excessive noise. Repeated disruptions would result in a referee's warning, followed by a 15-yard unsportsmanlike conduct penalty against the home team. This pressure often compelled the home team to urge their fans to quiet down, as the referee would ultimately enforce the penalty.

How drastically things have evolved, to the betterment of the game. The 12th Man phenomenon perfectly exemplifies what Edwin Schlossberg recognized as a new standard of excellence—one measured not by the quality of performance, but by the depth of participation.[4]

The 12th Man tradition started at Texas A&M's Kyle Field (College Station, Texas) in 1922. The Dixie Classic against Centre College is underway, and in the stands sits E. King Gill, a former football player who had left the team to focus on basketball. As injuries mount and the team's ranks thin, coach Dana X. Bible catches Gill's eye in the stands. Without hesitation, Gill descends from the crowd, dons a uniform, and stands ready on the sideline throughout the entire game.

Though Gill never stepped onto the field that day, his readiness to transition from spectator to participant created something far more significant than a mere football tradition. It established a new paradigm of fandom—one where the line between performer and audience blurs until it nearly disappears.

It took over half a century, but this participatory spirit has proven so powerful that it has spread far beyond College Station, Texas, to become one of the most iconic and celebrated traditions in the NFL. The Seahawks began actively cultivating the 12th Man identity in the 1980s. When the Seattle Seahawks' fans create their legendary wall of sound, they're not just cheering; they're actively affecting the game, forcing opposing teams into false starts and missed signals. The stadium becomes an instrument, and every fan becomes a player in a holographic performance. In fact, the Seattle Seahawks' stadium was intentionally designed with parabolic roofs over the stands that reflect and amplify crowd noise back onto the field, making it notoriously loud. This has led to multiple "loudest crowd roar" records and gives the team a significant home-field advantage.[5]

The 12th Man tradition revolutionized the relationship between fans and team by transforming the very notion of spectatorship. In today's NFL games, fans don't merely watch—they see themselves as active participants whose coordinated noise, energy, and presence can directly impact the outcome. This shift represents more than just enthusiastic support; it's a fundamental reimagining of the fan's role from passive observer to essential team component. The stadium becomes not just a venue but a collaborative space where the traditional boundary between athlete and spectator dissolves into a unified force.

Participation impacts the traditional sporting experience. In most entertainment venues, excellence is measured by what happens on the stage or field. But in the 12th Man tradition, excellence emerges from the synchronized standing of thousands of A&M students, ready to serve, or from the precisely timed roar of Seahawks fans creating their acoustic advantage. The fans aren't watching the game. They're playing their own crucial role in it.

> I love my ring. But as a Christian I want to win in the game of life where I receive a trophy that will never perish.
>
> LA RAMS WIDE RECEIVER COOPER KUPP WHEN ASKED ABOUT HIS SUPER BOWL RING[5]

This is what makes the 12th Man tradition such a perfect embodiment of the "P" in EPIC culture. Whether it's A&M students standing for entire games, Vikings fans braving sub-zero temperatures to support their team, or Saskatchewan Roughriders supporters bringing their "13th Man" energy to Canadian football, these traditions represent a fundamental shift from passive consumption to active participation.

In each case, the fans aren't just witnessing history—they're making it. They're not merely observing excel-

TWO MINUTE WARNING

lence—they're creating it. This is why Texas A&M so fiercely protects their trademark of the 12th Man concept. It's not just a slogan or a marketing tool; it's a testament to the power of participation, a living embodiment of Schlossberg's new standard of excellence.

This participatory spirit extends beyond the visible realm for people of faith. Just as the 12th Man tradition blurs the line between spectator and participant, Christians recognize they are surrounded by what Scripture calls a "great cloud of witnesses"—the communion of saints who have gone before. These ancestral spectators aren't passive observers but active participants in the ongoing story of faith, their testimony and witness adding another dimension to the crowd's energy. Like the physical fans in the stands, this unseen audience cheers on those of us still "running the race," their stories of faithfulness amplifying the courage and commitment of today's gospellers. The convergence of earthly and heavenly participants creates a particularly powerful dynamic in venues like Kyle Field, where the physical standing of thousands ready to serve mirrors the saintly posture of countless faithful witnesses standing with them.

The beauty of this participatory culture is that it transforms every game into a co-created experience. When Seattle's "12s" force an opposing quarterback to call a timeout due to crowd noise, or when the entire Texas A&M student body stands ready to serve, they're demonstrating that true excellence isn't about watching something amazing happen—it's about being part of making it happen.

This new faith offers what many seek: community, purpose, passion, and belonging. It unites cities in collective joy and shared suffering. The Steel Curtain dynasty of 1970s Pittsburgh didn't just win championships—it forged a civic identity that endures decades later. The '85 Bears' brief but brilliant reign still inspires Chicago's dreams of glory.

In every living room and sports bar across USAmerica, football has become what church once was—before pulpits and pews turned worshippers into passive listeners. The game restores what Protestant textuality diminished: a fully embodied participation in something larger than ourselves. While modern churchgoers sit quietly to receive the Word, football fans rise up, shout, embrace strangers, and become part of the drama unfolding before them.

> To live in the past is to die in the present.
>
> LEGENDARY COACH BILL BELICHICK
> SIX SUPER BOWL CHAMPIONSHIPS WITH NEW ENGLAND PATRIOTS

The game excites and engages. It offers rest to the weary and purpose to the adrift. It gives people something to believe in. Most crucially, it gives them a way to participate—to be part of the story, not just witnesses to it, much like the medieval faithful who experienced a multi-sensory faith through ritual, feast, and communal celebration rather than passive consumption of propositional content.

The Sports Bar as Fellowship Hall: Sacred Space in the Church of Football

In traditional faith communities, the fellowship hall serves as the heartbeat of community life—a sacred-secular space where Jesus humans share meals, stories, and life's rhythms. Today, this sacred function has found a new home in an unexpected sanctuary: the sports bar.

We see parallels between traditional fellowship halls and sports bars. Instead of potluck dishes, football fans gather around plates of wings and nachos. Coffee and conversation have given way to craft beer and passionate debates about last week's game. Yet, the essential function remains—creating space for communal experiences of the sacred.

When observed through theological lenses, sports bars reveal their profound significance. For fans, the bar is a temple of hope, with screens streaming revelations of truth—modern altars broadcasting moments of transcendence. Patrons aren't mere entertainment consumers but participants in sacred rituals.

Just as traditional fellowship halls strengthen religious communities between formal services, sports bars maintain communion among football faithful between game days. Everyone is a member of a vast congregation gathered to worship, rejoice, or commiserate.

The shared viewing experience creates a collective liturgy: gasps at near-misses, unified roars at touchdowns, and communal laments at defeats.

In a fragmented world, sports bars provide a sense of tribal identity, replacing weakened traditional religious ties. Jerseys are "articles of faith," marking belonging to a particular communion. Conversations are deeply meaningful exchanges about shared passion.

In these spaces, fandom transcends entertainment, becoming a means of activating faith. The sports bar creates space for true believers to pay tribute to heroes and witness miracles.

> My goal: to build a university of which our football team can be proud.
>
> A UNIVERSITY OF OKLAHOMA PRESIDENT[7]

The sports bar completes football's sacred spaces: if stadiums are cathedrals for high holy days, sports bars are fellowship halls where communities maintain bonds, practice rituals, and live out faith between game days.

And so we must ask: In this new USAmerican landscape, how does the ancient institution of the church—and the individual follower of Jesus—compare to this current colossus of the gridiron? What can each learn from the other about building community, inspiring devotion, and touching human hearts? More pointedly, how can the church reclaim its participatory spirit in an age when people no longer want to simply sit and listen, when both congregation and individual disciple yearn not just to witness but to embody their faith? These are the questions we must now explore.

Second Quarter
TACKLING LIFE'S CHALLENGES

Football combines two of the worst things in American life. It is violence punctuated by committee meetings.

COLUMNIST GEORGE WILL[1]

You typically score touchdowns on offense, not defense. Every offense has two key formations: the huddle and the field. But here's a painful truth: imagine an NFL team spending 85 percent of its budget on better huddles—cushioned turf for huddle circles, climate-controlled huddle spaces, professional huddle coordinators, advanced huddle technology—while leaving just pennies for the actual game equipment and field operations.

We'd call that insane. Yet that's exactly what we do in our

churches.

The average church pours 80–90 percent of its resources into maintaining and perfecting the huddle experience—buildings, staff, worship services, internal programs. Only 5–10 percent typically goes to actual field operations, the missional movement of advancing the divine presence in our communities. When we raise extra funds through capital campaigns, over 80 percent goes to upgrading our huddle facilities rather than expanding our field presence.

The huddle is vital. It's where teams strategize, unite, and prepare. But stay in the huddle too long? That's a delay of game penalty. And we're not just taking that penalty, we're investing heavily in making our delayed game more comfortable.

The huddle prepares us, but the field is where we score. Field formation means engaging our communities—serving at food banks, mentoring youth, supporting struggling families, building relationships with neighbors. While we invest heavily in better church programs, our true mission lies in these moments of real-world impact.

Field formation means meeting people where they are, then helping them grow. Like quarterbacks throwing to where receivers will be, we look ahead—seeing not just who people are, but who they could become with God's transforming love.

SECOND QUARTER

Our touchdowns aren't measured in points, but in lives changed. Scripture tells us heaven celebrates when one sinner repents (Luke 15:7). Maybe it's time we got as excited about restored lives as we do about perfecting our huddles. Maybe it's time our budgets reflected where the actual scoring happens: on the field.

It's kickoff time. The question isn't whether to huddle or play. We need both. The question is whether we're willing to put our money where our mission is, or be stuck in an endless huddle while the game clock runs down.

Game V

Breaking Huddle
STEPS OF FAITH

Quarterbacks cannot be wildebeests.
THE WEST COAST OFFENSE ARCHITECT BILL WALSH[1]

On the Serengeti Plains, a deadly drama plays out daily. A wildebeest, sensing danger, stands frozen—a fatal pause as golden predators circle. In that moment of paralysis, the animal seals its fate. Lions strike. Nature takes its course.

In the concrete jungle of the NFL, a similar dance of predator and prey unfolds. But here, where 300-pound defensive linemen stalk their quarry with the same lethal intent as African lions, a quarterback cannot afford such fatal hesitation. As the legendary Bill Walsh knew, the pocket is no place for prey mentality. A quarterback who freezes—even for a heartbeat—under the thundering pressure of an incoming rush might as well paint a target on his back.

The NFL graveyard is filled with talented arms attached to wildebeest hearts—quarterbacks whose careers were measured not in seasons but in snaps, their potential extinguished in that devastating moment of fright between fight and flight. In this league, survival demands more than instinct. It requires ice in the veins, clarity in chaos, and the courage to stand tall as the shadows of predators loom.

Every Sunday morning across USAmerica, millions gather in what might be the world's longest pre-game huddle. Trouble is, some churches have been huddling for decades without ever running a play.

Here is Pastor Len's favorite game-day demonstration. He'll call up a handful of volunteers—his impromptu offensive line, if you will—and watch human nature unfold like a well-worn playbook. First down: They form a circle. Then he asks: How can you make the circle better? Second down: They join hands. Again, he asks: Can you make a better circle? Third down: They squeeze tighter, cozier, safer. It's the spiritual equivalent of a group hug, and who doesn't love a good group hug?

But here's the million-dollar question: When was the last time you saw a football team score from inside a huddle? That's when Pastor Len drops his coaching bomb: "What if you turned around?" Or, "What if you expanded the circle?"

The revelation hits like a quarterback sneak—circles don't have to face inward. In fact, the most powerful circles face both ways, like a wheel with spokes, ready to roll into action. One arm locked with fellow gospellers, the other free to reach out to the world. Now that's what you call a formation!

The early church knew this playbook all too well. After Pentecost, the apostles were perfectly content running practice drills in Jerusalem. It took a full-blown persecution—think of it as divine special teams coverage—to scatter them across Judea and Samaria. Sometimes God's most effective play call is a good old-fashioned blitz.

Take a page from NFL legend Bill Walsh's book. He revolutionized football by seeing where players could be, not just where they were. His West Coast offense wasn't about huddling up—it was about spreading out, creating space, and throwing to spots before receivers even reached them. Joe Montana didn't throw to where Jerry Rice was; he threw to where Jerry Rice was going to be. In a world where everything is moving, you have to get ahead of reality, of where the receiver is, to complete a forward pass.

> It turns out that you cannot really "keep your eye on the ball" after all: skilled athletes anticipate as much as they observe.
>
> BRITISH DEVELOPMENTAL PSYCHOLOGIST SARAH H. NORGATE[2]

Huddle Formation and Field Formation

The huddle may be where we craft our strategy, encourage one another, and pat each other on the back. But eventually we must break formation and put our bodies on the line. Huddle formation is the ministry mode. Field formation is the missional mode. How telling that we invest endless resources in creating grander huddles, when they are merely preludes to the field—where our true mission awaits.

In field formation, players align themselves with purpose, their gaze fixed on distant cross bars. Here, they face the full force of opposition, the raw challenge of forward progress. While the huddle speaks of preparation and inspiration, the field demands action—turning knowledge into motion, and motion into mission.

The huddle reaches inward, gathering strength from

where we are. But the field beckons outward, calling us to where God envisions His people could be. In motion, we don't pass to where receivers stand, but to where they're destined to run. The huddle embraces the present—carpe diem. The field claims the future—carpe mañana.

This is the fundamental lesson of Quarterbacking 101: give your receivers a "lead," anticipating where they'll be, not where they are. Perhaps it's time for the church to embrace this wisdom—to stop playing it safe in the huddle and start leading God's people into tomorrow's end zone.

Church, are we running a static offense or a dynamic one? Is our Jesus a still photograph or a highlight reel? Our ministers are the quarterbacks of faith, reading the defensive formations, but even the greatest QB can't score from a perpetual huddle. Are we giving our people a "lead?"

Remember: The huddle is for calling the play, not playing the game. No one comes to a game to watch the huddles. It's time to break huddle, get into formation, and move downfield. After all, you can't spell "touchdown" without an internal "ouch" and an external "move."

Alonzo Smith "Jake" Gaither (1903–1994), legendary Florida A&M (FAMU) coach from 1945 to 1969, was a transformative figure who used football as a platform to advance social change. He trained his players to be "mobile, agile, hostile." Jesus wants his players to be mobile, agile, hospitable, not sterile, puerile, and senile. We write these words with the ache of someone who loves the church too much to watch it remain in an endless huddle when it was designed for the open field.

Conventional wisdom often produces conventional results.

MALCOLM FORBES AS QUOTED BY REVOLUTIONARY NFL COACH BILL WALSH WHO TRANSFORMED SAN FRANCISCO 49ERS INTO A DYNASTY

GAME TIME DECISION: YOUR DREAM SEASON

Allow us a hypothetical: You've got two different tickets in your hand, but you can only choose one destination.

Behind Door #1: Your NFL team just landed their dream quarterback—we're talking a generational talent who could make your Sundays electric for years to come. Multiple Super Bowl rings are practically glinting on the horizon.

Behind Door #2: There's this incredible church that's absolutely crushing it. The pastor's a natural leader who knows how to build up their team. Every Sunday the place is humming with energy—kids laughing in dynamic youth programs, life-changing outreach happening locally and globally, and a real sense that lives are being transformed.

Tough call, right? But here's where it gets interesting ...

A PLAYBOOK FOR FAITH IN MOTION

No football team could get away with running plays from 1985 against today's athletes. The result? Not just defeat—obliteration. Yet some people of faith, and faith communities cling to decades-old playbooks, wondering why they're losing ground in today's missional arena.

Let's cut to the heart of it: When was the last time you or your church broke formation? Really changed things up, not just moved worship outdoors, but stepped out of your personal comfort zone to serve in ways that scared you? When did you last let young leaders redesign a service, or better yet, when did you last let someone younger disciple you?

Are your young disciples warming the bench, or are they calling plays on key committees? Look around your leadership meetings. Are there voices under thirty shaping church vision? And personally, are you still playing the same spiritual position you've held for years, or are you learning new ways to follow Jesus?

Is your digital ministry still running on spiritual dial-up while your community streams at 5G? Does your church's idea of online presence stop at recording Sunday sermons? How about you? Are you connecting with other believers only inside church walls, or are you finding ways to build authentic Christian community throughout your week?

When did your congregation last dare to audible out of comfortable traditions into holy innovation? Have you tried new ways to serve your neighbors? And in your own walk with Christ, when did you last call an audible on your routine devotional habits or predictable patterns of service?

In football, there's no such thing as standing still—you're either driving downfield or getting driven back. The same truth echoes through sanctuary walls. The most vibrant churches, like championship teams, aren't just playing to survive—they're playing to break through, to glorify. They understand that God's playbook isn't carved in stone but written fresh each morning in the dew of divine mercy.

> Football is like life—it requires perseverance, self-denial, hard work, sacrifice, dedication, and respect for authority.
>
> VINCE LOMBARDI

But here's the harder truth: Across USAmerica, too many congregations have mastered what we might call the "eternal huddle"—that comfortable circle of familiar faces that's become not just a strategy session but a final destination. We've turned our huddles into bunkers, our preparation into procrastination.

Even the early church wasn't immune to this tendency. There is a revealing moment in Acts 8:1 (RSV):

> And on that day a great persecution arose against the church in Jerusalem; and they were all scattered throughout the region of Judea and Samaria, except the apostles.

Notice those last three words: "except the apostles." The apostles do not wish to leave the safety of their huddle. The apostles do not wish to "Go," the first word of Jesus' Great Commission. Even these apostolic giants, these first-round draft picks of the kingdom, had to be blitzed out of their comfort zone so they could hurdle the huddle. It took persecution—God's ultimate audible—to scatter the seed of the gospel beyond Jerusalem's walls.

So the question isn't just whether to choose between tradition and innovation. The real question burns deeper: Are you playing to advance in mission, or are you stuck in an endless huddle? Are your church's strategies designed to score touchdowns in eternity, or are you just trying to protect your home field?

Remember: In football, forward progress isn't just preferred—it's required. The game itself demands advancement. Why should we expect less from the greatest mission ever entrusted to humanity?

What's your next play going to be?

There are thirty-four quarterbacks in the NFL Hall of Fame (as of December 2024). Surprisingly, only four of them were #1 overall draft picks: Terry Bradshaw (1970 draft), John Elway (1983 draft), Troy Aikman (1989 draft), Peyton Manning (1998 draft).

Initial expectations and labels don't determine ultimate success on the gridiron of life. Many of the greatest quarterbacks weren't seen as the "best" prospects coming out of college, yet through dedication, development, and seizing opportunities, they achieved football immortality.

Our starting point doesn't define our potential for greatness.

DELAY OF GAME

In football, a team that lingers too long in the huddle faces a five-yard penalty, pushing them backward. Perhaps this offers a telling parallel to the church's current predicament. Many congregations seem almost to prefer this backward motion, yearning for the perceived safety of yesteryear, where change and challenge feel less threatening. "Delay of game" isn't just a penalty in football—it has too often become the church's defining stance.

But while a football team loses mere yards for such delays, the church faces far graver consequences: locked doors, shuttered windows, and "For Sale" signs on once-sacred ground.

This is no mere hypothetical. Each year, 4,000 churches across the United States write this ending to their story. Since 2010, this decline has accelerated, with church closures far outpacing new openings—a trend that COVID-19 only intensified. The mathematics of decline tell a stark story: just as we lose 1 percent of our churches annually, we lose 1 percent of those who self-identify as Christian. From 2010 to 2023, the percentage of USAmericans identifying as Christian plummeted from 77 percent to 64 percent—an unprecedented exodus in U.S. religious history.

It is time for the church to learn from the back-to-basics coaching philosophy of Vince Lombardi. One of his most famous moments came in 1961, when he stood before his Green Bay Packers team after a disappointing loss and began with the now-legendary line: "Gentlemen, this is a football." He would then proceed to teach the absolute fundamentals of the game to his professional players.

Church: this is a football. You don't leave the world to do church. You enter the world to be church. This is what being church in the world looks like. Here's how to know you are doing it vs. merely thinking you are doing it.

> God has battle tested me. I have the armor of God on me....
> I am blessed enough to wake up every day and to walk, to talk, to smell, to interact with people, and to play football.
>
> HOUSTON TEXANS QB AND PK C. J. STROUD[3]

SEMIOTIC BREAKDOWNS

But here lies the great paradox: How did an institution centered on history's most compelling figure become so utterly uncompelling? Jesus of Nazareth—the most influential person who ever lived—was a master of narrative, healing, and transfiguration. He was creativity incarnate. The Bible, His story, stands as Western civilization's foundational text, filled with humanity's greatest stories.

Yet somehow, congregants can occupy the same pew for decades while remaining virtually untouched by and illiterate in these revolutionary narratives. To borrow an expression from Kurt Vonnegut, "time quakes"[4] occur all too frequently in church pews when bored worshippers cannot keep their eyes open, the misery of tedium having so gripped them that they probably could not recall the intended message of that day's sermon even if their own lives depended upon it.

The huddle exists to call the next play, not to become the play itself. When we mistake communion for action, fellowship for mission, we risk turning the church into another social club—comfortable, perhaps, even spiritually nurturing—but falling far short of its divine calling to save the world.

Yet Sunday after Sunday, the cosmic drama of salvation shrinks to polite recitations and/or political incantations, as congregants sit in time-worn grooves of their pews, their spirits as unmoved as the hardwood beneath them. These revolutionary stories—which once inspired peasants to challenge kings and slaves to claim their freedom—now serve as little more than comforting background noise.

> God's blessed us very much. He gave us all the talents to be able to get here, so first and foremost, thanks to Him.... Thank God, thank you Jesus.
>
> PHILADELPHIA EAGLES COACH NICK SIRIANNI PRAISES GOD AFTER WINNING SUPER BOWL LIX.[5]

Where Sunday Morning Meets Sunday Afternoon

This is more than a hypothetical. It's Super Bowl Sunday. Two gatherings beckon:

- Behind Door #1: Wooden pews and familiar hymns

- Behind Door #2: The roar of 70,000 fans, electrifying plays, and a halftime show that'll be talked about for weeks.

Let's be honest—where would most people rather be?

Football has mastered what many churches have forgotten or haven't yet learned: the ritual art of creating EPIC community through shared experience. Every Sunday, millions flock to their TV-side sanctuaries, donning team colors like vestments, breaking bread/wine over nachos and beer, and witnessing moments of near-miraculous athletic grace. Meanwhile, many churches stick to their well-worn playbook, wondering why the stands—er, pews—aren't as full as they used to be.

The NFL, for all its flaws and controversies, has cracked a code that churches might do well to study. Rather than clutching our pearls about "misplaced priorities," what if we asked some tough questions:

- What makes football so magnetic while some

services feel mechanical?

- How does the NFL create such passionate communities while many congregations struggle to keep members engaged?

- Instead of dismissing Super Bowl Sunday as just another competitor for souls, what lessons could we learn from its ability to unite people across every demographic imaginable?

This isn't about condemning either institution. It's about acknowledging an uncomfortable truth: when given a straight-up choice between church and the Super Bowl, most USAmericans are voting with their remotes—and their hearts. Instead of wagging fingers, perhaps it's time for some divine inspiration from an unlikely source.

The question isn't whether football has become USAmerica's new civil religion (your authors think it has). The question is: what can the original keepers of the faith learn from this spectacular phenomenon?

GAME VI

RESILIENT ROOTS

THE ENDURING TRIUMPH OF FAITH AND FOOTBALL

> As I turned to survey the Coliseum, maybe for my last time, I felt the power and exhilaration of professional football. The world's fastest, strongest, toughest men facing off in collision combat inside the country's largest stadiums, packed to the limit with rabid fans. This is one hell of a great sport. It will never die.
>
> "HOLLYWOOD'S DOCTOR" ROB HUIZENGA, M.D.[1]

Your authors have two filing cabinets in two different offices. In one, Len methodically archives headlines declaring "The Death of Christianity." In the other, Chris collects obituaries for USAmerica's beloved NFL. Both collections grow thicker by the day, and both tell the same story—not of decline, but of resilience.

The Christian Church stands like an ancient redwood, its roots reaching deep into two millennia of human history. From the moment Jesus' disciples first stumbled and doubted, through centuries of storms that threatened to uproot it, this tree has not just survived—it has flourished. The French Revolutionaries sharpened their axes, Voltaire wielded his razor-sharp wit, and Marx declared it the "opium of the masses."[2] Nietzsche proclaimed God dead, while totalitarian regimes—from Hitler's Third Reich to Stalin's Soviet empire—tried to salt the earth where faith grew. Yet here stands the Church, its branches reaching ever skyward.

At its heart lies the ultimate paradox: the Cross—a tree stripped bare, tortured, and transformed. Like a seed that must die to bring forth life, this instrument of execution was meant to end a movement. Instead, it became an eternal wellspring. Every attempt to destroy it only proves its supernatural resilience. Cut it down, and new shoots spring forth. Burn it, and its ashes nurture fresh growth. Strip it bare, and it bursts with new life. In the divine economy, death becomes the source of life, and endings birth new beginnings. Jesus comes robed in paradox. Christianity wraps orthodoxy in the folds of paradox.

The cross is no mere symbol but a living reality that repeats itself through history: the more the Church is persecuted, the more it flourishes; the more it's stripped bare, the more abundantly it bears fruit.

Today's challengers arrive wearing lab coats instead of cloaks, brandishing bestsellers instead of swords. The New Atheists—Harris, Dawkins, Dennett—stride onto television screens and TED Talk stages, promising to finally disprove divinity and root our religion through pure reason.[3] Bill Maher launches his witty salvos from behind his HBO desk, expositing his brand of politics and espousing his sacrament of choice, marijuana.

A meaningless pile of ashes is what atheism inevitably leaves in its wake. Jesus, the bread of heaven, the vine of life, the living water, the light of the world, leaves in his wake sumptuous and scrumptious food and guiding light.

Yet all atheism, whether in its old-style or old-boys guise, faces three immutable truths.

First, atheism has no story to tell other than the story of "what you don't know doesn't exist." The only narratives it can come up with rely on the absence of evidence rather than affirmative proof. This is perhaps the Achilles' hell [sic] of atheism: its failure of imagination. The gospel story is that, despite everything, life is a gift. Atheists believe that life is a case of "just thereness," and there is no story to "just thereness."[4]

Second, atheistic arguments often presuppose the religious concepts they seek to refute. By defining itself in contrast to religious beliefs, atheism thereby inherits its theological framework. Psychologist Martin Seligman posed a question to philosopher Robert Wright on why he was moving toward Buddhism: "I thought you were a nonbeliever." Wright replied, "I was. I've never been able to choke down the idea of a supernatural God who stands outside of time, a God who designs and creates the universe. As much as I wanted to, I've never been able to believe there was meaning in life beyond what we choose to adopt for ourselves. But I'm beginning to think I was wrong."[5]

Third, human beings are hardwired for transcendence. As fast as they work to dismantle traditional faith, atheists inadvertently create their own secular religions, complete with prophets, dogmas, and absolute truths. Even Albert Camus, who rejected both religion and atheism in embracing "lucid indifference" to the question of God's existence, essentially summed up his own stance in absurdism's double negative: I do not believe in God and I am not an atheist.[6] Atheists fashion gods in their own image, and when they disappoint, they dethrone them—only to build new altars to different ideals that better match their hopes and dreams. These new altars—reason, science, humanity, progress—are treated with the same reverence once reserved to God.

When you cut down one altar, another rises in its place. The human heart, it seems, cannot bear a heaven stripped of meaning. The void will always be filled—if not with God, then with gods of our own making. This is why the Church, like the NFL, endures despite every prediction of its demise. They both satisfy something essential in the human spirit: our need for community, meaning, and moments that lift us beyond ourselves.

Even Oxford evolutionary biologist, ethologist, and evangelist for atheism Richard Dawkins, who calls the Bible Belt states in the U.S. "the reptilian brain of southern and middle USAmerica" in contrast to "the country's cerebral cortex to the north and down the coasts,"[7] gave these last words while proclaiming his atheism in the *Time Magazine* cover article on "God vs. Science:"

> If there is a God, it's going to be a whole lot bigger and a whole lot more incomprehensible than any theologian of any religion has ever proposed.[8]

Bingo! Or to cite the words of the brother of Jesus and the first Bishop of Jerusalem, "Let all mortal flesh keep silence."[9] The hymn's call for silence isn't demanding we never speak, but teaching us where true speech begins—in the fertile soil of holy stillness and humility.

The critics will keep writing their epitaphs, and we keep filing them away. Meanwhile, on Sundays, millions will still gather—some in pews, others in bleachers, some in homes around tables, some in homes in front of screens—seeking something larger than themselves, a reminder that in both divine and human stories, what appears to be an ending often proves to be just another beginning.

> How much boundlessly stupid naivete is there in the scholar's belief in his superiority, in the good conscience of his tolerance, in the simple, unsuspecting certainty with which his instincts treat the religious man as inferior and a lower type which he himself evolved above and beyond.
>
> FRIEDRICH NIETZSCHE, WHO HATED CHRISTIANITY, BUT WHO HATED ACADEMIC SMUGNESS EVEN MORE[10]

Through it all, ironically, Jesus' name is music and magic to even non-Christians in ways that many cultural commentators can neither understand nor adequately explain. Ahistorical fiction such as *The DaVinci Code*,[11] which presents the church and Christian history in a false and unfavorable light, was a wild best seller which became a cultural phenomenon and substitute "easy reading bible" for the tragically misinformed because it sought to alter the life story of an historical person of immense popularity—Jesus. As George Beverly Shea used to sing so beautifully on the Billy Graham crusades, in one of his three signature songs, "there's something about that name."[12]

In ancient pagan societies, and in much of paganism today, the individual was subordinate to the collective. The Christian emphasis on individual worth—including concepts like individual salvation, personal relationship with God, and inherent human dignity regardless of social status—represented a significant philosophical and theological shift from these earlier pagan worldviews.

Despite living in a brutal and corrupted world marred by various forms of prostituted principles—where press prostitutes ("presstitutes") distort truth, computational prostitutes manipulate data, institutional prostitutes prioritize power, substitute prostitutes spread falsehoods, political prostitutes abuse authority, prosecutorial prostitutes undermine justice, clerical prostitutes betray sacred trust, educational prostitutes manipulate curriculum for power and propaganda, medical prostitutes prescribe for greed, financial prostitutes trade ethics for gold and influence, ecological prostitutes sacrifice tomorrow's future for today's gain, and academic prostitutes trade academic freedom for political agendas—Christianity affirms that each person and place is loved and cherished by God

No earthly power, no matter how mighty, can extinguish the eternal flame of God's Word. Though human vessels may falter and fracture, Christianity's divine essence remains undiminished. Jesus transcends time itself, his presence an immovable cornerstone of human history. Prayer moves through the cosmos with a force beyond our comprehension, bending reality in ways science cannot measure. And when the powers and principalities of this world gather, the sword of the spirit cuts through deception with surgical precision, a divine blade against which no evil can stand.

> So when I'm down and at the half, honestly, I'm just thinking, "all right God, you've taken me here, and win or lose, I'm going to glorify you." That's my peace, that's the joy, that's the steadfastness, that's where I get it from. And that's the honest truth.
>
> 49ERS QB BROCK PURDY AFTER BRINGING HIS TEAM BACK FROM A 17-POINT DEFICIT IN THE SECOND HALF OF A PLAYOFF WIN OVER THE DETROIT LIONS[13]

FOOTBALL WITHOUT END, AMEN?

A chorus of voices, from Malcolm Gladwell, in the early 2010s, to Dr. Bennet Omalu of "Concussion" fame, to George Will, the conservative columnist, to Daniel Engber's columns in *Slate*, has sounded the death knell for the NFL. They ring hollow. While highly intelligent observers like Bob Costas sound dire warnings about football's future—citing mounting evidence that the sport "quite literally destroys brains"—they've joined an unlikely chorus of doomsayers who might as well be predicting the end times. Their predictions, however well-intentioned, dramatically underestimate the league's cultural resonance and relevance.

Even as concussion concerns mounted and controversy swirled during the 2016–17 season, the NFL's gravitational pull on USAmerican culture has only strengthened over the decades since the legendary 1958 Colts-Giants championship game. The league's most remarkable conquest? The other half of the population. Women, once considered peripheral to the sport, now comprise a staggering 45 percent of the NFL's fan base—a seismic shift from just twenty-five years ago.

The NFL's cultural entrenchment runs deeper than viewership statistics or merchandise sales. It has woven itself into the fabric of USAmerican life with a durability that makes predictions of its demise seem not just premature, but almost comically naive. The league's financial and cultural reserves aren't just healthy—they're fortress-like.

Challenges to the Game

The NFL's seemingly impregnable fortress faces two formidable self-inflicted assaults: a crisis of violence off the field and a growing awareness of devastating violence within the game itself. These dual challenges strike at the heart of the league's legitimacy and its future.

> All is not well, but all is not lost.
> FOOTBALL HISTORIANS ERIC A. MOYEN AND JOHN R. THELIN[14]

We pause for a moment to tell a New Jersey story in which both your authors participated. In 1990, after completing two terms in office as Governor of New Jersey, Thomas Kean became president of Drew University in Madison, New Jersey. In 1994 Len began working in the hallowed halls of Drew University, where he served as Dean and Vice-President of Academic Affairs under President Thomas Kean. Chris studied in the hallowed halls of Rutgers Law School-Newark, where among the echoes of legal discourse and the weight of jurisprudence at Rutgers, there walked a giant. Professor Alfred Slocum, fresh from his tenure as Public Advocate under Governor Thomas Kean's administration, commanded the classroom with an intensity that sent ripples through the student body. For Chris, crossing the threshold into Slocum's classroom meant entering an arena where mediocrity withered and excellence was the only currency accepted.

Like Professor Kingsfield from *The Paper Chase*, Slocum

wielded the Socratic method like a master swordsman, his questions precise and penetrating, cutting through the fog of uncertain knowledge to reveal the sharp edges of truth. But unlike the fictional character, Slocum's mastery was forged in the real-world crucible of civil rights law, where he had carved his legacy as a pioneer in the fight for justice.

It was during the tumultuous period of the O. J. Simpson murder trial when Chris found himself in Slocum's civil rights class. The nation was transfixed by the daily drama unfolding in that Los Angeles courtroom, but within the walls of Rutgers, Slocum offered a different perspective—one born from decades of observing human nature at its most volatile.

One day, as discussions of the trial and Simpson's football career swirled through the classroom, Slocum fell silent. The usual rapid-fire exchanges ceased. Then, with the gravity of someone who had witnessed the darkest corners of human behavior, he delivered words that would echo through time: "When you see someone with that level of violence in their lives, you walk to the other side of the street."

In that moment, the professor wasn't just teaching law. He was imparting wisdom that transcended legal theory, speaking not as an academic but as a guardian warning his charges about the realities that lay beyond the safety of classroom walls.

THE DOMESTIC VIOLENCE CRISIS

In 2014, the NFL's carefully cultivated image imploded when surveillance footage captured star running back Ray Rice knocking his fiancée unconscious in an elevator. Commissioner Roger Goodell's initial response—a mere two-game suspension—sparked national outrage. The fury intensified when Minnesota Vikings' Adrian Peterson faced child abuse charges for beating his four-year-old son with a tree branch. These weren't isolated incidents but rather high-profile examples of a deeper problem plaguing the league.

The NFL held its breath, particularly concerned about its hard-won female fan base—now 45 percent of its total audience. The league's tepid response to domestic violence seemed poised to alienate this crucial demographic. Yet remarkably, female viewership remained steady.[15] This resilience revealed an uncomfortable truth: fans' emotional investment in the game apparently outweighed their moral objections to the league's handling of violence off the field.

THE GATHERING STORM: VIOLENCE, CTE AND BRAIN TRAUMA

While the domestic violence crisis tested the NFL's public

relations machinery, a more existential threat looms: mounting evidence that football itself is so violent that it causes catastrophic brain damage. Your authors have already been criticized for even writing this book on the basis that the gospel should never be associated with such a violent sport in the first place.

Malcolm Gladwell has become the voice of those who denounce USAmerican football as a moral abomination.[16] Gladwell's core argument is that football, particularly at the professional level, is ethically problematic because it knowingly exposes players to severe health risks. The 2015 film *Concussion* thrust chronic traumatic encephalopathy (CTE) into public consciousness, but the real story lies in the growing list of football legends destroyed by the disease.

A toll of hall-of-famers and stars is revealing:

- Ken Stabler, the Raiders' "Snake," whose autopsy revealed a brain ravaged by CTE.
- Mike Webster, the Steelers' ironman center, who died homeless and disoriented at fifty.
- Junior Seau, who shot himself in the chest at forty-three, specifically preserving his brain for CTE research.
- Dave Duerson, the Bears' defensive anchor, who followed the same tragic script as Seau.
- Frank Gifford, whose CTE diagnosis posthumously

confirmed what many suspected.

- Andre Waters, Bubba Smith, and a tragically expanding roster of others.[17]

The NFL's initial response—years of denial and obfuscation—has only amplified the scandal. Critics like Bob Costas aren't merely questioning the league's policies; they're questioning its fundamental sustainability. Their argument is simple and devastating: a sport that "quite literally destroys brains" cannot maintain its cultural dominance in an increasingly health-conscious society.

Yet here too, fan loyalty seems to trump mounting evidence. Parents may be steering their children away from football—youth participation has declined significantly—but the NFL's television ratings and revenue continue to surge. The league has implemented rule changes and concussion protocols, but these measures raise another question: Can football be made safe without fundamentally altering what draws fans to the game?

The NFL now walks a precarious tightrope. It must somehow reconcile its violent essence with growing awareness of its consequences, both on and off the field.[18] Its success in threading this needle—or failure to do so—may well determine whether future generations view football as USAmerica's favorite sport or as a cautionary tale about the price of gladiatorial entertainment.

THE TRUE COST OF GLORY: LIFE AFTER THE NFL

The spotlight blinds us to a brutal truth: NFL careers don't end with a final whistle—they exact a lifelong toll. Former Super Bowl-winning coach Brian Billick captures this reality with haunting clarity: "Paying the price isn't just a slogan in pro football; the game clearly takes years off the lives of the men who play it, and to see these glorious athletes, so strong and seemingly indestructible in their primes, reduced to crippled shells in their forties and fifties is to understand what they have sacrificed to play the sport."[19]

Beyond Concussions: The Total Physical Toll: While concussions dominate headlines, they represent just one chapter in a broader story of bodily destruction. Former players navigate life with:

- Chronic joint pain from multiple surgeries
- Degenerative arthritis in their thirties
- Permanent nerve damage
- Mobility issues that transform simple tasks into daily challenges
- Addiction to painkillers that often begins during their playing days
- Cardiovascular problems from maintaining playing weight

The Psychological Battlefield: Perhaps even more insidious than the physical toll is the psychological warfare that begins the moment a player leaves the field. Former NFL quarterback Vince Evans draws a striking parallel: "It's like being a Vietnam vet. You go in and it's such a different world, and all of a sudden you come home and you're expected to be normal and you're not normal. You've been treated differently all along and now you're just supposed to fit in and you don't know how to fit in."[20]

This comparison isn't mere hyperbole. NFL players face a form of cultural whiplash as they transition from:

- Adoration to anonymity
- Structured intensity to unstructured routine
- Clear purpose to uncertain identity
- Team solidarity to individual survival
- Instant feedback to long-term ambiguity

What Paul Brown and Chuck Noll diplomatically called a player's "life's work" after their careers are over often becomes a desperate search for meaning and relevance in a world that no longer revolves around Friday Night Lights, Game Days, and Fundays. It has been said that professional football players suffer two deaths, the first when their playing careers are over.

Breaking the Cycle: A Generation Says, "No"

Witnessing this carnage firsthand, a growing chorus of NFL veterans now actively discourage their children from following in their cleated footsteps. This isn't mere paranoia—it's informed protest from those who've lived the true cost of the game.[21]

Yet some observers have leaped to an improbable conclusion: that this parental intervention will eventually starve the NFL of talent. Such predictions fundamentally misunderstand both human nature and social dynamics. Yes, some elite athletes may choose safer paths. Yes, middle-class parents might steer their children toward soccer or basketball. But as long as football offers a potential escape from poverty, as long as it promises glory and generational wealth, as long as it remains USAmerica's most dramatic stage, there will be young men willing to roll the dice with their future health.

Meditation on Mortality: Yet we must pause here to acknowledge an uncomfortable truth: all careers exact their toll. The "rolling of the dice" with future health isn't unique to football—it's inherent in human endeavor.

- The lawyer or professor whose sedentary life of reading and writing invites cardiovascular disease and metabolic disorders.

- The traveling executive or speaker logging millions of air miles, absorbing radiation exposure and disrupting circadian rhythms.
- The construction worker's joints and spine.
- The firefighter's respiratory system.
- The surgeon's stress-laden cardiovascular system.
- The night shift worker's shortened life expectancy.
- The coal miner's lungs.
- The professional driver's back and kidney problems.

What distinguishes football isn't the mere presence of risk—it's the certainty and severity of the damage. While other professions may plant the seeds of future health problems, football guarantees a harvest of pain. The question isn't whether injury will occur, but when and how severely.

But once again, that's the question of life itself. No one gets out of life alive. We're all killing ourselves, just at different speeds. "Committed suicide?" Strike that tired phrase. Death isn't a crime—it's our constant companion, and we're all accomplices in our own endings. Some of us sprint toward the exit, others take the scenic route, but we're all on the same roller coaster ride to eternity.

The genetic lottery spins its wheel, and we emerge: unwitting players in existence's grand carnival. Some of us begin the ride already leaning toward tomorrow's promise, while others grip the safety bar with white-knuckled uncertainty. Each rotation brings its choice—to lean into the spin or pull away, to embrace the dizzying dance or seek solid ground. In this way, our every action becomes a quiet ballot cast for or against prolonging our turn on life's bumper cars.

Survival is just suicide in slow motion. Watch us: flipping off death with every cigarette, every oversized portion, every skipped checkup. Some poison themselves with sugar, drowning their cells in sweet destruction. Others pickle their organs in alcohol, or let their muscles wither on the couch, remote in hand, as life ticks away in hour increments.

The question isn't if we're self-destructing—it's how we choose our poison. Fast or slow? Pleasure or neglect? A spectacular blaze of ashes or a quiet fade of dust? We're all giving death the finger. The only difference is how long we hold it up.

A Bottomless Well? The pipeline of talent may narrow, but it won't run dry. The NFL's talent pool won't evaporate—it will simply shift, perhaps drawing even more heavily from communities where the potential rewards of football seem to outweigh its documented risks. This isn't speculation; it's the pattern we've already seen in boxing, where middle-class flight hasn't ended the sport but has changed its demographics.

The real question isn't whether the NFL will find enough players. It's whether we, as a society, are comfortable with who those players will increasingly be, and what that says about our collective values. The game will continue. But its future may force us to confront uncomfortable truths about who pays the physical price for our delight and entertainment.

> As you get older, you slow down and the infielders back up because they've more time to throw you out at first. At the same time, you lose a little power so the outfielders move in because you aren't hitting the ball so far. When those two groups can shake hands it's time to retire.
>
> PAUL WANER, HALL OF FAME OUTFIELDER FOR THE PITTSBURGH PIRATES (1926-1940)

The NFL's Safety Net: Promises vs. Reality: The NFL's post-career care system presents a study in contrasts between public promises and private struggles. The league's primary support mechanisms include:

1) The NFL Player Care Foundation. Established in 2007, this organization offers assistance with: medical screening

programs; joint replacement surgery; prescription drug coverage; financial assistance for crisis situations; and mental health resources.

Yet former players often describe a byzantine bureaucracy that makes accessing these benefits feel like running a gauntlet. The application process for disability benefits is notoriously complex, with many players reporting denials for seemingly valid claims.

2) The 88 Plan. Named for Hall of Famer John Mackey (No. 88), who suffered from dementia, this program provides up to $130,000 annually for institutional care or $118,000 for in-home care for former players with dementia, ALS, or Parkinson's disease. While crucial, the plan's existence acknowledges the devastating neurological toll of the sport.

3) The NFL Pension Plan. Recent collective bargaining agreements have improved pension benefits, but they remain inadequate for many: Players who retired before 1993 receive significantly less than contemporary players. The "vesting" requirement of three credited seasons (recently reduced from four) still leaves many short-career players without coverage. Monthly payments often fail to cover the extensive medical care needed for football-related injuries.

4) The Health Reimbursement Account: Active players can set aside money tax-free for future medical expenses, with

the NFL matching contributions. Yet, the program requires proactive planning during playing days. Many young players, feeling invincible, don't maximize this benefit. The accounts can be depleted quickly given the cost of ongoing care

5) The NFL's Concussion Settlement. The league's $1 billion concussion settlement, while substantial, has faced criticism for: Complex qualifying requirements; the use of "race-norming" in cognitive testing (now discontinued after public outcry); delays in processing claims; exclusion of current players and future diagnoses; the requirement that players prove their conditions are specifically football-related

THE GAP BETWEEN SUPPORT AND NEED

The fundamental problem isn't just the adequacy of benefits—it's their accessibility. Former players describe a system that seems designed to frustrate rather than facilitate care.

There is the documentation challenge: Players must prove their current conditions stem directly from NFL play. Many teams' medical records from earlier eras are incomplete or missing. The burden of proof falls heavily on already-struggling former players.

There is the timing paradox: Many football-related health issues manifest years after retirement. Some benefits have strict time limits for filing claims. Players often don't recognize problems until it's too late to qualify for help.

There is the Knowledge Gap: Many players leave the game without understanding their benefits. The complexity of the system requires legal help many can't afford. Information about available programs isn't always effectively communicated.

There are the coverage holes: Dental problems from playing days often aren't covered. Mental health support remains insufficient. Pain management programs rarely address existing addictions developed during playing careers.

The NFL's response to these criticisms typically emphasizes the billions spent on player benefits. Yet this focus on total spending obscures the individual reality: former players still regularly face bankruptcy from medical bills, struggle to receive approved benefits, and often rely on charity from fellow players or outside organizations.

This gap between the NFL's touted support systems and the lived experience of former players reveals a deeper truth: the league's post-career care policies seem designed more for public relations than for comprehensive care. Until this changes, the true cost of football glory will continue to be borne primarily by the players themselves, long after the crowds have stopped cheering.

Communities like Orcas Island (WA), where Len lives, or Califon (NJ), where Chris lives, may opt out of football due to safety concerns. However, the NFL will remain unaffected. Historically, its talent pool hasn't come from better-off areas but from hardscrapple regions with grittier backgrounds, like Len's hometown in upstate New York (Gloversville) and his mother's home territory of West Virginia's Appalachian Mountains—where Len didn't grow up but spent a lot of time and always felt he was from in his heart.

Places like Texas and Pennsylvania are hotbeds of passionate football talent. Young athletes from these regions are driven to succeed, seeking fame, accomplishment, and recognition. They're fueled by determination and a desire for celebrity, wealth, and social status. No medical study or external concern will dampen their aspirations.

Attempts by the chattering classes to restrict football participation will face fierce grassroots resistance, particularly from those with skin in the game. People inherently resist external control, regardless of good intentions and sound arguments. This phenomenon transcends football, reflecting humanity's innate desire for autonomy.

The history of professional football leagues demonstrates why predictions of the NFL's demise are premature. While only the American Football League (AFL) achieved true success by forcing a merger with the NFL—demonstrated by the Jets' and Chiefs' Super Bowl victories—numerous other leagues have emerged and failed, including the AAFC, WFL, USFL, XFL, and UFL. The All-America Football Conference (AAFC) nominally merged with the NFL in 1949, but this so-called merger was more of a convenient absorption of the most prosperous teams in an otherwise struggling, feast-or-famine league, most notably Paul Brown's then perennial dominant Cleveland Browns (oh, how times have changed!).[22]

The CFL and Arena Football have survived but only in niche positions. What these leagues consistently proved is the inexhaustible supply of talented athletes eager to play professional football.

Here are some examples:

- Nick Buoniconti, initially overlooked by the NFL, started in the AFL and became a Hall of Famer who led the Dolphins' "no name defense" to the league's only perfect season[23]
- Len Dawson and George Blanda became NFL legends after getting their starts in the AFL
- Kurt Warner rose from the Arena Football League to lead two NFL franchises to Super Bowls. Without the Arena Football League and NFL Europe, the NFL's since abandoned developmental league,[24] Kurt Warner, a devout Christian and NFL Hall of

Famer, would have never led the St. Louis Rams' high-powered "Greatest Show on Turf" team to two Super Bowls and the upstart Arizona Cardinals to their first Super Bowl.

When you consider all the collegiate leagues in the U.S., there are almost 87,000 college students who play football every year (73,712[NCAA] + 6,000[NAIA] + 7,000[NJCAA] = 86,712 players). This deep talent pool was evidenced during the 1987 NFL strike, when owners quickly assembled entire replacement teams from eager candidates. For every athlete who might choose another sport due to concussion risks, there exists a vast reservoir of qualified replacements—undrafted college players, practice squad members, and athletes from smaller programs who weren't invited to the NFL Combine.

Another indicator of the growing appeal of the NFL is that Netflix, which once said it would never "go live" and stay on the streaming sports sideline, is now livestreaming the NFL in its Christmas line-up, as well as World Wrestling Entertainment Raw (WWE).[25] It would not surprise us to see a European Super Bowl in our lifetime.

While players now have greater awareness of long-term health risks (as exemplified by Buoniconti's later decision to donate his brain for CTE research), the allure of professional football's fame, fortune, and glory remains powerfully compelling. The combination of limited roster spots and an overwhelming number of capable, willing players ensures the NFL's sustainable future, regardless of growing safety concerns.

FOOTBALL AND POLITICAL CONTROVERSIES: THE INTERSECTION OF SPORT AND CIVIL RELIGION

The NFL once represented rare common ground in USAmerica's fragmented cultural landscape, as Michael MacCambridge noted in his magisterial *America's Game* (2005).[26] This unity, however, faced unprecedented challenges beginning in 2016 with the emergence of national anthem protests.

The national anthem has long held quasi-religious significance at sporting events, with performances scrutinized as rigorously as choirs or praise teams in church. While some renditions have achieved iconic status—like Whitney Houston's Super Bowl XXV performance—others have drawn criticism for perceived irreverence or poor execution.

The 2016 NFL season marked a turning point, with the league experiencing its first significant ratings decline in recent memory. While analysts cited various factors—from excessive penalties to concerns about domestic violence—one new variable stood out: Colin Kaepernick's decision to kneel during the national anthem to protest racial injustice. This act sparked intense controversy, drawing both passionate support and fierce criticism.

The intensity of this reaction needs to be understood through the lens of USAmerican civil religion—the reverence for national symbols, monuments, and historical figures that forms a civil religion that parallels the dominant traditional, faith religion. Just as USAmerica has its symbolic "trinity" (increasingly a quaternity) of Washington (Father), Lincoln (Son), and Kennedy/King (Spirit), complete with architectural shrines in Washington, D.C., that match their place in the Trinity (obelisk, temple, fire/water), it maintains deep emotional investment in patriotic rituals like the national anthem. Super Bowl half time has replaced the Fourth of July as the primary worship experience for USAmerican civil religion.

This controversy highlights the complex intersection between traditional faith, civil religion, and social justice. It raises fundamental questions about when and how to speak out against perceived injustice, and how to navigate conflicts between religious conviction and civic obligation—questions that resist easy answers even in civil discourse.

From Bell to Well: USAmerica's Great Divide

For generations, USAmerica resembled a Bell Curve society—a robust middle class flanked by modest extremes, like a comfortable hammock cradling the American Dream. Today, that curve has inverted into what Daniel Pink calls a "Well Curve," where the middle ground erodes like sand through an hourglass, leaving us with huge ends and weak middles.

This polarization plays out in fascinating microcosm within USAmerica's houses of worship, where Old Glory itself becomes a battlefield in the war between sacred and civil devotions. The U.S. flag in churches has long served as a litmus test for competing visions of faith and patriotism. While flag-burning protesters might represent an extreme edge of this debate, the mere suggestion of removing a flag from its sanctuary perch can ignite equally passionate conflicts.

In every local church, ministers often find themselves trapped between the Scylla of traditional patriotic expression and the Charybdis of theological purity. When someone launches a crusade to "de-flag" the sanctuary, the resulting controversy follows a script as predictable as a Sunday morning service: heated arguments erupt, church members retreat to their respective corners, and the congregation hemorrhages attendees—some decrying the assault on their patriotism, others lamenting the church's failure to transcend nationalism.

This tension between faith and civil religion isn't new, but it perfectly illustrates our broader social transfiguration:

the vanishing art of holding multiple truths in harmonious tension, replaced by the false comfort of absolute certainties. In our rush to plant our flags on one hill or another, we've forgotten how to meet in the valley.

The NFL: USAmerica's Newest Civil Religion

While churches have long wrestled with questions of patriotism and protest, the National Football League found itself in uncharted territory. The NFL had evolved into its own ersatz faith, complete with sacred Sundays, the high holy day of the Super Bowl, and ritualistic devotions that rival any established religion. Before 2016, this gridiron gospel existed in comfortable parallel with traditional USAmerican civil religion, its players generally limiting their public pronouncements to universally embraced sentiments like supporting our troops. Then came Colin Kaepernick's protest, which cracked the foundation of the NFL's carefully cultivated cultural consensus.

The league that had positioned itself as a bastion of traditional values—despite occasional player misconduct—suddenly found itself at the epicenter of USAmerica's cultural earthquake. The ubiquity of smartphone cameras and social media turned local incidents into global spectacles, while increasingly bitter political divisions transformed every gesture into a partisan battleground.

RESILIENT ROOTS

Kaepernick's decision to kneel during the national anthem exposed a fault line in USAmerica's sporting cathedral. For many fans, this perceived sacrilege against traditional patriotic observance proved too much to bear, leading some to abandon their Sunday bleacher-pews. Yet like any established religion, the NFL demonstrated remarkable resilience. Even as some faithful departed, Super Bowl LI still commanded an audience of 111.3 million viewers—the fourth-largest in the event's history.[27]

Today, the controversy has largely subsided, and the NFL's empire has never been more robust. The league now offers its devoted congregation an almost Byzantine array of viewing options across multiple platforms, knowing its flock will faithfully navigate these complex channels of devotion, however inconvenient or costly.

To appreciate the NFL's cultural supremacy, consider this: The celebrated finale of *M*A*S*H* in 1983 held the record for television viewership for nearly three decades with 106 million viewers. It took Super Bowl XLIV in 2010—featuring Drew Brees's Saints vanquishing Peyton Manning's Colts—to finally surpass it with 107 million viewers. That a "struggling" NFL could still deliver the fourth-most-watched broadcast in USAmerican history speaks volumes about its cultural permanence.

Like roots of an ancient oak, the NFL's hold on our national psyche may weather storms, but it remains deeply entrenched in USAmerican soil. The league has transcended mere sport to become a cultural institution, its rhythms and rituals woven inextricably into our national identity. Even when shaken by controversy, these roots prove remarkably resistant to upheaval, nourished by decades of tradition and an almost religious devotion from its followers.

THE POLITICAL GRIDIRON: WHEN PRESIDENTIAL POWER MEETS ATHLETIC PROTEST

The simmering tensions reached a boiling point when President Trump, addressing Kaepernick's continued unemployment, dramatically escalated the controversy. At a political rally, he called for NFL owners to "fire the SOBs" who refused to stand for the flag—a presidential match thrown into an already volatile cultural powder keg. The response was swift and massive: from fewer than ten kneeling players before President Trump's pronouncement to over two hundred the following Sunday, though these numbers gradually diminished over time.[28]

This presidential intervention, however, muddied the waters of protest. What began as Kaepernick's focused statement on racial injustice in law enforcement morphed into a Rorschach test of USAmerican discontent. Were players now protesting systemic racism, presidential overreach, or simply President Trump himself? The original message became lost in an expanding menu of moral stances and social causes, each claiming its own slice of righteous indignation.

History suggests presidents wade into sports at their peril. President Carter's 1980 Olympic boycott over the Soviet invasion of Afghanistan served mainly to shatter the dreams of U.S. athletes, their years of dedication sacrificed on the altar of symbolic gesture. President Trump's intervention, while politically calculated to energize his base (as evidenced by its inclusion in his State of the Union address), similarly produced unintended consequences—transforming a specific protest into a broader rebellion against perceived presidential overreach.

The controversy ultimately ended Kaepernick's NFL career, though his subsequent lawsuit against the league for collusion resulted in an unofficially reported settlement between $30–60 million. For the NFL, this substantial payout represented the cost of attempting to relegate a defining cultural moment to history's rearview mirror.

Perhaps most tellingly, the Kaepernick saga illuminates our culture's confused relationship with courage and virtue. We often mistake ideological alignment for moral courage, celebrating as "brave" those who share our views while dismissing opposing voices as "cowardly" conformists—regardless of the personal risks taken by either side.

This reflexive tribalism reduces complex moral stands to team sports, where we cheer our side and jeer the opposition without pausing to consider the authenticity or cost of either position.

This selective celebration of courage reveals less about the nature of bravery than it does about our own ideological entrenchments. In a Well-curve era of deepening divisions, we increasingly define virtue not by the courage of one's convictions but by the alignment of those convictions with our predetermined worldview—a troubling development in a nation founded on the premise of principled disagreement.

> Courage. Encourage.
> Two words, same origin.
> Heart. You gotta have heart.
>
> JIM KOUZES AND BARRY POSNER,
> *ENCOURAGING THE HEART* (2003)

THE PARADOX OF COURAGE: THE HEART OF THE MATTER

Although "courage" and "encourage" are distinct words, they share a common origin in the Latin root "cor," meaning heart. Originally, courage meant speaking one's truth, or "telling all one's heart." At its core, courage is heart-telling, and heart-telling is heart-healing.

There are three manifestations of courage:

> The courage to hold on
>
> The courage to let go
>
> The courage to venture where others fear to tread

Proactive courage embodies risk, danger, exhilaration and fulfillment.

In football, as in faith, playing it safe rarely leads to victory. While defensive touchdowns make for thrilling highlights, they account for a mere 2–4 percent of all scoring plays.

Of course, sometimes the best offense is a good defense. Jesus had a face-off with Satan in the desert and combated him with biblical bullets, each one-liner slug striking with devastating precision. This is what the church calls apologetics. While apologetics etymologically derives from the Greek "apologia" meaning defense, the most effective apologetics (think C. S. Lewis) actually operates as a forward-moving offensive approach that advances positive truth claims rather than merely responding to criticisms. Just as ancient Greek philosophers used apologias to persuasively advance their positions, apologetics is most compelling when it proactively sets the terms of discussion, builds confidence through strong positive arguments, and creates genuine dialogue rather than defensive posturing.

The math is clear: teams that want to win must have the courage to move the ball downfield, take calculated risks, and play offense.

Yet many churches today have adopted a defensive posture—building walls instead of bridges, protecting territory instead of lifting up the kingdom, and playing not to lose rather than playing to win. Rather than taking Jesus' message into challenging spaces—like addiction recovery centers, prisons, or marginalized communities—they limit their outreach to safe, controlled environments where they're already comfortable. We've become experts at defending against cultural incursion while forgetting that Jesus called us to go into all the world, not retreat from it. This is one of the reasons why one of your authors, Len, refuses to do "retreats" at his home on Orcas Island. He only conducts "advances."

> There are no retreats, just advances in different directions
>
> GENERAL LEWIS BURWELL "CHESTY" PULLER (1895–1971), LEGENDARY MARINE CORPS OFFICER AND ONE OF THE MOST DECORATED MARINES IN U.S. HISTORY

Let's drill down: You're the coach. It's the fourth quarter, two minutes left. You're up by three points. Your defense is tired, but you've got the ball on your opponent's 45-yard line. It's fourth and two. What play do you call?

It's the difference between flipping a coin for the chance to gain a dollar vs. flipping a coin to avoid losing a dollar we already have. Even though the mathematical odds are identical, our fear of loss makes us more protective of what we have than bold in pursuing what we might gain.

The conventional coach punts here—playing not to lose. They're more afraid of giving up good field position than seizing the chance to end the game. That punt is like clutching that dollar bill they gave you, too scared to risk losing it.

But the great coaches? They see something different. They see that two yards could win the game right there. Convert that fourth down, and your opponent never touches the ball again. Sure, you might fail and give them decent field position—but they'd need to score anyway to beat you.

This is where loss aversion kills you: when you're so focused on not losing what you have (the lead) that you hand the initiative to your opponent. You let them decide the game. And in football, like in life, playing defense forever is a losing strategy. The prevent defense only prevents one thing: winning.

The scoreboard might say you're ahead, but the moment you start playing "not to lose" instead of playing to win, you've already lost the mental game. And in football, that's usually when you lose the actual game too.

When churches succumb to loss aversion, they become like fortresses protecting their assets rather than embassies extending their influence.

You see it in church boards that clutch their financial reserves, perpetually waiting for a "rainy day" while their communities flood with immediate needs.

You see it when congregations resist updating their worship style, not because the traditional forms are more sacred, but because change might upset long-time members.

You see it when churches maintain pristine but empty buildings six days a week, fearing the mess and wear that community use might bring.

But playing offense in ministry means something radically different. It means churches investing in new outreach efforts even when success isn't guaranteed. It means engaging in difficult conversations about faith and society, not with harsh judgment but with grace and truth. It means allocating significant resources to mission rather than just maintenance.

> The critics are always right.
> The only way you shut them up
> is by winning.
>
> CHUCK NOLL, HALL OF FAME COACH OF PITTSBURGH
> STEELERS KNOWN FOR FOUR SUPER BOWL
> VICTORIES AND A STRONG CATHOLIC FAITH

When churches play offense, they're not pursuing mere survival or bigger numbers. They're pursuing changed lives, cultural influence through service, and communities healed through practical ministry.

The key distinction between courageous ministry and obnoxious behavior lies in the approach. Courageous churches lead with service rather than condemnation. They build relationships before challenging beliefs. They earn the right to be heard through consistent love and presence in their ZIP codes. When they speak truth, they do so with genuine humility and compassion, seeking first to understand before being understood. This isn't about being aggressive or confrontational. It's about being intentionally engaged in the messy work of loving people and lifting them up toward Jesus.

SWEET AND ERIKSEN

I never lost a game.
I just ran out of time.

QB BOBBY LAYNE, WHO LED THE DETROIT LIONS
TO THREE NFL CHAMPIONSHIPS IN THE EARLY
1950S (1952, 1953, 1957)

The 2014 NFC Championship Game between the Green Bay Packers and Seattle Seahawks provides perhaps the most painful example of loss aversion in football history.

The Packers, led by Aaron Rodgers, dominated most of the game and were up 19–7 with just over 5 minutes left. But instead of going for the kill, they went into ultra-conservative mode. Twice they faced fourth-and-goal situations from the 1-yard line earlier in the game, and both times they chose field goals instead of touchdowns. They played not to lose.

But the most telling moment came when they had the ball with about 5 minutes left. Instead of trying to get first downs to run out the clock, they ran three ultra-conservative plays and punted. They were playing to protect their lead rather than extend it.

The result? The Seahawks mounted a miraculous comeback, scoring 15 points in 44 seconds, and won 28–22 in overtime. The Packers' head coach Mike McCarthy later admitted, "We were trying not to lose the game instead of going to win the game." It's like holding a winning lottery ticket and being so afraid of losing it that you lock it in a safe ... only to find out later that you missed the deadline to claim your prize. The Packers' caution didn't protect their lead—it handed Seattle the opportunity to snatch it away.

The early church didn't achieve explosive growth by playing loss aversion or prevent defense. Peter, Paul, and the apostles moved the ball downfield aggressively, taking the gospel into hostile territory, risking imprisonment, persecution, and death to inhabit God's kingdom. They understood what every successful football coach knows: you can't win games by defense alone. Yes, playing offense means risking being offensive. It means some people won't cheer for your team. It means facing opposition, criticism, hatred, and the possibility of failure.

When we look at our comfortable sanctuaries and carefully curated programs, we must ask ourselves: Would the apostles recognize our version of church as the movement they gave their lives to build? They didn't grow the church by protecting their reputation or avoiding conflict. They didn't measure success by building maintenance or budget surpluses.

Instead, they took the gospel into the heart of hostile Athens, into the streets of resistant Jerusalem, into the households of Gentile Rome. They risked everything—

safety, status, and life itself—not to preserve an institution but to gospel the world.

Today's challenge is clear: Are we willing to take similar risks? Are we ready to engage in the difficult conversations in our workplaces, to build relationships with those who oppose our beliefs, to invest our resources in ventures that might fail but might also heal lives? Are we prepared to face criticism for standing with the marginalized, for challenging injustice, for loving those whom society rejects? This isn't about being needlessly controversial or seeking persecution. It's about choosing kingdom impact over institutional comfort, choosing mission over maintenance, choosing bold love over safe silence.

The early church didn't have the option of playing it safe. Neither do we, if we're serious about fulfilling our great commission. The only question is whether we'll embrace the risk of presencing God's kingdom or continue retreating into our comfortable defensive positions.

Look at our own life choices. Are we playing spiritual prevent defense—carefully protecting our Christian reputation, avoiding difficult conversations, staying safely within our believing bubble? The apostles didn't spread the gospel by keeping their faith private or sharing it only with those who already agreed with them. They didn't live transfigured lives by limiting their relationships to the like-minded or speaking up only when it was comfortable.

What would it look like for us to play spiritual offense? It might mean being the one person in the workplace willing to gently share your faith perspective when difficult issues arise. It might mean building genuine friendships with people whose lifestyles challenge our comfort zone. It might mean risking our social standing by standing up for someone being marginalized or mocked. It might mean investing time and resources in helping someone who may never be able to repay you or even thank you.

The first Christians didn't have the luxury of compartmentalizing their faith into a safe Sunday morning nod-to-God hour. Neither can we, if we're serious about gospelling. Every day, we face a choice: Will I presence Jesus in my sphere of influence, even at personal cost, or will I retreat into the comfortable defense of silent faith? The apostles chose to risk everything to move the gospel forward. What will we choose?

Moving the Chains: From Defense to Divine Offense

In the game of football, a team stuck perpetually on defense finds itself in an exhausting position—constantly reacting, never initiating, growing more tired with each play. The question before us isn't whether to engage, but how to shift from a defensive crouch to an offensive mindset that moves the chains down the field.

The challenge lies partly in our hesitation to advance. We've become more comfortable playing "Devil's Advocate" than "Jesus Evangelist," as if questioning and doubting were somehow more sophisticated than bold proclamation. When we constantly play devil's advocate, we inadvertently end up advocating for the devil, surrendering precious days of our lives to defensive positioning rather than forward progress.

Søren Kierkegaard identified this defensive mindset as more than just tactical error. He saw it as profound misunderstanding of Christianity itself. To defend Christianity, he argued, is to inadvertently disparage it, treating it as "some poor, miserable thing that in the end has to be rescued by a champion." It's like having a warehouse full of gold and spending all your time justifying its value instead of distributing its wealth, he said.[29]

But perhaps our defensive posture stems from a deeper complexity: sometimes the battle isn't simply between good and evil, but between competing goods. This nuanced reality can paralyze us. When facing clear evil-like spectral evidence, where the devil could potentially take the form of an innocent person that so troubled Increase Mather at the Salem witch trials—the path forward seems clearer. Mather ultimately declared it better for ten suspected witches to escape than for one innocent person to be condemned. But what about when the lines aren't so clear?

Reinhold Niebuhr's insight, famously quoted by President Barack Obama, acknowledges "serious evil in the world," but also reminds us that evil resides within ourselves.[30] This recognition should temper any crusading certainty about "ridding the world of evil." Evil remains both visible and inscrutable, an ineradicable mystery that defies simple solutions.

This complexity, however, shouldn't leave us paralyzed on defense. Gospellers need audacity, bravura, more daring and more "demure"—the word of the year for 2024. We need the confidence to look rampaging evil in the eye, poke it in the chest, and declare, "You've got to get by me first!" This can't be done by just a "bowling alone" spirituality; it requires organized religious formation to counter evil's tendency to organize itself into pseudo-religious systems of false salvation.

The path forward requires discernment rather than disarmament or defensiveness. When we understand that evil has already been defeated-as celebrated in that old camp-meeting song "This is the week of the Devil's defeat"-we can move with both confidence and humility. We don't need to defend the warehouse of gold; we need to distribute it. We don't need to prove our worth; we need to advance the ball and move the chains.

But the chains only move forward when you're on offense. The church scores no touchdowns on defense (save the rare "pick 6" interception or fumble recovery for a touchdown). We need to shift from protecting what we have to actively pursuing new opportunities. This will require making difficult choices between competing priorities, moving forward even when we don't have perfect information, and maintaining confidence in our long-term success based on our preparation and capability.

Moving the chains isn't about perfect execution or absolute certainty. It's about faithful forward progress, one play at a time, with both the audacity to advance and the humility to acknowledge the complexity of the field before us.

Jesus' message was so offensive to the religious establishment of His day that they crucified Him—yet His offensive play called "The Cross" became the greatest scoring drive in history, winning salvation for all who believe. Perhaps it's time for the church to take a page from both our spiritual and sporting playbooks: strap on our helmets, move out of our comfortable defensive formation, and start calling some offensive plays for the kingdom that move the gospel down the mission field.

> The least important fact in life is the score at half-time.
>
> ANONYMOUS

Through shattered walls and scattered stones, the ancient Hebrews lifted their voices in Psalm 118, declaring what every earthly sign denied: "The right hand of the Lord is winning." Their temples lay in ruins, their prophets in graves, their armies in defeat—yet still they sang of victory, of triumph through tears, their faith undiminished by disaster.[31]

Physical vs. Moral Courage

Courage wears many masks. Physical courage—the willingness to face bodily harm—can exist entirely separate from virtue, as history's gallery of infamous figures attests. John Dillinger's brazen bank robberies required undeniable nerve, yet served no noble purpose. More chillingly, Hitler's Wehrmacht demonstrated remarkable physical courage while advancing an agenda of unprecedented evil, their territorial conquests briefly rivaling Genghis Khan's empire before their eventual defeat.

Yet moral courage presents a different calculus altogether. One can hardly claim virtue without the backbone to defend it.

This brings us to crucial questions for religious institutions today: Do our churches more closely resemble Pete Rozelle's visionary leadership or Roger Goodell's reactive fumbling? Are we sustaining ourselves on the diminishing returns of past glory? Can we develop robust conflict resolution mechanisms to prevent inevitable disagreements from becoming institutional catastrophes? How might an empowered laity provide stability during periods of questionable leadership and succession? And perhaps most crucially, how do we compassionately confront failure within our faith communities while preserving both truth and unity?

The answers to these questions demand both moral courage and practical wisdom—a combination as rare as it is essential for navigating our increasingly complex cultural landscape. The answers may determine whether our faith institutions remain vital forces for personal and social transfiguration or become mere museums of departed glory.

GAME VII

HEAVEN'S SCOREBOARD
MEASURING WHAT MATTERS

Who in their right mind, Kevin, could possibly deny that the twentieth century was mine? All of it, Kevin. All of it. Mine.

AL PACINO, AS JOHN MILTON/SATAN TO HIS "SON,"
KEVIN LOMAX (KEANU REEVES)
IN *THE DEVIL'S ADVOCATE* (1997)

THE DEVIL'S GAME

When Al Pacino played Satan as a Manhattan power lawyer in *The Devil's Advocate*, he wasn't just chewing scenery, he was serving theological commentary with a side of irony. As a member of the New Jersey bar since 1993, one of your authors (Chris) found particular delight in this portrayal, though it never quite reached the heights of

Pacino's Michael Corleone in *The Godfather* saga. The film's premise—Satan as a prestigious attorney—plays like a cosmic joke, especially for those like Chris who believe in law's noble potential to undergird democracy and help ordinary people ("Mom, if you're watching from Heaven, I see you nodding," Chris says).

The screenplay's suggestion that lawyers have their "glomming fingers in every pie" finds an unexpected echo in Scripture itself. When it came to calling out the establishment, Jesus pulled no punches. To lawyers, he delivered a devastating one-liner in Luke 11:52 (KJV): "Woe unto you lawyers! For ye have taken away the key of knowledge: Ye entered not in yourselves, and them that were entering in, ye hindered." Two millennia later, the legal profession is still recovering from that burn.

But if lawyers got singed, the clergy got scorched. Jesus unleashed a nuclear arsenal of metaphors on the religious leaders: "blind guides" stumbling through their own hypocrisy, a "brood of vipers" poisoning the faithful, and "children of hell" leading others to damnation. But his pièce de résistance? The "whitewashed tombs" takedown—beautiful on the outside, but inside full of rotting bones and decay.[1] It was the ultimate ancient Middle Eastern way of saying "all hat, no cattle."

Both professions shared a common sin in Jesus' eyes: they had become gatekeepers who slammed the door on those seeking truth and justice, whether legal or divine. The lawyers hoarded knowledge; the clergy monopolized access to God. Two thousand years later, his words still sting—and still ring true.

But beyond this professional ribbing lies a deeper question about evil's nature and presence in our world. First of all, since morality is not the same as legality, you can do the devil's work without ever breaking a law. Second, hyper-sophisticates often dismiss Satan as medieval folklore, reducing the Prince of Darkness to a Halloween costume or heavy-metal mascot. C. S. Lewis saw through this intellectual sleight of hand, noting that demons must surely celebrate when people either deny their existence or become unhealthily obsessed with them. Those who mockingly ask about horns and pitchforks miss Lewis' crucial insight: if you go looking for the Devil, you'll find him—though perhaps not in the form you expect. And that encounter, whatever its shape, leaves permanent scars on the soul.[2]

This isn't merely theological speculation. Great fiction often illuminates profound truths, and Pacino's sulfurous, uriniferous attorney raises a disturbing question that atheist Norman Mailer ironically wrestled with in his final book, *On God, An Uncommon Conversation* (2007): Is evil actually winning? Are we witnessing a cosmic offensive that demands, like the Old Testament prophets, our vigorous resistance?

Which brings us to football—USAmerica's most successful sport and, perhaps, its most morally ambiguous. The NFL's prosperity is undeniable, but profit alone doesn't confer virtue. Where does this gladiatorial spectacle fall on the spectrum between good and evil?

Or is it tragedy in the Sophocles tradition, where "goods collide and evils gather?" The meaning of "goods" here is not "things" but the "good." To choose one good is to choose often against another good, so you cannot escape evil, because in choosing one good, you inevitably create or enable some evil through the negation of another good.[3]

Or is it a celebration of human excellence and strategic brilliance, or a contemporary coliseum where we sacrifice young men's bodies and minds for our entertainment?

As we explore these questions, we might find that the line between virtue and vice in USAmerica's favorite game is as blurry as the hash marks on a rain-soaked field.

THE SACRED AND THE STADIUM: WHERE PIGSKIN MEETS PROVIDENCE

Imagine sitting in the Roman Coliseum with Augustine's friend Alypius, who was addicted to the bloodshed of gladiators clashing in mortal combat. Now fast-forward to today's NFL stadium, where today's warriors battle on artificial turf under stadium lights. Same bloodlust, different millennium? Not quite.

The game of football, like humanity itself, lives in the tension between glory and grit, virtue and violence, and the wild exploits chronicled in books like *Pros and Cons*,[4] *Foul Play*,[5] and *Boys Will Be Boys*.[6] It's enough to make any thoughtful gospeller pause and ask: Has our world become filled with Romans, thumbs up or down, feeding our appetite for controlled violence?

THE MOON AND THE MARGIN

A pivotal year: 1966 witnessed a remarkable historical juxtaposition. The United States raced towards the moon, a symbol of technological advancement, while simultaneously grappling with the profound social and racial inequalities highlighted by Martin Luther King Jr.'s powerful testimony before a Senate subcommittee. He pointed out "the striking absurdity in committing billions to reach the moon where no people live … while the densely populated slums are allocated minuscule appropriations." When Neil Armstrong took his giant leap for mankind, many in Harlem's bars didn't even watch. "There ain't no brothers in the program," one patron noted, adding that "the whole thing uses money that should be spent right here."[7]

Was King right? Was he wrong? The answer isn't simple. The space program gave us technological advances that benefit humanity daily. The Apollo mission stood as humanity's greatest leap into the cosmos—a breathtaking triumph of imagination that united a nation and inspired a world. Yet beneath this soaring achievement lay a darker shadow, one that forces us to confront uncomfortable truths about the price of progress.

At the heart of USAmerica's space triumph stood Wernher von Braun, whose brilliant mind had previously served a far more sinister purpose. Before he directed rockets toward the stars, he had aimed them at London's heart. His V-1 and V-2 "vengeance weapons" rained terror from above, claiming thousands of innocent lives in service of the Nazi war machine. The same hands that would later guide humanity to the moon had worn the insignia of the SS, a fact that would only emerge years after Apollo's triumph.

The irony proved too raw to ignore. At the Apollo 11 launch press conference, von Braun stormed out when a reporter dared ask if a falling rocket stage might be bound for London—a pointed reminder of his haunted past. His story embodied Operation Paperclip's bargain with the devil: American authorities, in their cold-blooded calculus, decided that Nazi scientific genius could be repurposed for national glory.

HEAVEN'S SCOREBOARD

This stunning technological achievement, this monument to human potential, was built in part upon a foundation of moral compromise. As we gaze in wonder at footprints on lunar dust, we must also confront an unsettling question: What price are we willing to pay for progress, and can the advancement of human knowledge ever truly be separated from the darkness of its origins? King's words ring with prophetic truth—what profit a nation to gain the moon but lose its soul to systemic injustice?

The same tension exists in football. While some see a billion-dollar industry that could feed the hungry, others recognize how the sport creates opportunities, builds communities, and yes, even lifts people out of poverty. Truth is absolute, but our view of it shifts with our vantage point—whether we're watching from the luxury box or the nosebleed seats. Like a football field seen from different angles, the eternal truths remain unchanged while our perspective reveals different aspects of their meaning.

> And mystic sweet communion
> with those whose race is won.
> "THE CHURCH'S ONE FOUNDATION" (1866)[8]

BEYOND THE BREAD AND CIRCUSES

Football isn't just about bone-crushing hits and testosterone-fueled drama. Like the "Great Cloud of Witnesses" in Hebrews 11—that divine roster of imperfect saints—football tells a more nuanced story of redemption. Take Peyton Manning, dubbed "an offensive coordinator in pads,"[9] whose mental acuity rivals any chess grandmaster. Or listen to Green Bay Packers' guard Jerry Kramer's passionate defense: "We're not subhuman beasts ... trained animals clawing at each other for amusement."[10]

The game mirrors our own spiritual journey: moments of triumph and failure, teamwork and individual responsibility, sacrifice and celebration. It's a parable played out in four quarters.

THE JOY DEFENSE

Some well-meaning critics suggest that enjoying football distracts us from "real" problems—poverty, injustice, family struggles. But this argument mirrors the moonshot debate. Must we choose between joy and justice? Between play and progress? The Divine Coach doesn't demand perpetual hand-wringing. Sometimes, the most spiritual act is finding harmony between celebration and service.

Think about it: Who's more likely to change the world—someone paralyzed by constant anxiety about global problems, or someone who knows how to combine purpose with pleasure? Joy isn't just permitted; it's prescribed. Yet that joy must never blind us to others' pain.

HEAVEN'S SCOREBOARD

> I love football. I don't need a lot of motivation from the outside world or inspiration. I wake up, I love what I'm doing, I'm grateful to still be playing, and I want to go out and compete and light up the defense every day.
>
> JETS QB AARON ROGERS IN 2024 INTERVIEW[11]

THE ULTIMATE SCOREBOARD

Remember Pontius Pilate facing Jesus? The Roman governor thought he held all the power. History—and eternity—proved otherwise. Within four centuries, the empire that crucified Christ knelt before Him. The scoreboard isn't always what it seems.

Like the space program, football has evolved beyond its literal achievements—beyond yards gained and games won—into something more profound: a living narrative that helps us understand ourselves. Just as Star Wars isn't really about lightsabers and hyperspace, or Harry Potter about spells and wizardry, football isn't just about touchdowns and tackles. It's become one of our culture's great storytelling vehicles, a lens through which we examine human ambition, resilience, and connection.

On any given Sunday, we're not just watching athletes

compete. We're witnessing chapters in an ongoing saga. Each season brings its classic hero's journeys: the undrafted rookie defying odds, the veteran seeking redemption, the small-market team challenging dynasties. These stories resonate because they reflect universal themes of struggle, growth, and transformation that extend far beyond the field.

What makes football particularly powerful as a cultural narrative is that it unfolds in real time, with genuine stakes and unscripted outcomes. Unlike fictional universes, its drama emerges organically from authentic human experience—making its lessons about leadership, teamwork, and perseverance all the more compelling.

THE FINAL PLAY

When we view football—or any cultural phenomenon—through the lens of redemption, we recognize that God can use anything, even a physical sport, to showcase grace, build community, and tell His story. Yet we must never stop asking the hard questions, never cease examining our priorities, never quit working toward a more just and equitable playing field on the gridiron of life.

HEAVEN'S SCOREBOARD

The essentially tragic fact is not so much the war of good with evil as it is the war of good with good.

GERMAN IDEALIST PHILOSOPHIER
G. W. F. HEGEL (1770-1831)[12]

LIVING LIFE ON A WIDER FIELD OF FAITH:

The year was 1979, and Raymond Berry stood on the practice field at California Lutheran College, something nagging at his football-trained instincts. Berry wasn't just any coach. He was a legend; the man who had caught passes from Johnny Unitas in what many consider the greatest quarterback-receiver combination in NFL history. And now, as he watched the Dallas Cowboys' receivers running their sideline patterns, something felt off.

"I think the field is too narrow."

Everyone laughed. After all, this was an established college field, one the Cowboys had used for six straight summers of training camp. Who was he to question what everyone had accepted as normal? But Berry persisted, even as the snickers grew louder. He called for a measuring tape, and in that moment, demonstrated a truth that transcends football: sometimes our greatest limitations are the ones we never think to question.

Sure enough, the field was more than a foot too narrow. For years, players had been running their routes, scoring their touchdowns, and playing their games—all while operating in a space smaller than it should have been.

How many plays were never made?

How many touchdowns were never scored?

How many victories were made more difficult simply because everyone assumed the boundaries they saw were the boundaries they had to accept?

This story strikes at the heart of how many of us live our lives of faith. We operate in fields made narrow by our assumptions, our fears, and our comfortable habits. We accept the boundaries that others have drawn for us, or worse, the ones we've drawn for ourselves. "This is just how things are," we tell ourselves. "This is how it's always been."

But God's vision for our lives is never confined by our limited perspective. When God called Abraham, God didn't show him a small plot of land. God told Abraham to look at the stars and imagine his descendants. When God spoke to Moses, God didn't offer a minor adjustment to the Hebrew people's conditions. God promised complete deliverance. When God anointed David, He didn't see a shepherd boy. God saw a king.

As Paul wrote to the Ephesians, God "is able to do immea-

HEAVEN'S SCOREBOARD

surably more than all we ask or imagine." The question isn't whether God has given us a full-sized field to play on. God has. The question is whether we're willing to question our assumptions about where the boundaries lie.

Think about the dreams you've set aside because they seemed too big. Consider the calling you've ignored because it didn't fit within your comfortable boundaries. Reflect on the prayers you've never prayed because they seemed beyond what's "reasonable." Are you playing on a field that's too narrow?

Isaiah's words ring through the centuries: "Enlarge the place of your tent, stretch your tent curtains wide, do not hold back."[13] This isn't just poetic language. It's a divine invitation to step into the fullness of what God has prepared for you.

Raymond Berry's expertise as a receiver gave him the confidence to question what everyone else had accepted. Our gospel faith should do the same for us. After all, if we truly believe in an infinite God who loves us and calls us to abundant life, how can we be content playing on a narrow field?

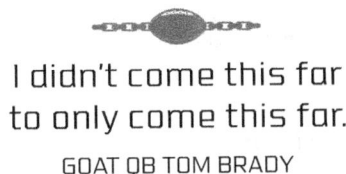

> I didn't come this far
> to only come this far.
>
> GOAT QB TOM BRADY

The time has come to get out the measuring tape. To question our assumptions. To challenge our comfortable boundaries. To ask ourselves: Are we living our faith on a field that's too small? And if so, isn't it time to step into the full dimensions of what God has prepared for us?

We often limit our faith to comfortable spaces—perhaps serving in familiar church roles, praying for safe outcomes, or sharing our beliefs only with those who already agree. But what if God is calling us to expand our vision?

Here are signs your faith might be operating in too small a field:

- You haven't felt spiritually challenged or uncomfortable in months
- Your prayers focus mainly on personal comfort rather than transformation
- You rarely encounter people whose beliefs differ from yours
- Your service to others stays within predictable boundaries

Expanding your field might mean:

- Having honest conversations with people who question your faith
- Serving in communities outside your comfort zone
- Praying for outcomes that seem impossible

- Taking spiritual risks that require genuine trust in God's provision

If you're not gonna go all the way, why go at all?

LEGENDARY QB JOE "BROADWAY JOE" NAMATH WHO LED JETS TO A HISTORIC SUPER BOWL III VICTORY

The question isn't just whether we believe, but whether we're willing to live out that belief in ways that stretch us beyond our self-imposed limits.

Because just like those missed touchdowns at Cal Lutheran, we'll never know what victories we've missed until we're willing to question the boundaries we've accepted for so long.

Halftime
The Second Wind

I'm not here to make kicks or miss kicks. I think I'm here to spread the love of Jesus. So, however long he gives me this stage, that's what I plan to do.

DETROIT LIONS KICKER JAKE BATES[1]
DISTINGUISHING THE CAREER OF FOOTBALL
FROM THE CALLING OF DISCIPLESHIP

Halftime comprises "exhortations" on the sidelines and in the locker rooms.

There is a difference between a coach who pulls a player aside during practice vs. one who yells across the field. A true "exhortation" approach would be more like:

- A coach taking a player aside during a water break to quietly discuss their technique

- A team captain putting an arm around a discouraged teammate after a tough play
- A veteran player mentoring a rookie in private after practice
- A coach having a one-on-one meeting in their office rather than criticizing a player in front of the team

This approach aligns more with Paul's usage of *"parakaleo"* (the Greek word often translated as "exhort")—it carries the sense of coming alongside someone, rather than speaking down to them. It's more about encouragement and guidance than harsh criticism.

How different these two scenarios feel:

- A coach screaming "YOU'RE NOT HUSTLING!" from the sidelines
- A coach quietly saying during a private moment: "I've seen how hard you can work, and I know you have another gear. Let's figure out together what's holding you back."

The second approach—the true "exhortation"—is more likely to build trust and motivate genuine change. It respects the dignity of the player while still pushing them toward excellence.

What follows in Halftime are exhortations in the Pauline sense of "I exhort you:" a calling to the side and speaking lovingly to you, not yelling at you.

GAME VIII

THE LOMBARDI LEGACY
DISCIPLINE AS DEVOTION

You stay at the foot of the cross.

VINCE LOMBARDI TO HIS "PRODIGAL SON," THE DISSOLUTE BUT TALENTED AND HARD-DRIVING HALFBACK PAUL HORNUNG, AFTER LEARNING THAT THE NFL WAS SUSPENDING HORNUNG FOR HAVING GAMBLED ON FOOTBALL GAMES.

You walk into the Green Bay Packers' locker room, glancing at your watch. It reads 8:46 a.m. for a 9:00 a.m. meeting. You're early, right? Wrong.

In Lombardi's world, you're already late. Welcome to "Lombardi Time"—a parallel universe where being fifteen minutes early is just barely on time. It's like showing up to a party exactly when the invitation says to arrive—you know you're actually late.

Before the Super Bowl trophy bore his name, before he became football's patron saint of excellence, Vince Lombardi was the ultimate organizational turnaround artist. Think of him as the Steve Jobs of football—taking failing franchises (the "Apple Computers" of their day) and transforming them into championship dynasties. The Green Bay Packers were the equivalent of a tech startup on life support: eleven straight losing seasons, with a dismal 1–10–1 record. Then came Lombardi, their entrepreneurial savior in a fedora and overcoat. He did the same with the Washington Redskins, leading them to a winning season in 1969, thereby ending Washington's long and futile streak of fourteen consecutive non-winning seasons before Lombardi died suddenly of a particularly virulent form of cancer the following year.

You've probably heard "Winning isn't everything, it's the only thing." It's like the "Just Do It" of the 1960s NFL—everyone knows it, but few understand its deeper meaning. While this quote (borrowed from UCLA's Red Sanders) became Lombardi's trademark, it's like judging a book by its cover quote. The real story lies in the pages beneath.

Here's where it gets interesting. Imagine a coach who could make grown men tremble with a glare but also stood as an unwavering champion for racial equality in the segregation era. It's like finding out your strict high school principal secretly ran a youth center for underprivileged kids.

Lombardi operated with a zero-tolerance policy for discrimination that would make today's DEI consultants look lenient. In an era when using racial and other slurs was as common as helmet-to-helmet hits, Lombardi declared that anyone using derogatory language would be "through with this team."[1] Period. No appeals process, no second chances.

Think of Lombardi as the Professor Snape of football—harsh, demanding, sometimes seemingly cruel, but ultimately driven by a deeper purpose. His words could cut like a laser, leaving marks that players like Bob Brunet would carry for decades.[2] But like a tough-love parent, his ultimate goal wasn't to hurt but to build character through challenge.

> Competitive sport keeps alive in us a spirit and vitality. It teaches the strong to know when they are weak and the brave to face themselves when they know they are afraid. To be proud and unbowed in defeat yet humble and gentle in victory. And to master ourselves before we attempt to master others. And to learn to laugh, yet never forget to learn how to weep. And to give the predominance of courage over timidity.
>
> VINCE LOMBARDI IN *THE SPEECH*[3]

In today's world of participation trophies and "everyone's a winner" mentality, Lombardi's philosophy stands out like a flip phone at an iPhone convention. He believed in the hunt for excellence—not as a destination but as a never-ending journey. It's like having a GPS that never says "You have arrived" but keeps pushing you toward a better route.

His speech about modern ideology could have been ripped from today's social media debates about educational standards and merit-based systems. Lombardi wasn't just ahead of his time; he was timeless.

> Today we have a new ideology—that is to be homogeneous, no letter grades, no classification. The only line that some of our people seem to want today is a line between passing and failing. There is no hunt for excellence, in other words. And you and I both know that this is the easy way. The prevailing idea today is to take the easy way—and that effort and work are unnecessary.[4]

What makes Lombardi's story relevant today isn't just his winning record (.758—try finding that kind of success rate in today's NFL), but how he won. He was like a master chef who insisted on both perfect presentation AND perfect ingredients—no cutting corners, no cheap shots, no compromises on integrity. His players blocked and tackled with the ferocity of lions but played with the honor of

THE LOMBARDI LEGACY

knights. Celebration dances in the end zone? You'd have better luck finding a vegetarian at a barbecue competition. As Paul Hornung put it, anyone showing off after a touchdown would find themselves "on the first plane out of Green Bay."[5]

Lombardi wasn't perfect. He was more like a masterpiece painting with visible brush strokes. His intensity could burn, his words could sting, but his principles stood as solid as the frozen tundra of Lambeau Field. In an era of instant gratification and shortcuts to success, perhaps we need a dose of Lombardi time—where excellence isn't just encouraged, it's expected, and where being early isn't just polite, it's mandatory.

Imagine walking into a church where the pastor wears a fedora instead of a collar, where the pulpit is a sideline, and where the congregation wears helmets and cleats. In a world obsessed with Ted Lasso's feel-good coaching style, Lombardi was more like the Nick Saban of spirituality—demanding excellence while building character.

In today's world of ChatGPT-generated inspiration and BeReal authenticity moments, Lombardi's old-school teaching methods might seem as outdated as a Blockbuster membership card. But like Jesus with his parables, Lombardi knew that repetition wasn't just about memorization—it was about transfiguration. Vincent Lombardi and Martha Stewart were the original influencers, but instead of chasing likes, he was chasing excellence.

> When we don't use our abilities to the fullest, we're not only cheating ourselves and the Green Bay Packers, we're cheating the Lord; He gave us our ability to use it to the fullest.
>
> VINCE LOMBARDI[6]

Remember that parable about the talents? Lombardi turned it into a playbook. In an era where "quiet quitting" trends on LinkedIn and "work-life harmony" fills TED Talk streams, Lombardi's message hits harder than a Travis Kelce touchdown celebration—God didn't give you gifts to keep them in bubble wrap or save them for your side hustle. God's gifts aren't meant to be stored like photos taking up space in your iCloud—they're meant to be shared like Mr. Beast's money giveaways, multiplied like loaves and fishes, spreading hope and changing lives with every generous click of your heart's "share" button. Gifts are given to be given away.

Before Taylor Swift united Swifties worldwide, before BTS created the ARMY, Lombardi was building his own passionate community on the frozen tundra of Green Bay. His theology of team love wasn't about Discord servers or Slack channels—it was about loving the unlovable, supporting the struggling, being present in the pain. Think less Reddit karma, more real-life dharma.

While today's spiritual seekers might find their peace through Headspace meditation apps or Peloton mindfulness rides, Lombardi found his in the pre-dawn quiet of daily Mass. Like a spiritual version of Apple's "Screen Time" report, he kept a daily accountability with his Creator. Daily Mass was a divine huddle that helped him better yell at himself, and his players, "Get out of the huddle!"

Lombardi was like the latest iPhone Pro Max—sleek and powerful on the outside, but complex and sometimes glitchy on the inside. His son called him a paradox,[7] much like we all are—posting our Spotify Wrapped successes while privately wrestling with our Apple Music guilty pleasures.

In an age when some treat prayer like DoorDash for divine intervention, Lombardi's approach was refreshingly authentic. No praying for touchdowns here—just thanksgiving and protection. He understood that God isn't your Spotify algorithm, curating perfect playlists for your life. The Almighty is your head coach for eternity, calling the plays down the mission field of life.

The Game of Life

There is a wonderful story about a college football game which turned out to be a terrible mismatch. One team outweighed the other by thirty pounds per man, was more experienced, better coached, etc. The lighter, weaker team was being terribly beaten, not only on the scoreboard but also on their bodies. They were bruised and cut and bleeding and several first-stringers had already left the game because of injuries.

As they gathered 'round in their huddle late in the final period, the quarterback noticed that they had twelve men on the field, one more than the eleven allowed by the rules. That's all they needed. If the referee discovered the extra man, he would assess a penalty, thereby adding to their already deep humiliation.

"Look," the quarterback said to his teammates, "We'll try a running play that will take us past the bench. In the confusion, as we pass the bench, I want one of you to drop out. If we can do this fast enough, the referee may not notice and we can avoid the penalty at least."

Whereupon, amidst great confusion, they succeeded in running the play right past the bench. When they returned to the huddle to decide on their next play, the quarterback discovered, to his amazement that six men had dropped out.

The easy path beckons us all. When the blows rain down and our spirits break, the sidelines whisper our names. But true discipleship isn't measured in moments of triumph—it's forged in the furnace of adversity. Christ didn't call us to comfort, but to commitment; not to escape, but to endurance. Jesus calls us to a give-it-all discipleship. His cross wasn't optional, and neither is ours.

> Take it [all]! Let my lord the king
> do whatever pleases him.
>
> 1 CHRONICLES 21:23 (NIV)

THIS BRUTAL BEAUTIFUL GAME

Lombardi knew football is violent. But like watching Wednesday Addams navigate Nevermore Academy, he saw beauty in the darkness, redemption in the struggle. In an age of cushioned comfort and instant gratification, Vince Lombardi's legacy offers a bracing reminder: true growth demands more than good intentions. It requires the courage to embrace difficulty. Lombardi understood that football, like faith, is both brutal and beautiful. Its value lies not in spite of its demands, but because of them.

Lombardi's genius wasn't just his winning record. It was his understanding that excellence emerges through:

- Mastery of fundamentals, practiced until they become second nature
- Disciplined dedication to daily improvement, not sporadic bursts of effort
- Patient endurance through setbacks and failures

- Community forged through shared struggle and sacrifice

While today's self-help gurus peddle frictionless paths to success, Lombardi's philosophy was uncompromising: greatness costs everything. Every practice was a crucible for character formation. Every drill was an opportunity for spiritual growth. Every game was a test of not just skill, but soul.

This vision transformed football into more than sport. It became a laboratory for human development. In Lombardi's hands, the game became a universal language for teaching deeper truths about discipline, perseverance, and purpose. His players learned that excellence isn't a destination but a daily choice, that character isn't inherited but forged through consistent correct choices under pressure.

Today, as we navigate a world of artificial intelligence and algorithmic ease, Lombardi's message becomes more crucial: there are no shortcuts to significance. Whether in faith, family, or profession, meaningful growth happens only through committed practice, patient endurance, and willing sacrifice.

His legacy reminds us that our daily work—on field, in office, or at home—is sacred space where heaven and earth meet. Like the early Christians who elevated their world through faithful presence and patient endurance,

Lombardi showed how ordinary moments, approached with extraordinary commitment, become opportunities for transformation.

In our culture of quick fixes and filtered reality, Lombardi calls us to a deeper game—one where victory isn't measured in likes or follows, but in lives transformed through persistent dedication to excellence and truth.

The Universal Language

Think football talk is just sports chatter? In our world of AI chatbots and algorithm-curated echo chambers, where even ChatGPT can be prompted to agree with everything we say, football remains one of the few topics that can still bridge the divides like a Patrick Mahomes cross-field touchdown pass.

"Sports talk," particularly around football, has long served as a universal language in USAmerican culture, transcending traditional barriers of race and class. While critics once dismissed sports metaphors as exclusionary "male Swahili," this characterization has become outdated. The surging involvement of women in sports, especially the NFL, has transformed football talk from a male-centric dialect into a truly universal cultural lexicon. Like the English language itself—which readily absorbs and naturalizes new expressions—football terminology has evolved into an authentic lingua franca of USAmerican social interaction, fostering genuine connections across demographic lines.

Today, Lombardi's statue at the Pro Football Hall of Fame has a nose worn smooth by countless touches. In an era where even Andrew Tate can build a following and Mr. Beast makes millions giving away money, Lombardi's legacy upload has staying power.

What Lombardi called "heart power,"[8] we might today call emotional intelligence or authentic leadership. But unlike today's LinkedIn influencers selling quick-fix solutions between #ThoughtLeadership posts, Lombardi's version came with calluses and grass stains. It was earned through sweat equity, not social-media equity.

The world has changed since Lombardi's time. We've traded clipboards for iPads, playbooks for apps, and chalkboards for Zoom calls. But in a world where Elon Musk can rename Twitter to "X" and Mark Zuckerberg can challenge him to a cage match, some things remain wonderfully constant: the need for a life story, the call to mission, the hunger for connection, the power of love.

Lombardi's message isn't just relevant. It's revolutionary. It's a call to excellence in an age of "good enough," a demand for authenticity in a world of filters and deepfakes, and a reminder that true greatness isn't measured in followers and views, but in the lives you touch and the legacy you leave.

THE LOMBARDI LEGACY

> For physical training is of some value, but godliness has value for all things, holding promise for both the present life and the life to come.
>
> 1 TIMOTHY 4:8 (NIV)

It may seem strange to end a chapter on Vince Lombardi with a Tom Landry story, but Lombardi and Landry actually worked together on the New York Giants coaching staff in the 1950s. From 1954 to 1958, Lombardi served as the Giants' offensive coordinator while Landry was the defensive coordinator under head coach Jim Lee Howell. Their time together on the Giants' staff is often considered one of the most remarkable coaching combinations in NFL history—two future Hall of Fame coaches working together before going on to define different aspects of professional football's golden age.

This period was crucial in the development of both coaches' philosophies and systems. Lombardi was developing what would become his famous "Packer Sweep" while Landry was innovating defensive schemes, including the 4–3 defense that would revolutionize the game. Both would go on to become legendary head coaches—Lombardi with the Green Bay Packers (1959–1967) and Landry with the Dallas Cowboys (1960–1988). They faced each other in two of the most famous NFL Championship games in history: the 1966 NFL Championship and the famous "Ice Bowl" in 1967. Both games were won by Lombardi's Packers in dramatic fashion.

Lombardi and Landry shared similar values about discipline, preparation, and character-building, though their personalities were quite different. Lombardi was known for his fiery, passionate approach, while Landry was famously stoic and analytical. Both men helped shape the modern NFL and are considered among the greatest coaches in football history.

Landry innovated a scouting and development system that was as controversial as it was successful. Gil Brandt, the Cowboys' chief talent scout, was known for finding "diamonds in the rough" and converting athletes from other positions into successful NFL players. One such "diamond" was Drew Pearson. His story is a gridiron gospel that greatness is not grabbing all you can for yourself, but giving away of yourself all you can.

Pearson played quarterback in high school and running back in college. No NFL team drafted him when he graduated from the University of Tulsa in 1973. But Landry saw his potential as a wide receiver, and signed him as an undrafted free agent. Landry's system was designed to develop not just great players, however, but also people of character.

Drew Pearson became one of the Dallas Cowboys' greatest wide receivers—and was one of their most beloved players, which is no small feat given the franchise's storied history. From 1973 to 1983, #88 exemplified excellence both on and off the field.[9] Pearson became one of the NFL's elite receivers, earning three Pro Bowl selections (1974, 1976, 1977) and three First-team All-Pro honors. He was a key part of the Cowboys' Super Bowl XII championship team in 1977. His most iconic moment came in the 1975 playoff game against the Minnesota Vikings, when he made the legendary "Hail Mary" catch from Roger Staubach—a play that added a new term to football's lexicon.

What truly set Pearson apart was his character. Drew Pearson held the record for having caught a pass in every game. He was about to break another record, but with just a few seconds to go in the game, the Cowboys were ahead by one touchdown, and they had the ball. Roger Staubauch realized that Drew Pearson had not caught a pass all day. So they went back into the huddle for the final play of the game. The normal thing to do was to call a play, fall on the ball, and let the clock run out. But Staubach called a pass play, with the pass going to Drew Pearson. When Pearson heard the play, he said, "That's not a good play." Ends don't ever tell the quarterback what's a good play, especially when Tom Landry had sent in the play. But Drew Pearson said again, "You ought to do what you know you ought to do." So Staubach called a play, kept the ball, fell on it, and the clock ran out.

In an era when players might have insisted on padding their stats, Pearson chose the right thing over the record books. He chose the team's interests above personal glory. This moment between him and Staubach, under Coach Tom Landry's watchful eye, exemplifies the values that made those Cowboys teams special.

After years of waiting, Pearson finally received pro football's highest honor with his induction into the Hall of Fame in 2021. He was also inducted into the Cowboys Ring of Honor in 2011. His legacy isn't just about spectacular catches or championships—it's about being a legendary human being who understood that how you play the game matters just as much as what you achieve.

One reason why coaches like Vince Lombardi and Tom Landry put such emphasis on perfect execution is that each moment of play, just as each moment of life, is precious. You only have about eleven minutes of actual game action to determine the outcome of a three-hour event.

In an average NFL football game, while the game clock runs for sixty minutes (four fifteen-minute quarters), the actual time the ball is in play is remarkably brief—only about eleven minutes of actual action.

A typical three-hour broadcast breaks down roughly like this:

- Actual play time: eleven minutes
- Time between plays/game clock running: about sixty-seven minutes
- Replay reviews, timeouts, and halftime: about forty-two minutes
- Commercial breaks and advertisements: about sixty minutes

The 11 minutes of actual play consists of around 120–140 individual plays, each lasting about 4–6 seconds on average. The rest of the time is spent with teams in the huddle, lining up for plays, timeouts, official reviews, and other stoppages.

The contrast between 11 minutes of action and 3 hours of total time is the gridiron gospel in a nutshell.

First, gospellers must learn the importance of preparation and readiness. Just as football players spend hours preparing for mere minutes of actual gameplay, our faith lives often require extensive preparation for pivotal moments. The time spent in prayer, study, or meditation may seem disproportionate to the brief moments when we're called to act, but that preparation is essential for those crucial moments.

SWEET AND ERIKSEN

> The sensational accomplishments
> in life are the result of
> unsensational preparation.
>
> HALL OF FAME QB AND DEVOUT CATHOLIC
> ROGER STAUBACH[10]

Second, gospellers must remember that our most significant moments are often brief. Just as a single 5 second play can determine the outcome of an entire football game, life's biggest moments—decisions, encounters, and opportunities to show love or courage—are often surprisingly brief. But these moments carry outsized importance because of all the preparation that preceded them.

Third, gospellers are disciplined about patience and persistence. Most growth in faith, like most of football, is about the "downtime"—the quiet moments between the action. It's about showing up consistently, staying ready, and maintaining focus even when nothing dramatic seems to be happening. Just as football players must stay mentally engaged during the long periods between plays, gospelling requires sustained attention during ordinary times.

Finally, there is a profound truth about time and legacy. Just as those 11 minutes of football action continue to inspire millions decades after the players have left the field, our brief moments of gospel faithfulness—small acts of kindness, quiet decisions to choose right over recognition, moments of selfless courage—can bear fruit long after we're gone. We may never see the full harvest of the seeds we plant in those brief moments. Like Drew Pearson's choice of team over personal glory, which still teaches character to new generations fifty years later, every moment, no matter how brief, carries the potential for eternal impact. We are often called to be faithful in small moments that may only bear their full fruit in lives we'll never see and generations we'll never know.

GAME IX

THE BELICHICK BLUEPRINT

STRATEGY AND SPIRIT

Join me, and together we can rule
the galaxy as father and son.

DARTH VADER TO LUKE SKYWALKER[1]

For what shall it profit a man, if he
shall gain the whole world, and lose
his own soul?

JESUS[2]

In the cathedral of professional football, where gladiators clash beneath stadium lights that shine like stars, few figures loom as large or enigmatic as Bill Belichick. Wrapped in his trademark grey hoodie—a kind of modern-day sackcloth that marks him as both penitent and prophet—Belichick has rewritten the gospel of football success. But like all gospels, this one comes with both glory and cost, resurrection and fall, triumph and temptation.

Belichick's revolutionary approach centered on a few key principles that transformed modern football:

1) Situational Adaptability: Instead of having a fixed "system," Belichick completely reimagined his game plan each week based not only upon his opponent's specific weaknesses, but upon their perceived vulnerable strengths as well. This was radical in an NFL where teams typically stuck to their established identity. He might run fifty times one week and pass fifty times the next. And on defense, it was unknown week-to-week which strength Belichick would target or "take away," turning it into a weakness, and simultaneously getting into the head of his opponent through this type of unpredictable and asymmetrical psychological warfare. Rookie quarterbacks usually had no serious chance against a Belichick-coached team. Sam Darnold, then playing for the New York Jets, once infamously stated that playing against Belichick's defense was like "seeing ghosts."

What can gospellers learn from this? Rather than clinging to rigid formulas, maturity of faith means adapting our approach based on different situations and people we encounter. Just as Paul became "all things to all people,"[3] effective faith often requires flexibility while maintaining fixed core principles.

2) Position Versatility: Belichick famously used players in unexpected ways. Linebackers became tight ends, and receivers became defensive backs. He valued adaptable players who could fill multiple roles over specialists who excelled in just one area.

What can gospellers learn from this? Instead of limiting ourselves to traditional religious roles or expressions, we might develop multiple "spiritual skill sets"—being able to serve, teach, listen, or lead as different situations require. Recognizing our "strengths" is important, but even more is the recognition that God's strength is made perfect in our weaknesses more than our strengths. So we must be open to being summoned to change positions at the point of our greatest weakness, not strength.

3) Value in the Overlooked: Belichick consistently found value in players other teams dismissed—sixth-round draft picks, undrafted free agents, players considered "too small" or "too slow." He focused on what they could do rather than what they couldn't.

What can gospellers learn from this? Are we looking for God's presence and purpose in unexpected places and people, recognizing that divine work often happens through those the world overlooks?

4) Preparation Beyond the Obvious: While other teams practiced standard situations, Belichick had his teams prepare for highly unlikely scenarios—rare weather conditions, obscure rules, unusual game situations. This preparedness often proved decisive in critical moments.

What can gospellers learn from this? Are we developing spiritual depth that goes beyond surface-level practices, preparing ourselves for challenging seasons of life before they arrive?

5) Process Over Personality: His famous mantra "Do Your Job" emphasized systematic execution over individual stardom. Every person's role, however small, was crucial to the larger mission.

What can gospellers learn from this? Understand that authentic faith isn't about personal spiritual stardom but faithful execution of our specific calling within God's larger purposes.

READY, SET, WHATEVER

Long before he became the architect of football's greatest dynasty, young Bill Belichick sat at the feet of his father Steve, engaging in what can only be described as a form of football lectio divina. Like the ancient practice where monks would read, meditate, pray, and contemplate sacred texts, young Bill studied game film with monastic dedication. At age nine, while other children played at games, he was already developing what would become a supernatural understanding of football's sacred texts.

His father Steve, author of a revered book on football-scouting techniques, passed down not just knowledge but wisdom. "Focus not on weakness, but strength," he taught his son. This paradoxical insight would later become the cornerstone of the Belichick way—a philosophy that mirrors Paul's understanding that God's strength is made perfect in weakness.[4]

Like the young prophet Samuel hearing God's voice in the temple, Belichick's early years showed glimpses of future glory. In 1976, as an intern with the Detroit Lions, he demonstrated his first football miracle. Against the mighty New England Patriots, who had just demolished the eventual Super Bowl champion Oakland Raiders 48–17, Belichick suggested an unprecedented two-tight-end formation. Like David choosing five smooth stones against Goliath, this unconventional strategy proved devastatingly effective, leading to a 30–10 victory.[5]

> Before honor is humility.
> PROVERBS 15:33 (NKJV)

Belichick's path to greatness first led through failure. In Cleveland, where he compiled a 37–45 record over five seasons, Belichick learned the bitter taste of defeat. Art Modell, who had once fired the legendary Paul Brown, now dismissed Belichick—a parallel to how prophets are often rejected in their own time and territory.

But as in all great spiritual narratives, this wilderness experience wasn't wasted—it was preparation. Just as Moses needed forty years in Midian before leading the Exodus, Belichick's time in Cleveland shaped his understanding of both football and human nature.

Like Paul studying under Gamaliel, Belichick's apprenticeship under Bill Parcells proved crucial to his development. As Giants' defensive coordinator, he crafted the game plan that helped defeat the Buffalo Bills in Super Bowl XXV—a plan so brilliant it now resides in the Pro Football Hall of Fame. His strategy of allowing Thurman Thomas to gain yards while preventing the Bills' passing attack was like Solomon's wisdom—paradoxical yet profound.

When Drew Bledsoe fell injured in 2001, few could have known they were witnessing a pivot point in football history. Bledsoe, like Saul, was the established king with a massive contract ($103 million). Tom Brady, like David chosen over his more impressive brothers, stepped onto the field. In Brady, Belichick found his football Samuel—a partnership that would reshape the landscape of professional football.

Their bond became a kind of covenant relationship, reminiscent of David and Jonathan. Together they forged what became known as "The Patriot Way"—a system of beliefs and practices that transformed a mediocre franchise into a dynasty. This "way" demanded sacrifice, much like the early Christian church—players often accepting less money to remain part of the community.

The initial proof of the power of "The Patriot Way" was New England's first Super Bowl championship in 2002, Super Bowl XXXVI, the franchise's first league championship of any kind. Former NFL quarterback and learned ESPN football commentator Ron Jaworski, in his outstanding and informative book on football strategy, *Games That Changed The Game*, dedicated a chapter to Bill Belichick, focusing upon this particular Super Bowl matchup, under the heading of "Bull's Eye Game Plan."[6] Jaworski, who is an avid historian of the game of football who has a coach's voracious appetite for game film, has referred to Belichick's coaching performance in Super Bowl XXXVI as the best coaching job that he had ever seen in any single NFL game.[7]

Death is swallowed up in victory.

APOSTLE PAUL[8]

In the Hollywood havens of football films, there's a moment in *Any Given Sunday* (1999) when Al Pacino's

Coach D'Amato preaches what might be called the Gospel of Inches. "Life is a game of inches," he thunders, every word a hammer striking truth's anvil. "The inches we need are everywhere around us." Super Bowl LI transformed this silver screen sermon into flesh-and-blood testimony.

No moment better encapsulates the spiritual dimensions of Belichick's "Patriot Way" legacy, however, than Super Bowl LI. Down 28–3 to the Atlanta Falcons in the third quarter, the Patriots faced what appeared to be certain death. The statistical probability of victory was infinitesimal.

The Patriots found themselves in their own garden of Gethsemane—a moment when giving up seemed not just reasonable, but rational. No team had ever scaled such a mountain in Super Bowl history. The victory margin seemed as wide as the sea Moses faced at the shores of Egypt.

The Patriots began to claim their inches. Each completion, each defensive stop, each small victory became a mustard seed of possibility planted in the soil of seeming defeat. They gathered these inches like manna in the wilderness:

- 28–9: An inch of hope
- 28–12: Another inch of faith
- 28–20: An inch of momentum
- 28–28: The inches becoming yards, becoming a miracle

This wasn't just football anymore. It became a parable for every soul facing their own impossible deficit: the addict fighting for one more clean day, the student struggling through one more page, the parent trying one more time to reach a wayward child, the believer holding on through one more dark night of doubt.

The Patriots showed us faith in cleats: not the mountain-moving kind that happens in an instant, but the inch-claiming kind that persists in the face of impossible odds. They reminded us that resurrection doesn't always come in dramatic flashes of light, but often arrives one heartbeat at a time, one play at a time, one inch at a time.

Shifting Sports for a Moment

A baseball diamond is where the difference between a solid career and legendary status can be measured in mere inches. A dependable hitter who maintains a .250 average—connecting with the ball once in every four attempts—earns respect, at least as an average player, in the major leagues. Yet those who ascend to the hallowed realm of .300 hitters achieve something transcendent: they succeed just three times in ten attempts.

The mathematics of excellence here are striking. Among hundreds of professional players, scarcely a dozen reach this threshold of greatness in a season. These elite few, the .300 hitters, inhabit a rarified atmosphere. Their reward?

Commanding salaries, coveted trading cards, and lucrative endorsements that reflect their exceptional status.

But here lies metaphysical author Eric Butterworth's masterstroke of insight: what truly separates the great from the good? In twenty at-bats, the .250 hitter connects five times. The .300 hitter? Just once more—six hits. A single successful attempt—one more well-timed swing, one more precise adjustment, one more moment of perfect connection between bat and ball—marks the boundary between competence and greatness.[9]

This razor-thin margin reminds us that excellence doesn't always demand monumental leaps. Sometimes, greatness whispers in the spaces between heartbeats, in the fraction of an inch between a foul ball and a line drive, in that single extra mile (as Jesus would put it) that transforms the good into the extraordinary.

In those moments when spreadsheets show no path to victory, when statistics say surrender is sensible, when the scoreboard mocks our efforts—that's when we most need to remember Super Bowl LI. Not just as a football game, but as a holy reminder that God often works in inches, that persistence is a form of prayer, that no deficit is too deep for divine comeback stories.

For in the end, the game of life, like football, is won in the inches. And as the Patriots proved on that sacred Sunday, if we fight for them with everything we have—those inches add up to miracles.

Julian Edelman's miraculous catch, surrounded by defenders like Daniel in the lions' den, became a symbol of divine intervention in human affairs. The overtime drive to victory became a testimony to resurrection power.

THE FALL: SPYGATE AND THE PRICE OF GLORY

> Pride goes before destruction.
> PROVERBS 16:18 (NKJV)

Yet even in the midst of glory, the tempter lurked. In 2007, the NFL fined Bill Belichick $500,000 and the Patriots $250,000, plus docked them a first-round draft pick, after catching them videotaping the New York Jets' defensive signals from an unauthorized location during a game, a practice that was against NFL rules but that Belichick claimed he had misinterpreted.

The Spygate scandal revealed the shadow side of excellence. Like King David with Bathsheba, success bred a certain hubris. The penalties listed above were severe, but the worst punishment of all was a perception of the stained legacy.

Unlike Vince Lombardi, who maintained an almost priestly

relationship with Commissioner Pete Rozelle, Belichick's relationship with Roger Goodell became adversarial—a reminder that integrity often matters more than victory. Winning may be everything, but losing with grace is the real championship. To sacrifice honor for gain is to trade gold for dross. Even in football, grace is found between the vertical reaches of human striving and the horizontal bounds of earthly limitation.

When the Patriots were caught videotaping opponents' signals in 2007, they learned that shortcuts to victory often exact a steeper price than honest defeat. Their Super Bowl wins became tainted, raising questions that persist years later.

But integrity isn't just about avoiding scandal. It's about the small daily choices that shape our character. It's choosing to:

- Admit our mistakes rather than shift blame
- Give credit to others when we succeed
- Put in the hard work instead of looking for shortcuts
- Stand by our principles even when it costs us
- Tell difficult truths instead of comfortable half-truths

THE BELICHICK BLUEPRINT

> When you win, say nothing.
> When you lose, say less.
>
> COACH PAUL BROWN
> NAMESAKE OF CLEVELAND BROWNS AND
> ONE OF THE GREATEST COACHES IN NFL HISTORY

These moments rarely make headlines. They're the quiet victories won in ordinary moments—when we choose the harder right over the easier wrong, when we lift others up instead of stepping on them to advance, when we remain faithful to our commitments even when no one is watching.

In these choices, we find that real victory isn't just about the scoreboard of life. It's about becoming the kind of person who can face both success and failure with grace, knowing we've competed with honor.

THE MYSTERY: THE BUTLER BENCHING

Super Bowl LII presents us with what theologians might call a mystery of "calling." It remains one of the most perplexing decisions in NFL history. Coach Belichick decided not to play Malcolm Butler, hero of Super Bowl XLIX. Butler wept over the decision during the national anthem, knowing he wouldn't play. The decision defied human logic and understanding. The Eagles scored forty-one points against a defense that desperately needed Butler's skills.

Why did Coach Belichick not field his best team for the biggest game of the year? Belichick offered no explanation for this puzzling decision. Not then. Not now. We are still waiting. We probably will never have one. Indeed, if you want to anger Bill Belichick, ask him this question again.

Life isn't fair, even in football. Some of us swim into this world into the arms of love. Other of us are spit out onto the ground. Some of us are born into stadium lights and cheering crowds, caught by sure hands and cradled in victory's embrace. Others arrive like a wobbling punt in the rain, bouncing hard on uncertain ground, with no blockers to clear our path. The cosmic game plan often seems inscrutable—a divine scenario we cannot decode, no matter how many hours we spend in life's film room. Malcolm Butler lived this brutal truth, as will we. No explanation. No justice. No fair catch to signal. Just the hard landing of reality's punt, bouncing unpredictably before us.

Yet here lies the deeper mystery of faith: Can we trust the divine Head Coach even when His game plan and play "calls" seem to make no earthly sense? Can we believe, as Butler had to, that there is meaning beyond our understanding—that even our benching might serve some greater purpose in God's eternal playbook?

The Butler benching reminds us that faith isn't faith until it's tested in the crucible of confusion. Like Job who lost everything yet refused to curse God and like Joseph thrown into a pit by his brothers only to rise to greatness, we're called to trust not in our understanding but in God's unfailing love—even when the play call seems to defy all football logic.

For in life's toughest moments, when the game plan seems written in a language we cannot read, perhaps what matters most is not our position on the field, but our posture before the One who sees the whole game, from opening kickoff to final whistle, in God's eternal now.

THE PROPHET'S BURDEN: BELICHICK AND THE PRICE OF EXCELLENCE

Like the prophets of old who found no honor in their hometown, greatness often attracts both followers and fierce critics. Bill Belichick's legacy mirrors this ancient truth—that success, far from silencing critics, often amplifies their voices. As Jesus himself was jeered, "Isn't this the carpenter's son?"[10] so too do Belichick's critics ask, "Isn't this just Brady's beneficiary?"

The six camps of Belichick criticism reveal a deeper truth about human nature and the burden of excellence:

1) The New Sanhedrin: The Lombardi Primacy Advocates: Like those who clung to Moses' law while questioning Christ's authority, these traditionalists hold fast to Lombardi's pristine legacy. They scrutinize Belichick's wilderness years in Cleveland as the Pharisees questioned

Jesus' Nazareth origins. Their argument echoes an eternal truth: we often measure new prophets against the sanctified memories of those who came before.

2) The Keepers of the Temple: The Saint Lombardi True Believers: These are the zealots of football orthodoxy, for whom Lombardi remains the untouchable saint of the gridiron gospel. Their resistance to Belichick's achievements mirrors how religious authorities often resist new interpretations of ancient truths. The "cheater" narrative they promote becomes their stone of stumbling, their way of maintaining the old order.

3) The Dual Covenant Theorists: The Dynamic Duo Approach: Like scholars debating whether grace or works save us, these analysts cannot decide whether Brady or Belichick deserves more credit. Their struggle reflects humanity's eternal desire to perfectly apportion credit and blame, even when dealing with mysterious partnerships of divine design.

4) The Apostles: The Belichick Paladins: Every prophet has their devoted followers. These believers see in Belichick not just a football coach but a revolutionary who has transformed the sport itself. Their fervor reminds us that transfiguration often requires both vision and devoted disciples willing to spread the new gospel.

5) The Converts: The Lord of the Rings Advocates: Like Paul on the road to Damascus, these former critics were struck by the undeniable light of six Super Bowl rings. Their conversion reminds us that sometimes truth must be demonstrated repeatedly before it can be accepted.

6) The Eternal Critics: The Belichick Iconoclasts: Like those who demanded signs from Jesus while dismissing the miracles before their eyes, these critics attribute Belichick's success to luck and circumstance. Their skepticism serves as a reminder that some will never believe, no matter how many victories they witness.

Excellence that Withstands the Heat of Criticism

This chorus of criticism reveals a profound spiritual truth: success does not shield us from doubt, scrutiny, or opposition—it often intensifies them. As the psalmist wrote, "Many are the afflictions of the righteous."[11] In Belichick's story, we see echoed the timeless pattern of prophetic figures:

- The more light they bring, the more shadows they cast
- The higher they rise, the more critics they attract
- The more they achieve, the more their methods are questioned

Yet perhaps this is the very crucible in which greatness is refined. Like gold tested by fire, true excellence must withstand the heat of criticism. Belichick's legacy, debated and dissected from every angle, reminds us that the path to greatness is never smooth, and the crown of achievement often comes with the thorns of criticism, thorns of the Genesis curse that Jesus wore on the cross when he turned that curse into a blessing.

In the end, the multitude of perspectives on Belichick's legacy serves not to diminish but to illuminate his impact. For as with all transformative figures, the very intensity of the debate proves the significance of his contribution. The critics, whether they intend to or not, help write the gospel of his greatness.

*If the world hates you,
keep in mind that it hated me first.*

JESUS[12]

THE DEEPER GAME

Every prophet faces their critics, every innovator their skeptics, every leader their doubters. Moses had his murmuring masses, David his suspicious brothers, Jesus his religious critics. The presence of criticism often confirms the significance of the calling—not because opposition validates truth, but because meaningful change invariably disturbs the comfortable status quo.

THE BELICHICK BLUEPRINT

Like Belichick, we're called not to silence our critics but to let our work speak louder than their words. When Belichick reimagined how football could be played—valuing versatility over specialization, adaptability over tradition—many dismissed his methods as unsustainable or unorthodox. His response wasn't to argue but to execute, letting results build his case over time.

This holds profound implications for people of faith today. In an age of social media arguments, virtue signaling, and culture war posturing, we're tempted to measure our impact by how effectively we can shout down opposition. But authentic faith, like genuine innovation, proves itself through patient, persistent action rather than loud defense. It's seen in:

- The quiet consistency of living our convictions when no one is watching.
- The steady work of serving others without requiring recognition.
- The humble willingness to let transfiguration speak for itself.
- The courage to stay focused on our calling despite criticism.
- The patience to let time validate truth rather than rushing to defend it.

The goal isn't to win arguments but to live answers. Not to

prove critics wrong, but to prove the calling right through faithful execution. In this way, criticism becomes not a burden to fight but a backdrop against which authentic faith becomes more clearly visible.

Belichick's innovations changed football's landscape not through argument but through demonstrated effectiveness. Likewise, our faith journey might persuade most when we live it with such compelling authenticity that results speak for themselves.

> Blessed are you when people insult you, persecute you and falsely say all kinds of evil against you because of me.
>
> JESUS[13]

The Eternal Game

In Bill Belichick, we see reflected both the glory and the struggle of the human condition. Like Jacob wrestling with the angel, his legacy leaves us both blessed and limping—marked by both victory and struggle, excellence and imperfection.

Perhaps that's the most important lesson: our greatest achievements come not from our perfection, but from our willingness to persist in the face of our imperfections. In both football and faith, the true victory lies not in never falling, but in how we rise again. As of 2024, Bill Belichick is now the head coach at the University of North Carolina with a five-year contract, fulfilling his dream of college coaching ever since his father was an assistant coach at UNC.

> But we have this treasure in earthen vessels, that the excellency of the power may be of God, and not of us.
>
> APOSTLE PAUL[14]

A TALE OF TWO TITANS: THE LOMBARDI-BELICHICK PARALLEL

We have argued that, in the pantheon of NFL coaching legends, Vince Lombardi and Bill Belichick stand as twin peaks, their shadows stretching across different eras but cast by the same eternal sun of excellence. Though their methods differed as dramatically as thunder from silence, their common ground reveals essential truths about leadership, legacy, and the price of greatness.

As a concluding coda to this part of the book, let's explore their similarities which run deep beneath surface differences:

- Both built dynasties through unwavering systems they believed in absolutely
- Both made tough personnel decisions without sentiment
- Both fought relentlessly against complacency
- Both despised showboating and self-promotion
- Both demonstrated exceptional teaching abilities
- Both demanded total commitment to team over individual.

Lombardi built his legacy on uncompromising integrity, while Belichick's brilliance occasionally cast shadows of controversy. Yet their contrasts illuminate different paths to greatness:

Leadership Style?

- Lombardi: A volcanic force of nature, psychology's master practitioner, penetrating hearts through sheer force of personality.
- Belichick: A glacier of quiet intensity, system's architect, earning respect through results rather than rhetoric.

Relationship with Rules?

- Lombardi: Absolute adherence to both written and unwritten laws, earning the Commissioner's trust and respect.

- Belichick: Occasional willingness to probe gray areas, leading to conflicts with authority and tarnished triumphs.

Path to Success?

- Lombardi: Never experienced a losing season, his excellence immediate and sustained.
- Belichick: Rose from early failures in Cleveland, his greatness forged in the furnace of setbacks.

The paradox lies in their shared destination reached by divergent paths. Yet both achieved what few others have: they changed not just how the game is played, but how it is conceived.

Their story offers a profound lesson. There are countless routes to achievement, but integrity has only one path: unwavering commitment to truth. In the end, both men's legacies force us to wrestle with essential questions about the relationship between means and ends, between winning and virtue, between greatness and goodness.

THIRD QUARTER

GAME ON: THE FIELD NOT THE SIDELINES

Third Quarter introduces athletes in action, those who live and love the game on the field not just the sidelines, including those whose vital contributions often go unnoticed. Baseball offers us almost as good a lens as football for this theme.

Many today have never experienced the legend of Sandy Koufax, whose fabled fastball seemed to sing through the summer air, striking fear into batters before they even stepped to the plate. When Koufax took the mound, dugouts fell silent, players straining to catch that mythical hum before stepping into the box, already half-beaten. The poetry of his motion, that balletic stretch and magnificent release, made him one of baseball's immortals. Yet his brilliance required a foundation—a partner in the dirt whose role, though less celebrated, was equally crucial.

John Roseboro, Koufax's batterymate from 1957–1966, exemplified this essential truth: greatness often rests on those who work in the shadows. Without his steadfast presence behind the plate, Koufax's lightning might have struck wild. While crowds marveled at the pitcher's elegant arc, victory was forged in the catcher's humble squat—not in the glamor of the high stretch, but in that low, gritty fortress where brilliance found its foundation.

The football equivalent of the catcher is the center—the player who starts every offensive play by snapping the ball to the quarterback. Like a catcher, they're in a physically demanding crouch position, operate in the trenches, and are essential to every play while rarely getting the spotlight. Just as catchers need intimate knowledge of their pitchers' tendencies and opposing batters' weaknesses, centers need to understand their quarterbacks' cadence, timing preferences, and how to identify defensive formations. Both positions require a unique combination of mental sharpness and physical toughness.

This dynamic—of spotlight and shadow, star and enabler—carries us perfectly into our exploration of football's stage, where similar partnerships shape every play, even if we don't always see them all.

Down in the dirt is where games are won.

GAME X

CROSSING THE GOAL LINE
WHERE HEAVEN MEETS EARTH

Love is the force that ignites the spirit and binds teams together.

BASKETBALL COACH PHIL JACKSON[1]

When heaven touches earth, it rarely announces itself with trumpets. More often, it arrives in moments that seem, at first glance, like endings rather than beginnings. A rookie's shattered knee. A linebacker's torn deltoid. A perfect season that refuses to become a dynasty. Yet in these moments of apparent defeat, something divine often stirs—if we have eyes to see it.

Divine Adaptation: The Madden Testament

> And we know that in all things God works for the good of those who love him, who have been called according to his purpose.
>
> ROMANS 8:28 (NIV)

John Madden's journey to football immortality began with what seemed like disaster. The year was 1958. Philadelphia Eagles' training camp, and a rookie's dreams, were shattering with his knee in an era when orthopedic surgery was more medieval than modern. But God specializes in turning endings into new beginnings.[2]

While other injured players retreated into self-pity, young Madden noticed something extraordinary: the Eagles' star quarterback, Norm Van Brocklin, obsessively studying game film. Hour after hour, reel after reel, the veteran quarterback analyzed every play, every pattern, every possibility. Instead of ignoring the injured rookie, Van Brocklin did something unexpected. He invited Madden to join him. In that act of grace, what seemed like a career-ending injury became a divine classroom.[3]

Those hours of film study with Van Brocklin shaped more

than just Madden's understanding of football; they forged his future.

By 1969, at the audacious age of thirty-two, Madden did something that seemed as unlikely as young David challenging Goliath. He walked straight into Al Davis's office and campaigned for the Raiders' head coaching position. His three commandments became Raiders Scripture:

> Be on time (honoring the sacred)
>
> Pay attention (practicing presence)
>
> Play like hell when I tell you (answering the call)[4]

Under Madden's leadership, the Raiders weren't just a team; they were a tribe. Like David's mighty men, they were society's castoffs transformed into warriors. His .763 winning percentage stands as testament to how divine wisdom often works through simple truths and authentic leadership.

When health concerns forced Madden from coaching at just forty-two, he faced what many would consider another career crisis. Instead, he found new ways to translate football's mysteries to the masses. Partnered with Pat Summerall, he didn't just announce games—he turned them into parables. His "All-Madden Team" celebrated the game's unsung warriors, particularly the offensive linemen, football's forgotten servants.

Then came the video games, where Madden proved that

ancient wisdom could speak through today's technology. Madden brought football's gospel to new generations through pixels and programming. Each transformation reached more people than the last, not because he abandoned his core principles, but because he found new ways to translate them.

GRACE UNDER FIRE: THE TAYLOR PARADOX

The year is 1988. The place? New Orleans Superdome. Lawrence Taylor takes the field with a torn right deltoid muscle—an injury that would sideline most athletes for weeks. The Saints' offensive line sees weakness, opportunity. They don't know LT. For the next sixty minutes, Taylor transforms pain into power. Three sacks. Two forced fumbles. Seven tackles. One deflected pass. A defensive performance Bill Parcells would later call Taylor's finest hour. Like Jacob wrestling the angel, Taylor seemed to grow stronger through his wound.

This wasn't an isolated incident. In 1989, he played with a fractured ankle. Another season, he battled through a hairline fracture in his tibia and a hamstring injury that, as teammate Karl Nelson noted, "would have put most athletes on crutches."[5] Each morning, his body would "sound like popcorn"[6] just walking to the bathroom. Yet Sunday after Sunday, he left everything on the field.

Lawrence Taylor's life story is draped in a plethora of "do not follow" signs. His excesses and dangerous indiscretions have, by his own admission, involved substance abuse and, in general terms, living an accelerated life in the fast lane. Like the prodigal son who squandered his inheritance yet never lost his father's love, Taylor's story forces us to wrestle with deep questions about talent, grace, and redemption. When God gives extraordinary gifts, does that come with extraordinary latitude? Where do we draw the line between understanding human frailty and enabling destructive behavior?

A rookie linebacker steps onto the NFL stage and immediately starts "eating the wolves," as Bill Parcells famously noted.[7] While most rookies struggle to survive, Taylor revolutionized the game from day one, becoming the only rookie ever named NFL Defensive Player of the Year. Like young David facing Goliath, Taylor possessed a supernatural confidence that transformed the impossible into routine.

The key to adapting the Parcells approach to the "Taylors" in your life is the harmony between uncompromising standards and unconditional worth. Show someone they matter enough for you to maintain boundaries while assuring them they matter too much for you to enable destructive behavior.

Actionable elements of Parcells' approach with Taylor that apply to all the "Taylors" in our lives: 1) consistent communication even during Taylor's lowest points; 2) clear boundaries set with real consequences; 3) always distinguish between the person and their struggles—Parcells famously said about Taylor, "This is a good kid with bad habits;" 4) accountability structures in place that played to Taylor's strengths; 5) prophesying forward with leadership responsibilities that show trust while creating positive pressure to stay clean; 6) the use of humor and tough love rather than shame; 7) a focus on small wins and incremental progress; 8) combining high standards with second chances—each day was a fresh opportunity to do better and start over.

A clarification and caveat about "tough love." If there is not a loveliness to love, even to "tough love," then it is merely toughness or punishment masquerading as care. This "LOVE TOUGH" philosophy was developed by Dan Quinn during his tenure as the head coach of the Atlanta Falcons, and was further implemented in his subsequent roles, including as head coach of the Washington Commanders. Quinn emphasizes that the foundation of tough love should be love, not toughness. Without genuine care, he argues, tough love can be misinterpreted or misconstrued. So he fostered empathy, connection, and loyalty to create a "LOVE TOUGH" tight-knit team culture, and often uses prayer, biblical scriptures (Isaiah 27 and Psalm 133 come to mind) and spiritual themes of unity and brotherhood to motivate his players.[8]

> Faith is a very important part of my life, and I think it's helped me be the person I am. It's helped me make decisions, it's helped me go through trials and tribulations ... I think it's very important to have faith, to believe in something bigger than yourself ... You can get through even the toughest of circumstances because God is on your side.
>
> LEGENDARY NEW YORK GIANTS COACH
> BILL PARCELLS
> WITH TWO SUPER BOWL VICTORIES

In this arena, Bill Parcells ("The Big Tuna") emerges as a master of redemptive leadership. He approached Taylor with what we might call "prodigal grace"—the kind of love that neither condemns nor enables, that sees the person beneath the behavior. Like the father in Jesus' famous parable, Parcells kept watch for his prodigal, maintained standards while extending mercy, and created space for transformation without demanding perfection.

"God loves sinners," Taylor would often say, "and He tells even people like me, 'For now, do what you have to do ... but when this is over, you belong to me.'"[9] These words, part profound theology and part dangerous rationalization, capture the eternal tension between grace and accountability. They echo through church halls and locker rooms alike, challenging our understanding of how exceptional talent intersects with exceptional grace.

Taylor's life embodied an almost biblical tension:

- The warrior who could play through impossible pain
- The genius who knew everyone's defensive assignment
- The leader who could take over games at will
- The lost soul who battled constant demons off the field

Even his confrontations with Bill Belichick (showing up handcuffed to a team meeting, challenging his coach's authority) revealed both the audacity of his talent and the depth of his struggles. Yet like the biblical Samson, Taylor's strength seemed undiminished by his lifestyle—until it was.[10]

> But one thing I do: Forgetting what is behind and straining toward what is ahead.
>
> PHILIPPIANS 3:13 [NIV]

Perfect Storm: The Bears' Miracle

Some miracles aren't meant to be repeated. Certain moments of glory stand alone in sacred history. The 1985 Chicago Bears were such a miracle—a convergence of personalities, power, and purpose that created one perfect season of football divinity.

There was once a defense so dominant that John Madden, who had battled the legendary Steel Curtain dynasty, declared, "These guys were more dominant than the Steelers."[11] Not long ago, ESPN ranked the 1985 Bears as the best team for a single season in NFL history. The defensive coordinator, Buddy Ryan, was loved with such fierce devotion that his players petitioned ownership to keep him. A head coach, Mike Ditka, fought with Ryan at halftime yet couldn't deny the holy fire Ryan brought to the team.

The numbers tell a sacred story:

- 18–1 record
- Two playoff shutouts
- A Super Bowl massacre where the Patriots gained -19 yards by halftime
- A 44–0 dismantling of Tom Landry's Cowboys that ended an era

The Bears' demolition of the Cowboys reads like an Old

Testament battle. In what Ron Jaworski called "more autopsy than film breakdown,"[12] Chicago's defense unleashed years of pent-up fury on America's Team. It wasn't just a victory; it was a changing of the guard, marking the end of Landry's twenty-year run of excellence as surely as David's stone marked the end of Goliath's reign.

Yet the '85 Bears' collapse offers a study in how great things fall apart. Their descent wasn't sudden but systematic, a series of fractures that turned champions into cautionary tales.

The Defensive Gospel Lost:

- Buddy Ryan's departure to Philadelphia stripped more than schemes—it took the soul of the defense.
- The fierce "46 defense" that terrorized quarterbacks gave way to a tepid "bend don't break" philosophy.
- In 1986, despite a 14–2 record, the Bears' defense lost its holy fire.
- Washington's Joe Gibbs exposed the new vulnerability, spreading his offense to defeat the Bears 27–13 in the playoffs.

The Quarterback Curse:

- Jim McMahon's leadership extended beyond statistics—he had the rare charisma that united both offense and defense.

- Green Bay Packer Charles Martin's notorious cheap shot (throwing McMahon on his injured shoulder) ended more than a season.
- Doug Flutie's arrival revealed the locker room's fragility.
- McMahon's cruel nickname for Flutie ("America's midget")[13] split the team's solidarity.

The Celebrity Seduction:

- Like Israel demanding a king to be like other nations, the Bears chased worldly glory.
- Players prioritized commercials over commitment.
- The "Super Bowl Shuffle" went from celebration to distraction.
- Book deals and public appearances fractured focus.
- Team unity dissolved into individual brands.

By 1987, the Bears still had talent but had lost their mystique. No longer did teams fear them. The swagger became hollow. The defense played without its former fury. The brotherhood that made them special had splintered.

The Digital Cathedral: When Fandom Becomes Faith

Imagine a contemporary cathedral where millions gather not just on Sundays, but every day. This sanctuary isn't built of stone and stained glass, but of statistics and shared dreams. Welcome to fantasy football, where virtual teams create real community and digital competition builds authentic relationships.

When your authors hear the word fantasy, they're immediately transported back to the heyday of *Fantasy Island* (1977–1984). In its prime, with a plum slot, the show was a cultural phenomenon. Now, seen on nostalgia channels, it feels nearly unwatchable. Yet the brilliance of its creators and writers lay in recognizing a universal truth: people crave the chance to live out their fantasies. This yearning—to see dreams realized, even if only by proxy—speaks to a fundamental human desire.

The numbers tell a fantasy story that would make even John Madden's eyebrows dance:

- Over 40 million Americans participate
- The industry generates over $18 billion annually
- 89 percent of fantasy players use mobile apps to stay connected
- Fantasy sports drives 35 percent of NFL viewership

Former Ravens coach Brian Billick revealed something stunning: "I got more statistical data off the internet generated by gamblers and fantasy players than we as a team could possibly generate on our own."[14] Think about that: millions of amateur analysts creating more insight than professional NFL teams.

The phenomenon spreads across every sector of society:

- Corporate leagues transforming office culture
- Prison leagues building community behind bars
- Military leagues connecting deployed soldiers with home
- Family leagues spanning generations
- Church leagues creating new forms of fellowship

Like medieval cathedral builders who created community through shared purpose, fantasy football provides:

- Ritual and Routine
- Weekly lineup decisions become liturgy
- Trade discussions become fellowship
- Draft day becomes high holy day
- Stats become Scripture

The explosive success of fantasy football presents an uncomfortable mirror for the church today. Here are some revealing parallels:

The Engagement Gap:

- Fantasy players eagerly spend 6.9 hours weekly studying statistics; many Christians struggle to find 10 minutes daily for prayer[15]

- League members check apps 30+ times daily; weekly church bulletins go unread

- Draft preparation involves weeks of research; Bible study attendance declining

- People arrange schedules around game day; Sunday attendance becomes optional

Why do people invest so deeply in Fantasy Football? Looking closer, we see an EPIC interface that John Wesley might have embraced under his mantra "Plunder the Egyptians."[16] Len has explored the EPIC interface that connects with digital culture in many of his books, but to summarize here in shortand:

E: Experience over Logical, Linear, Theoretica, Abstract

- People seek experiential meaning
- Details matter in creating experiences
- Community forms around shared passion
- Investment follows interest

P: Participation over Representation

- People want to be players, not spectators
- Analysis deepens engagement
- Community requires interaction
- Interactivity is the new standard of excellence

I: Image-rich over Word-based

- Visual storytelling drives connection
- Stats become compelling narratives
- Graphics make data memorable
- Live scoring creates dramatic tension
- Team logos build identity

C: Connection over Individualism

- Daily engagement beats weekly meetings
- Shared activities build relationships
- Competition can strengthen community
- Technology can enhance tradition

Perhaps it's time to ask: What if we created church experiences as engaging and EPIC (Experiential, Participatory, Image-rich, Connective)[17] as fantasy football? What if our communities were as Missional, our fellowship as Relational, our participation as Incarnational (MRI)?[18]

> But he said to me, "My grace is sufficient for you, for my power is made perfect in weakness."
>
> APOSTLE PAUL[19]

Sacred Choices: The Fuel That Drives Us

Here is a scene from 1919: A brash young rookie named George Halas, batting a measly .091, is compensating with his mouth. His target? The legendary Ty Cobb, baseball's most feared competitor and notorious hothead.

"Hey punk," Cobb growls after enduring Halas's stream of insults, "I'll see you after the game. Don't forget, punk!"[20]

Young Halas, who would later become "Papa Bear" and lead the Chicago Bears to six NFL titles, feels his bravado drain away. He delays leaving the ballpark, imagining the beating that awaits. But when he finally emerges, he encounters something unexpected: not Cobb's fists, but his wisdom.

"I like your spirit, kid," Cobb says, displaying a grace that history rarely attributes to him. "But don't overdo it. Direct your energy positively. Don't waste yourself being negative."[21]

That moment, when expected violence presented as unexpected mentorship, reveals a truth that echoes through football history: our choice of fuel determines our destiny. History offers us two men who seemed touched by divine protection, each making radically different choices about how to use their apparent invincibility:

George Washington rode through bullets that shredded his uniform but never touched his flesh. Leading from the front, he transformed protection into purpose:

- Keeping the Continental Army together against impossible odds
- Turning defeat at New York into victory at Trenton
- Walking away from power not once but twice
- Building a legacy of servant leadership

Adolf Hitler survived over forty assassination attempts, interpreting each survival as divine endorsement. His choice of hate as fuel led to:

- Initial victories that seemed to validate his approach
- Growing megalomania that proved ultimately self-destructive
- A legacy of ashes and apocalypse

One man's legacy built a nation; the other's burned a continent.

> Faith, family, and football is how I prioritize my life. And they all go together, but they go in that order.
>
> SEVENTEEN-SEASON NFL QB PHILIP RIVERS[22]
> EIGHT-TIME PRO BOWL SELECTION

A fundamental truth about both sports and faith? Our choice of fuel determines our destiny. Like a football team choosing between a power running game or a spread offense, every player must choose their motivational fuel. The NFL's sidelines have seen multiple approaches:

- Bill Parcells building through tough love.
- Tony Dungy leading through quiet strength.
- Buddy Ryan fueling his '85 Bears defense with controlled fury.
- Chuck Noll building the Steel Curtain with disciplined determination.

Each chose their fuel, and their choices shaped not just games but lifelines and legacies. For people of faith, several distinct types of "fuel" can power the journey:

1) Contemplative Fuel: Drawing strength from silence,

meditation, and deep prayer. This is the fuel of monastics and mystics, those who find God most clearly in stillness and solitude. It's like a slow-burning ember that provides steady, lasting warmth.

2) Relational Fuel: Finding energy through fellowship, mentoring, and walking alongside others in faith. This fuel comes from seeing God's face in others and participating in the divine through community.

3) Justice and Mercy Fuel: Being energized by working to align the world more closely with divine ideals of righteousness and equity. This was the fuel of prophets and reformers, those who found their deepest connection to God through confronting injustice.

4) Wonder Fuel: Drawing inspiration from nature, art, music, and beauty as windows into transcendence. This is the fuel of poets and artists who see divine glory reflected in creation.

5) Service Fuel: Finding spiritual sustenance through practical acts of care and compassion. This powered figures like Mother Teresa, who encountered God most directly in serving "the least of these."

6) Study Fuel: Being energized by deep engagement with scripture, theology, and religious thought. This intellectual fuel powered many of the great teachers and theologians.

The most resilient lives of faith often draw from multiple types of fuel, like a hybrid engine. Different seasons might require different fuel mixtures. What's fascinating is how these various fuels can either complement or clash with each other—the contemplative's need for silence might conflict with the activist's drive for engagement, for instance. The art seems to be in discerning which fuel best serves one's unique calling and season of life.

When Hospitality Meets Holy Ground

It's Sunday morning at Heavenly Heights Church. Sarah, a first-time visitor, wraps her hands around a Styrofoam cup filled with what the welcome team proudly calls their "fellowship blend." One sip and her face tells the story—this coffee could make angels weep, and not in a good way.

Meanwhile, across town at Mammoth Stadium, Tom, a lifelong football fan, savors an artisanal pour-over at the new premium coffee bar. The barista knows his name, his team, and his precise brewing preferences. Who would have thought that the NFL would become a beacon of hospitality while some churches seem stuck in the bitter dregs of welcome?

Len's friend once quipped, "If Jesus showed up at today's megachurches, He'd be flipping espresso machines instead of money tables!" We chuckle, but there's a deeper truth brewing here. In our caffeine-powered world, a cup of coffee isn't just a drink. It's a handshake, a hug, a way of saying "you matter." When we serve bitter, burnt coffee in dented urns, are we unconsciously telling our visitors they're not worth the good stuff?

The NFL gets it. They've transformed USAmerican Sundays from simple game days into immersive experiences where every detail counts. Their playbook is simple but profound:

- Quality speaks volumes about how much you value your guests.
- Experience creates connections that statistics can't measure.
- Details aren't just details—they're the whole game.
- Welcome is a verb, not a sign on the wall.

While the NFL has turned their venues into modern-day gathering spaces, too many churches are stuck in a *Fantasy Island* time warp, serving up programs as outdated as Mr. Roarke's white suit or as songlike as Ricardo Montalban's accent. The plane may still be landing, but nobody's rushing to get that kind of fantasy anymore.

The truth is, hospitality is holy ground, whether it's served in a cathedral or a stadium. Maybe it's time for churches to wake up and smell the coffee—literally.

When we serve bitter coffee, we risk brewing something

far worse than a bad cup of joe. We risk cultivating bitterness in the very places meant to dissolve it. The NFL's coffee revolution isn't just about better beans; it's about better belonging. They've learned that hospitality, like a perfectly-pulled espresso shot, requires both pressure and precision, heat and heart.

Perhaps it's time for churches to filter out the grounds of complacency and percolate something new. After all, every Sunday presents a choice: We can serve up bitterness, both in our cups and our hearts, or we can brew something better. Choose bonds over bitterness. Choose the quiet grace of connection over the clamor of hatred. For sometimes our greatest lessons come from surprising sources—even a cup of coffee, or a game where men chase a leather ball across painted grass.

> "For I know the plans I have for you," declares the LORD, "plans to prosper you and not to harm you, plans to give you hope and a future."
> JEREMIAH 29:11 (NIV)

THE POWER OF RESONANCE: BEYOND WIN OR LOSE

The only thing that promotes engagement more than

enragement is resonance—that deep, vibrating truth that hums in perfect harmony with our being. In today's world of hot takes and heated rivalries, it's easy to fuel our passion with fury. We see it in stands divided by team colors, on social media platforms split by tribal loyalties, and yes, even in church pews separated by doctrine and denomination and devotional rituals. But fury creates discord; resonance creates symphony.

Like young George Halas discovering an unexpected note of grace in Ty Cobb's wisdom, we face daily choices about what frequency we'll tune our lives to:

- Will we choose love's deep bass note or hatred's jarring static?
- Will we build up harmony or tear down with dissonance?
- Will we welcome new voices to the chorus or exclude them?
- Will we adapt our rhythm or stagnate in old melodies?

The frequency we choose today determines who we become tomorrow. Every NFL stadium tells this story—where this weekend's bitter rivals become next week's traded teammates, finding a new harmony in unexpected places. Where old feuds give way to new alliances, creating fresh rhythms of relationship. Where the game's greatest lessons often come from its hardest hits, teaching us that even life's discordant moments can lead to deeper resonance.

Perhaps that's the deepest truth hidden in this game we love: that sometimes heaven touches down not in our moments of victory, but in how we tune our hearts for the journey. In how we play our part in the greater symphony, not just what we win. In how we unite our voices, not just who we beat.

> Choose you this day whom ye will serve ...
>
> JOSHUA 24:15 (KJV)

In the end, the life of faith is not about the score on the board but the resonance in our hearts. For in this great game of life, as in football, our greatest victories often come not from the points we score, but from the grace we share, the bonds we build, and the love we choose to fuel our journey toward that eternal goal line—each step a beat in the universal rhythm, each choice a note in the cosmic symphony of faith.

Game XI

Red Zone Redemption
From Fumbles to Faith

When I speak of love I am not speaking of some sentimental and weak response. I am not speaking of that force which is just emotional bosh. I am speaking of that force which all of the great religions have seen as the supreme unifying principle of life. Love is somehow the key that unlocks the door to ultimate reality.

MARTIN LUTHER KING, JR.[1]

When Heaven Celebrates: Scoring Touchdowns in Eternity

> I tell you, there is rejoicing in the
> presence of the angels of God over
> one sinner who repents.
>
> LUKE 15:10 (NIV)

Once upon a time, American politics was like old-school football—a muddy battle between the 40-yard lines, where success meant grinding out three yards and leaving cleat marks in the moderate middle. How quaint that seems now.

Today's political playbook reads more like a Vegas oddsmaker's fever dream: all Hail Marys and quarterback sneaks to the end zones, no rest stops in the middling middle. The moderate middle has become no-man's land, where careful centrists get blitzed from both directions.[2]

Like modern football itself, politics has abandoned the art of the methodical march. No one dreams of being the steady fullback anymore; everyone wants to be the touchdown dancer in the end zone. The middle of the field has become a ghost town, with both teams camping out in their red zones, loading up their political shotgun formations. It's all explosive plays and end-zone dances

RED ZONE REDEMPTION

now—either you're spiking the ball in triumph or watching your dreams get picked off by the opposition. Three yards and a cloud of dust? Please. Today it's touchdown or turnover, with the moderate middle serving as nothing but a fly-over zone between two warring end zones.

Think about it: In football, a single touchdown sends shockwaves of joy through eighty thousand souls. Complete strangers become instant family, leaping into each other's arms as if gravity itself has been suspended by pure joy. The roar of celebration can be heard from outer space (or at least from the parking lot).

But in the kingdom of heaven? When one soul turns toward home, the celebration dwarfs any Super Bowl moment. Angels don't just cheer. They throw a cosmic party. Heaven doesn't just roar. Heaven erupts with the kind of joy that makes stadium celebrations look like polite golf claps.

Here's the gut check: Would any self-respecting football player ever brag, "Hey, I played fifteen seasons and never once scored or helped score a touchdown"? Even the greatest quarterbacks know their job isn't just to cross the goal line themselves. It's to put the ball in the hands of someone who will.

Yet somehow, we've convinced ourselves that spiritual spectating is a legitimate sport. We sit in our comfortable pews, clutching our rulebooks, more interested in throwing flags than throwing perfect spirals of grace to searching hearts. We've become expert refs in a game we were meant to play, debating the finer points of Roberts Rules of Order while the Spirit's playbook of goodness, beauty, and truth gathers dust on our bench.

Every day, God hands us the ball. Every day, we have a clear shot at the end zone or—better yet—the chance to spot someone wide open for the gospel pass or lateral of their life. Every day, heaven leans forward, waiting to erupt in celebration, not just when we score, but when we help others find their way home.

The question isn't whether we have the opportunity to carry the ball or help someone else carry it into glory. It's whether we'll ever trust the Spirit's offensive line, leave our comfortable sidelines, and get in the game of eternal consequence.

THE PITTSBURGH PLAYBOOK: WHEN WARRIORS BECOME WITNESSES

Can you imagine the 1970s Pittsburgh Steelers, either as the NFL's team of the decade, or as God's gathering of spiritual warriors? The truth is they were both.

While their archrivals, the Oakland Raiders, celebrated breaking rules, these Steelers were breaking something far more significant: the stereotype that faith and football couldn't mix.

In their locker room, a different kind of game plan unfolded:

- Donnie Shell mentoring rookie Tony Dungy
- Bible study replacing trash talk
- Prayer warriors wearing Super Bowl rings
- Champions more concerned with eternal victory than temporal glory

THE DUNGY FORMATION: A DIFFERENT KIND OF VICTORY

Tony Dungy represents a long list of active and retired Christian NFL players and coaches who have lived and breathed Jesus. Dungy started out as a quarterback, then turned defensive back. He became the NFL's first African American head coach to win a Super Bowl, leading the Indianapolis Colts to victory in 2007.

But beyond the scoreboard, Dungy revolutionized leadership in the NFL with his calm, Christ-centered approach dubbed the "Dungy Way"—proving you could win without yelling or cursing, succeed without compromising values, and lead through quiet strength and unwavering faith. An incredulous reporter once asked Tony Dungy how it could be possible to be an NFL Coach without cursing, to which Dungy replied "Why not?"

His coaching tree, which includes the natural semiotician Mike Tomlin and the calm and collected Lovie Smith, carried forward this philosophy. Despite personal trials, including the tragic loss of his son James to suicide in 2005, Dungy's faith never wavered. He used his platform to mentor players both in faith and football, wrote multiple bestselling books about life and leadership, and developed a prison ministry that continues to impact lives. His legacy transcends football statistics, as he demonstrated that success in professional sports doesn't require sacrificing one's faith or family values, ultimately becoming as well-known for his Christian ministry and mentorship as for his coaching achievements.

Dungy's coaching career rewrote the NFL playbook:

- Sending coaches home to their families while others worked obsessively[3]
- Putting faith first when others prioritized only winning
- Building eternal legacy while others chased temporal glory
- Scoring touchdowns in prison ministry while others sought only sporting victory[4]

RED ZONE REDEMPTION

> As much fun as it was to be winning, we tried not to get too caught up in it. We knew that our family life and faith walk were more important.
>
> TONY DUNGY[5]

Heaven's Highlight Reel

The roar of Three Rivers Stadium during the Steelers' Super Bowl victories (1975, 76, 79, 80) was legendary—a thunderous celebration that seemed to shake the very Red Beds of Pittsburgh. But high above the steel and concrete, beyond the confines of earthly championships, a different kind of celebration was taking place.

In heaven's grand arena, the angels weren't watching the scoreboard. Their eyes were fixed on moments that would never make ESPN's highlight reel:

- They celebrated that quiet afternoon when "Steel Curtain" safety Donnie Shell took young Dungy under his wing, planting seeds of wisdom that would bloom across decades.
- They celebrated when offensive tackle Tunch Ilkin, the NFL's first Turkish player,[6] discovered "men's men" living faith deeper than any gameplay strategy.

- Their cheers echoed through the celestial stands each time a prisoner found hope and redemption through Dungy's ministry.

The heavenly hosts erupted in joy for victories that would never be recorded in sports almanacs—for every coach who chose family over fame, every player who demonstrated grace in defeat, every life redeemed by radical love. While earthly stadiums might hold tens of thousands of cheering fans, heaven's arena pulsed with the celebration of eternal victories.

In this divine playbook, the rules were different. True victory wasn't measured in yards gained or points scored, but in lives touched and hearts warmed. Leadership meant serving others, not commanding them. Faith spoke loudest when it was lived, not preached. The impact of these moments rippled through eternity, far outlasting the gleam of any championship ring.

When earthly touchdowns brought fleeting joy to the Pittsburgh faithful, heaven celebrated the touchdowns that would echo forever—souls turning toward light, hearts opening to grace, lives redirecting toward mission. The stadium cheers would fade into memory, but heaven's rejoicing resonated through eternity.

Even in the bleakest moments, like when Dungy and his wife Lauren faced the devastating loss of their son James, they continued to move the eternal chains forward.

Through their prison ministry, their advocacy for families, their living testimony, and their radical grace, they scored touchdowns that mattered most in heaven's playbook—touching lives, healing hearts, investing in others, and spreading hope in ways that no football victory ever could.

In heaven's highlight reel, these were the plays that made the angels lean forward—not for feats of athletic brilliance, but for moments when eternity touched time. Each act of kindness, each moment of grace, each life transfigured became a touchdown that swept The Wave of joy through heaven's courts, where earthly acclaim fades but love's victories set the crystal sea ablaze.

> Most of the men were into football, and I found that I had a common bond with them—they read the sports page and the Bible.
> TONY DUNGY DISCUSSING HIS PRISON MINISTRY[7]

The Pro Football Hall of Fame may celebrate Dungy's earthly achievements, but heaven's hall of fame records different statistics: lives changed, souls saved, families restored, hope renewed. Every time a prisoner opens a Bible, every time a coach chooses family over fame, every time faith rises above fear, heaven's hosts erupt. The wave sweeps over wanderers, waywards, and wayfarers who have found The Way. In God's grand stadium, the celebration is unceasing, and the victories endure forever.

UNEXPECTED TOUCHDOWNS: WHEN GRACE OUTSCORES JUSTICE

While Tony Dungy's story shows us the beauty of consistent faith, Ernie Holmes' story reveals something equally powerful: how divine grace can score touchdowns in the most unlikely end zones.

Imagine a man so fierce that teammate L. C. Greenwood said, "Ernie wanted to see blood."[8] A player who would crack open a roasted pig's skull to devour its brains.[9] Not exactly the stuff of inspirational posters. But God specializes in impossible plays and players.

On a cold Pennsylvania highway in 1973, Ernie Holmes drove toward what should have been his ending. Armed with a shotgun and pistol, the Pittsburgh Steelers' defensive tackle succumbed to an emotional breakdown and turned the interstate into his personal shooting gallery. Truckers swerved to escape his bullets. Police helicopters circled overhead as Holmes, lost in a haze of confusion and rage, opened fire on them too. When the chaos settled, an officer lay wounded, and Holmes' promising NFL career seemed destined for ruin.

By any earthly measure, this story should have ended in tragedy. But divine grace had drawn up a different playbook for disaster tackling faith and faith tackling disaster.

THREE PLAYS OF GRACE THAT CHANGED THE GAME

The first miracle came through the restraint of law enforcement. Despite Holmes giving them every justification to respond with lethal force, the officers chose mercy. "We could have killed him a dozen times," one later recalled,[10] yet not a single shot was fired at the troubled player. In that moment of choosing life over justified force, heaven's scoreboard lit up: Grace 7, Vengeance 0.

The second divine play came through the legendary Rooney family. Where others saw a liability, the Steelers' ownership saw a soul worth saving. They didn't just post bail—they invested $45,000 in Holmes' treatment and freedom. Art Rooney Jr. made regular visits, later reflecting, "We all thought he needed mercy."[11] The scoreboard flashed again: Grace 14, Abandonment 0.

The third touchdown of grace came through community. Rather than reject the man who had endangered so many, teammates and fans embraced Holmes' transformation. What could have been a story of permanent exile became one of restoration, as he evolved from liability to leader, from danger to defender, from outcast to integral part of the Steelers' family. Heaven's scoreboard glowed once more: Grace 21, Rejection 0.

SWEET AND ERIKSEN

When a teammate fumbles, the true spirit of the team emerges: players rally around their fallen comrade, offering encouragement and support rather than scorn. They lift up rather than tear down, understanding that any one of them could be in those shoes tomorrow. Yet ironically, in the church—where grace should reign supreme—we often witness the opposite. "Only the church shoots its wounded," the saying goes, replacing the healing balm of mercy with the salt of judgment.

THE VICTORY FORMATION

Within months of his highway rampage, Holmes traded firing at police for firing off the line in training camp. By Super Bowl IX, his redemption story had reached its athletic apex. As part of the legendary "Steel Curtain" defense, Holmes dominated the Minnesota Vikings' offense, helping hold them to a mere 17 yards rushing and securing a championship in both game and life.

Holmes' later years wrote an epilogue of incomplete but powerful redemption. As a 400-pound (not 688-pound as some said) Baptist minister, with his own church in Wiergate, Texas, he used his darkest moment to illuminate God's grace, preaching about divine providence and second chances. His testimony continued until his final day, when at age 59, a single-car accident near Beaumont, Texas, brought his earthly journey to an end. He was not wearing a seatbelt, and was ejected from the vehicle.

Yet the story of Ernie Holmes endures—not just as a tale of football greatness, but as a testament to the transfigurative power of mercy when the world has every reason to condemn. His life reminds us that sometimes, even on our darkest highways, grace can redirect our course from bondage to liberation, from shadow to light.

Heaven's Highlight Reel:

- Every time Holmes told his story from the pulpit: Touchdown in eternity!
- Every time an officer's mercy was remembered: Touchdown in eternity!
- Every time the Rooneys' grace was recounted: Touchdown in eternity!

The Eternal Playbook

Holmes' story teaches us:

- No one is beyond grace's reach.
- Mercy scores more than judgment.
- Investment in broken lives pays eternal dividends.
- God's game plan often surprises us.

> For I will forgive their wickedness
> and will remember their sins no
> more.
>
> HEBREWS 8:12 (NIV)

Holmes never became a saint. But his story reminds us that heaven celebrates not just the perfect plays, but the messy victories of grace over guilt, welcome over walls. Sometimes the biggest touchdowns in eternity come from the most unlikely players, and plays, on the field.

In the annals of NFL history, Fran Tarkenton of the Minnesota Vikings revolutionized the quarterback position with his legendary "scrambling" ability. When carefully designed plays collapsed under defensive pressure, Tarkenton transformed these broken patterns into opportunities, dancing away from defenders and turning chaos into victory. His book *Broken Pattern* (1971) speaks to a profound truth that extends far beyond the football field: sometimes our greatest moments emerge from our most challenging setbacks.

Just as Tarkenton found possibility in broken plays, God specializes in redeeming what appears shattered and lost. Through divine creativity and resurrection power, God takes our fractured lives—our failures, disappointments, and missteps—and weaves them into something more beautiful than we could have imagined. Like a master kintsugi artist who creates masterpieces from broken pieces of pottery, God doesn't simply repair what's broken; God transfigures it, making our wounds into stained-glass windows reflecting the divine light.

The parallel between Tarkenton's improvisational genius and God's redemptive work reminds us that what we perceive as broken patterns in our lives may actually be the very moments when divine providence is most powerfully at work. In God's hands, our brokenness becomes the raw material for resurrection, and our setbacks become setups for God's greatest displays of grace.

Sacred Touchdowns: When Forgiveness Outgains Revenge

*Forgive us our debts,
as we also have forgiven our debtors.*

JESUS[12]

While Warrick Dunn rushed for over 10,000 NFL yards in his storied career, his most significant gains came in a different kind of end zone—the sacred red zone of redemption, radical forgiveness, and transfiguring grace.

On 07 June 1993, in Baton Rouge, Louisiana, Betty Smothers, a police corporal and single mother of six, was working an extra security detail, one of many jobs she took to provide for her family. In the darkness of night, ambushers waited. In moments, six children, including high school senior Warrick Dunn, lost their mother.

His devastation went beyond grief. Overnight, young Warrick had to become head of his household, carrying a weight no teenager should bear. Inside him, pain and rage warred with responsibility and love.

But God's playbook often writes glory through tragedy. When Dunn arrived in Tampa Bay as a first-round draft pick in 1997, he found more than a team. He found a family. Tony Dungy, himself a testament to faith lived out loud, became more than a coach. He became a father figure, showing Dunn how to navigate both football and life with grace.

Lauren Dungy, understanding the void in Dunn's life, stepped in with what Dunn calls "a mother's touch," helping him manage family responsibilities and personal struggles. Through their love, Dunn learned the crucial lesson that would define his legacy: "He couldn't do it alone."[13]

> Lord, what is it that You're trying to do in my heart in this season? Patience? Forgiveness? Do they deserve it? Doesn't matter. He didn't ask me if they deserve it. That wasn't on the agenda for me. The agenda for me was just "forgive."
>
> QB DEREK CARR[14]

THE FORGIVENESS FORMATION

The most remarkable play in Dunn's life came far from any football field. In 2007, he walked into Angola State Prison, seeking answers from his mother's killer. The scene could have turned ugly—especially when the death row inmate, still appealing his case, denied any involvement in the murder.[15]

But instead of rage, Dunn offered grace: "If you didn't do it, I don't know why you are here today, but I know why I'm here today. I am here because I need to forgive somebody … It is time for me to move on."[16]

Like Jesus converting an instrument of death into eternal life, Dunn turned his tragedy into ministry and mission. Through his Homes for the Holidays program, he began providing fully furnished houses to single-parent families.

SWEET AND ERIKSEN

Each home becomes more than shelter—it becomes a testament to how pain can birth purpose. More than 150 families have now found stability and hope through this ministry.[17] Each key handed over, each door opened, each life changed becomes another touchdown in eternity's end zone.

While earthly records celebrate Dunn's rushing yards and Pro Bowl appearances, heaven's highlight reel features different victories. Each time a family finds shelter, angels cheer. Each time forgiveness defeats bitterness, heaven touches down. Each time tragedy transforms into blessing, eternal touchdowns are scored.

Dunn's story isn't just about football or philanthropy. It's about the divine alchemy that turns lead into gold, wounds into wisdom, and pain into purpose. His journey teaches us that forgiveness isn't weakness but ultimate strength, that loss can birth legacy, and that grace gains more yards than grievance ever could.

> But Joseph said to them, "Don't be afraid. Am I in the place of God? You intended to harm me, but God intended it for good to accomplish what is now being done, the saving of many lives."
>
> GENESIS 50:19-20 (NIV)

Game XII

Playing Injured
Grace Under Pressure

For I determined to know nothing among you except Jesus Christ, and Him crucified.

APOSTLE PAUL[1]

Visit Cooperstown during Hall of Fame week. Empty chairs sit where legends should be; their names erased not by lack of achievement but by chemical enhancement. Barry Bonds' 762 home runs, Mark McGwire's 70-homer season, Sammy Sosa's supernatural surge—all marked with asterisks, all tainted by the shadow of synthetic strength.

These fallen icons tell a story older than sports. Like Adam and Eve reaching for forbidden fruit to become "like gods," athletes reach for syringes promising superhuman power. The needle promises what the fruit promised—transcendence without transfiguration, glory without growth, divinity without devotion.

In NFL locker rooms, they tell stories of players who chose "the juice"—their statistics soared, their contracts swelled. Then came the consequences: shortened careers, damaged organs, shattered legacies. Like Esau trading his birthright for a bowl of stew, they exchanged tomorrow's legacy for today's glory.

TODAY'S ICONS: THE FALL FROM GRACE

The morning fog hasn't yet lifted from Venice Beach when Arnold Schwarzenegger pushes through the doors of Gold's Gym. Weight plates clink like communion chalices, metal bars gleam like altar rails. In this cathedral of iron, where human transfiguration is measured in pounds and percentages, a drama of enhancement vs. authenticity is about to unfold.

Lou Ferrigno, massive but still living in Arnold's shadow, moves through his routine. The air is thick with more than chalk dust and sweat—it's heavy with the unspoken knowledge of what builds bodies this size, what turns men into gods. "I'm watching you, Lou," Arnold says, his voice carrying both prophecy and warning.

These priests of the iron temple make no secret of their chemical sacraments. Like the first riders of the Tour de France, who openly and almost proudly doped on amphetamines as a part of bicycling's athletic craft,[2] their transparency about steroids stands in stark contrast to your authors' era, where we hid our helps, masked our methods, and denied our dependencies. In their honesty about enhancement, they reveal something profound about human nature—our perpetual quest for shortcuts to glory.

Watch the young Arnold pose before the mirror. His physique is a masterpiece painted in both dedication and chemicals, a testament to both human achievement and human compromise. In him, we see our own reflection—how we too try to synthesize salvation, manufacture miracles, and engineer enlightenment.

> Dying and losing ... they're the same thing.
> LANCE ARMSTRONG[3]

Churchill's Bottle: The Illusion of Control

Imagine you are in the war rooms beneath London, 1940. Air raid sirens wail while Winston Churchill stands defiant, whiskey in one hand, cigar in the other. "I got more out of alcohol than alcohol got out of me," he declares, his words echoing through history like thunder after lightning.

Here stands one of history's pivotal figures, leading Britain through its darkest hour, his speeches rallying a nation. Yet even as he masters the art of war, he remains servant to his bottles. Even as he directs the fate of nations, he cannot direct his own dependencies.

A lady from the Women's Christian Temperance Union once confronted him about his lifetime consumption of whiskey. Churchill's response revealed both his wit and his rationalization: "My dear woman, if I had not drunk so much whiskey, I would not have lived so long, and you would not have had the pleasure of knowing me!" And then he looked up at an imaginary line in the wall and said, "So much to do, so little time to do it in."

Like the rich young ruler approaching Jesus, Churchill's proclamation of mastery reveals the very chains he refuses to acknowledge. "All these commandments I have kept from my youth," said the ruler. "All these bottles I have mastered," says the addict. Both statements ring with the hollow certainty of self-deception.

Arnold's Needle: The Promise of Power

That summer of 1977, *Pumping Iron* pulled back the curtain on bodybuilding's chemical communion. What made this moment remarkable wasn't just the drama between titans of testosterone, but the raw honesty about enhancement that seems almost innocent now, like finding ancient cave paintings of forgotten rituals.

Arnold stood as their high priest, his five Mr. Olympia titles forming a rosary of achievement. His trajectory from bodybuilding to Hollywood to Sacramento's governor's mansion tells a larger story—one of ambition fulfilled through drive and discipline. Yet the tabloid headlines and personal scandals remind us that enhancement always demands its price.

This chemical covenant reveals our indwelling temptations which put Christians at such risk:

- We seek drive-through discipleship, wanting transfiguration at the speed of fast food.

- We adopt a microwave mentality in faith formation, impatient with the slow cook of authentic growth.

- We cultivate Instagram faith: filtered, enhanced, artificial—more concerned with appearance than essence.

THE CROSS VS. THE CHEMICAL: A DEEPER THEOLOGY

Several years before his imprisonment in a Nazi cell, Dietrich Bonhoeffer wrote of a danger more subtle than the regime that would later hold him captive: "cheap grace."[4]

Cheap grace is grace without the cross. It is forgiveness without repentance, baptism without disciplined discipleship, communion without confession, absolution without personal confession. Cheap grace is grace without growth in a relationship with the living and incarnate Jesus Christ.

Bonhoeffer contrasted "cheap grace" with "costly grace," which demands our whole life and acknowledges the full weight of what Christ's sacrifice means for how we live. The cheap grace he warned against is essentially comfort without change—a Christianity that demands nothing of us while promising everything to us.

When Bonhoeffer wrote about grace that "costs a man his life," he couldn't have known exactly how prophetically preparatory those words would be for his own journey. His rejection of cheap and easy grace prepared him for the moments when he had to choose between comfort and conscience, between security and solidarity with the persecuted. The theological framework he developed around costly grace became the lens through which he interpreted and found meaning in his own suffering.

Like performance-enhancing drugs promising strength without struggle, cheap grace whispers sweet deceptions to our souls. At Gethsemane, facing his moment of truth, Jesus had options. He could have called twelve legions of angels—the ultimate performance enhancement. Instead, he chose the cup of suffering over the chemical of shortcuts. "Not my will, but yours be done" becomes the ultimate rejection of spiritual steroids.

- In the weight room, steroids promise paradise without process.
- In the prayer room, cheap grace promises heaven without holiness.
- In the gym, chemicals offer glory without gutting it out.
- In worship, easy faith offers redemption without repentance.

THE CHAMPION'S CHOICE: A DESERT PARABLE

Every morning at 5 a.m., in gyms across USAmerica, athletes face their moment of decision. The weight feels heavier today. The mirror shows less progress than hoped. A teammate whispers about a "helper," a shortcut, a way to accelerate destiny. In this predawn moment, character reveals itself more clearly than any spotlight could.

This same drama played out in another desert, long ago. Jesus, weakened by forty days of fasting, faced the ultimate performance enhancement dealer. Satan's offers came wrapped in Scripture, gilded with logic:

- "Turn these stones to bread"—why suffer when you could satisfy?

- "Jump from the temple's height"—why wait when you could wow?
- "Bow once and own it all"—why work when you could win instantly?

Only through fire can the smith
pull and stretch
Metal into the shapes of his design.

Only through fire can the
artist reach
Pure gold which only furnaces
refine.

MICHELANGELO, SONNET LIX[5]

Today, we face our own desert moments. The Instagram prophet promises prosperity without pain. The YouTube guru offers enlightenment without effort. The podcast preacher sells salvation without sacrifice. The prosperity gospel offers wealth without waiting. Like street-corner dealers offering clean needles and dirty shortcuts, they promise enhancement without engagement, growth without grief, power without process.

Standing before a bathroom mirror, we face our own small compromises. The sleep aid promises rest without addressing our racing thoughts. The appetite suppressant offers weight loss without changing how we eat. The energy drink sells alertness without confronting our exhaustion. The supplement bottles promise health without the hard work of lifestyle change. Like rows of plastic promises on the drugstore shelf, they tempt us with chemical shortcuts around the real work of living—the patience of proper sleep hygiene, the discipline of mindful eating, the commitment to managing stress at its roots.

There is need for some nuance here. Steroids do not replace the necessity of hard, regular workouts; rather, they amplify the outcomes of such rigorous training. However, they represent a shortcut because they allow athletes to achieve results that are beyond what is typically attainable through even the most demanding and disciplined training regimens. While "normal" training is already enormously difficult and challenging, steroids push the performance envelope further, providing an unfair advantage by altering the natural limits of human physiology.

Watch the athlete training naturally. See how they embrace the plateau, the pain, the persistent grind of gradual growth. Now watch the Jesus disciple walking the narrow way. See how they welcome the desert, the doubt, the darkness, the daily death to self that nonartificial, true transfiguration demands.

> Sex won't satisfy you. Fame won't satisfy you. Drugs won't satisfy you. Money won't satisfy you. Alcohol won't satisfy you. Success won't satisfy you. Life is empty without Jesus. He is the only one who can satisfy your heart.
>
> "PRIME TIME" DEION SANDERS
> INSTAGRAM POST 16 AUGUST 2023[6]

WHEN SHORTCUTS CAN'T REPLACE THE CROSS

When the sports pages read like crime blotters and scoreboards tally dollar signs instead of points, your authors turn to a different kind of champion—Eric Liddell, the "Flying Parson" who ran not for gold, but for God.

Paris Olympics, 1924. While others chased medals, Liddell chased conviction. He stunned the world by refusing to run the 100-meter race—his best event—because it fell on Sunday. The Sabbath wasn't a rule to be bent, but a relationship to be honored. Yet here's the miracle: in choosing God over gold, he found both. He switched to the 400-meter race and not only won, but shattered the world record.

For Liddell, the track was more than dirt and chalk lines.

It was holy ground. He ran with a peculiar joy, head tilted back, mouth open in what observers called a "beatific smile." He lived what we've forgotten: true sportsmanship isn't about crushing opponents, but lifting them up. Fair play. Hard work. Level field. Generous spirit. Camaraderie.

But *Chariots of Fire* only tells half the story. The real test of Liddell's character came not on an Olympic track, but in a Japanese prison camp called Weihsien—a pressure cooker of human suffering where hope went to die. There, amidst cramped squalor and crushing despair, Liddell became a different kind of champion. He taught kids to play games. He smuggled extra food to the sick. He gave away his own meager supplies. When someone needed to stand in the gap, he stepped forward.[7]

The brain tumor that took his life before liberation wasn't in the script anyone would have written. He never got to embrace his wife again or see his daughters grow up. But even in death, Liddell teaches us something profound: sometimes the greatest victories aren't marked by medals, but by the lives we touch when no one's keeping score.

In an age of steroids and scandals, Liddell's legacy still runs ahead of us, challenging us to be better than our worst impulses, to resist the spiritual steroid shortcuts. His life asks us a simple question: What race are you really running?

> There are no secrets to success: don't waste time looking for them. Success is the result of perfection, hard work, learning from failure, loyalty to those for whom you work and persistence.
>
> GENERAL COLIN POWELL,
> SPEAKING AT DREW UNIVERSITY'S DREW FORUM ON
> 12 SEPTEMBER 1996.

THE ETERNAL SCOREBOARD: BEYOND THE ASTERISK

When the final whistle blows, heaven's record books will show:

- Not our shortcuts but our scars
- Not our enhancements but our endurance
- Not our supplements but our surrender

Christ's victory came not through avoiding the suffering of the cross but through embracing it. His strength was perfected not in enhancement but in weakness. His glory emerged not from shortcuts but from submission.

Consider Moses, who chose suffering with God's people over Egyptian enhancement.

Consider Daniel, who chose vegetable-fueled faith over royal refinements.

Consider Paul, who learned to boast in weakness rather than seek strength through shortcuts.

The champion's choice isn't made once in the spotlight. It's made daily in the shadows.

- In the early morning when no one watches.
- In the quiet moments when shortcuts seduce.
- In the painful places where enhancement beckons.

When facing our own medicine cabinet of quick fixes and spiritual steroids, always remember: authentic advancement has no shortcuts. Just as Christ walked the long road to Calvary, bearing every step with perfect intention, so must we embrace the sacred slowness of genuine growth. Human weakness becomes the very vessel of divine strength, our struggles the crucible of God's grace. For it is precisely in our desert moments, when we resist the siren call of instant solutions, that we discover the deepest truth: "My grace is sufficient for you, for my power is made perfect in weakness."[8]

The path to beauty was never meant to bypass the ugliness of the cross.

GAME XIII

THE ULTIMATE CHAMPIONSHIP

BUILDING GOD'S TEAM

I believe God created sports for a good reason. To build strong men and women, to bring people together, and to have good, clean fun.

COLLEGE FOOTBALL LEGEND TIM TEBOW
KNOWN FOR HIS "TEBOWING" PRAYER POSE AND
TEBOW FOUNDATION

In the beginning, there was a rubber ball. Not the cosmos-creating Word that John's Gospel proclaims, but a simple toy in the hands of Lamar Hunt's daughter, Sharon.

The year is 1966. Kansas City Chiefs owner Lamar Hunt is in his living room, watching his children bounce a Wham-O Super Ball against the walls. The rubber sphere soared and ricocheted with almost supernatural spring, delighting his kids and sparking something in Hunt's mind. At the time, he was neck-deep in merger talks between his American Football League and the rival National Football League, wrestling with what to call their upcoming championship game. The official suggestions were stiff and formal—"The AFL-NFL World Championship Game" felt about as exciting as reading a tax form.

Then, watching that Super Ball's trajectory, Hunt had his eureka moment. "Super Bowl," he suggested at the next owners' meeting, almost as a throwaway placeholder.[1] The other owners weren't impressed, preferring their formal title. But reporters and fans latched onto Hunt's catchier name, and it spread like wildfire through sports columns and radio shows. By the third championship game in 1969, the unofficially official "Super Bowl" became the official official name of USAmerica's most sacred sporting ritual: The Super Bowl.

Hunt would later joke that the most significant innovation in sports history was inspired by a fifty-nine-cent toy. Sometimes the best ideas don't come from boardrooms. They bounce right into your living room. Like the mustard seed in Jesus' parable, this tiny beginning grew into something that overshadows all other sporting events, providing shelter for millions of passionate devotees.

Sacred Signals: Reading the Signs of Our Times

The Super Bowl has become our contemporary burning bush—a spectacle that demands we remove our shoes, for we stand on ground that our culture has deemed holy. Unlike Moses's encounter, though, this fire burns not from divine presence but from our collective passion, consuming hours of preparation, billions of dollars, and the hopes and dreams of cities and their faithful.

What does it say about our cultural theology that more women watch the Super Bowl than any other television event? Perhaps it echoes Paul's declaration that in Christ there is neither male nor female. The kingdom of God, like today's NFL, breaks down traditional barriers of gender and culture, creating a new community united in common worship.

The Symphony of the Sacred

Every cathedral needs its choir, and the Super Bowl delivers with a symphony that would make Bach envious. The rhythm begins with the meditative silence before a game-winning kick—a moment when 70,000 people hold their breath in unified anticipation, much like the holy silence before the breaking of communion bread. The crowd's response erupts in either exultation or lamentation, reminiscent of ancient Israel's celebrations and dirges.

The halftime show serves as our contemporary praise band, with A-list celebrities leading what amounts to a secular doxology. Like David dancing before the Ark of the Covenant, these performers command attention, with a performance that can serve as our entertainment, God's glory, or sometimes both.

Sacred Signs and Symbols

Watch carefully as the Lombardi Trophy processes onto the field. Former champions carry it with the reverence of priests bearing the Ark, and players reach out to touch it like medieval pilgrims seeking healing from a holy relic. The NFL may not intend this parallel, but the human hunger for transcendent meaning creates it nonetheless.

Team jerseys function as contemporary vestments, marking out the priests of our secular sanctuary. Each player's number becomes a kind of ecclesiastical designation, their statistics a measure of their standing in this peculiar priesthood. The stadium itself rises like a postmodern cathedral, its architecture designed to draw eyes and hearts heavenward, even as its luxury boxes create a hierarchy of access that Jesus might have challenged.

Where Heaven Meets Hashmarks

The fusion of sacred and secular reaches its apex in the rituals surrounding the game. What is the pregame feast if not a form of communion? We break chips instead of bread, share beverages in fellowship, and gather in homes and bars that become temporary sanctuaries. The liturgy unfolds with precision: the national anthem as opening hymn, the coin toss as invocation, the game itself as the main service.

But it's in the stories of saints and sinners that we see the deepest theological parallels. Adam Vinatieri becomes our patron saint of clutch performance, his game-winning kicks transformed into miracles worthy of canonization. Scott Norwood bears his wide-right cross with a dignity that should remind us of grace, though our culture offers little. Jackie Smith's dropped pass becomes a kind of original sin, passed down through generations of highlight reels.

THE GRACE GAME

Perhaps the most powerful theological moment in recent championship history came not during any game, but in the aftermath of the reverse of the Chicago Cubs seemingly interminable championship curse in Major League Baseball. When the Chicago Cubs offered Steve Bartman a World Series ring in 2017, fourteen years after he became their scapegoat during the 2003 NLCS for having as a fan interfered with a ball in play, they enacted a parable of grace that Jesus might have told. Here was restoration offered freely, healing extended to the wounded, community rebuilt from the ashes of blame.²

Here in a nutshell is the theme of the book: What if we treated our faith lives with such passion? What if we celebrated conversions like touchdowns, treated every baptism like a Super Bowl victory, approached worship with the enthusiasm of a fourth-quarter drive? Jesus, after all, is the ultimate quarterback, calling audibles in our lives, reading the defense of our doubts, threading the needle of grace through the tightest coverage of our sin.

> Scoring a touchdown is the ultimate feeling. It's like you're on top of the world, everything slows down, and you just feel pure joy.
>
> UNKNOWN NFL PLAYER

THE FINAL SCORE

In our winner-take-all culture, the Super Bowl holds up a mirror to our collective soul. We worship winners with an intensity that should be reserved for God alone. We crucify losers with a fervor that makes us uncomfortable when we remember Jesus' words about the last being first. We seek redemption stories because they echo the greatest

THE ULTIMATE CHAMPIONSHIP

redemption story ever told.

But beneath the spectacle and the sponsorships, the commercials and the ceremonies, lies a deeper truth: our hunger for transcendence cannot be satisfied by even the greatest game. The Super Bowl's true gift may be how it reveals this hunger, pointing beyond itself to the God who designed us for deeper worship and truer victory.

Remember: Jesus never promised a winning season, only abundant life. He never guaranteed a Super Bowl ring, but offered a crown of glory that won't tarnish. In God's playbook, every soul can be a champion, every life can score eternal touchdowns, and the victory parade never ends.

Both of your authors gather with friends and family for this annual civil religious ritual. But we recognize the Super Bowl for what it is: not an idol to be worshipped or an enemy to be condemned, but a cultural liturgy that points to our deeper spiritual needs. Let it remind us that while touchdowns may bring temporary joy, true victory was secured not on any field of play, but on a hill called Calvary.

In the end, the greatest super bowl of all might be the one Jesus described—a heavenly banquet where all are welcomed, where the price of admission was paid on the cross, and where the celebration never ends. Now that's a game worth the watch and wait.

The Ultimate Scoreboard: Playing for Eternal Stakes

Imagine Walter Payton's heartbreak after Super Bowl XX—watching Refrigerator Perry score a touchdown while he, one of football's greatest running backs, never reached the end zone in his only Super Bowl appearance. That pain was real, tangible, memorable, yet ultimately temporal.

Now consider this: Every day, Christians walk past eternal end zones without even attempting to score.

Let that sink in.

> I think football is a great way to spread the word of God. And that's what I'm all about.
>
> DEFENSIVE END REGGIE WHITE (13 PRO BOWL SELECTIONS)

Touchdowns for Eternity: Real Stories of Kingdom Impact[3]

The Sideline Conversation: Sarah wasn't a football fan, but she understood game-changing moments. As a barista at a busy coffee shop, she noticed one of her regular customers seemed increasingly distressed each morning. Instead of just serving coffee, she felt the Holy Spirit's nudge to reach out.

"I don't normally do this," she said one morning, "but would you like to talk? I'd love to listen."

The first act of evangelism is listening—bending the ear to God, Scripture, others, and culture.

That simple question led to a conversation about depression, loneliness, and eventually, faith. Today, five years later, that customer not only found healing through counseling and church community but now leads a mental health ministry that has touched hundreds of lives.

"I almost didn't say anything that morning," Sarah recalls. "I was afraid of overstepping. Now I realize that was God's two-minute drill—a crucial moment when eternal stakes hung in the balance."

The Fourth Quarter Comeback: James, a high school football coach, saw beyond the scoreboard. When his star quarterback lost his father to cancer, James didn't just offer condolences—he became a spiritual mentor. For two years, he spent extra time after practice, not working on plays, but listening, praying, nudging, and sharing his own journey of faith.

That quarterback never made it to the NFL, but today he runs a youth ministry that impacts thousands. "Coach James showed me that real victory isn't about touchdowns on the field," he says. "It's about the lives you touch for eternity."

The Special Teams Play: Maria wasn't a starter in any ministry. She worked in accounting and lived alone. But she understood kingdom opportunity. When she inherited $50,000, instead of upgrading her car, she felt a divine nudge to invest in missions. Her "spiritual touchdown" funded wells in three villages in Africa, leading to churches being planted in each community.

Twenty years later, those three churches have spawned fifteen more. Thousands have come to faith. "I never left my hometown," Maria says, "but God showed me how to score in places I'll never visit until heaven."

The Goal Line Stand: Tom, a recovering addict, worked as a janitor at a megachurch. One Sunday, he noticed a young man sitting alone in the parking lot long after services ended. Instead of finishing his cleaning routine, Tom felt the nudge to sit down next to him. "I know what rock bottom looks like," Tom said. "I've been there."

That conversation prevented a suicide and launched a recovery ministry that has helped hundreds find freedom from addiction. "People see my former addiction as a fumble," Tom says. "God turned it into a touchdown for His kingdom."

The Two-Point Conversion: Linda, an elderly widow,

couldn't attend church anymore due to health issues. But she turned her phone into a ministry tool. Every day, she calls three people from her church directory to nudge them with encouragement and to pray with them.

Over ten years, she has prayed with over 5,000 people. Marriages have been saved, prodigals have returned, and faith has been renewed through her faithful intercession. "I may be homebound," she says, "but God's prayer line is always open. Every prayer is a play call from heaven's playbook."

The Unexpected Interception: David, a business executive, was focused on closing a major deal when his meeting was interrupted by a cleaning staff member whose son was in crisis. Instead of rescheduling, he felt God's nudge to stop and pray with her.

That moment led to him starting a workplace ministry that has since spread to thirty companies, creating space for faith conversations in corporate settings. "I almost missed God's call," he says. "Now I realize every interruption could be heaven's trick play."

Training Camp Tips from Kingdom Athletes

- Stay spiritually alert—eternal opportunities rarely announce themselves.

- Don't despise small beginnings—kingdom touchdowns often start with simple obedience.
- Use what's in your hands—God can turn any resource into eternal impact.
- Share your failures—your greatest fumbles might become someone else's breakthrough.
- Keep eternal stats—count lives touched, not personal recognition.
- Play through pain—your current struggle might be tomorrow's ministry.
- Watch for divine audibles—God's best plays often come through interruptions.

THE SCOREBOARD THAT MATTERS

These stories remind us that eternal touchdowns often look nothing like we expect:

- Sometimes they're quiet conversations
- Sometimes they're sacrificial giving
- Sometimes they're simply being present
- Sometimes they're sharing our brokenness
- Sometimes they're just faithful prayer

But they all have one thing in common: someone chose to get in the game rather than watch from the stands or stay in the huddle.

Your Next Play

Every day brings new opportunities to score for eternity:

- That difficult coworker? Potential kingdom impact.
- Your social media platform? An eternal end zone waiting to happen.
- Your past struggles? God's trick play in disguise.
- Your current resources? Kingdom field position.

Remember: No one in heaven will regret the eternal touchdowns they scored. They'll only regret the plays they were too afraid to run.

The game clock is running. Your number is being called.

What's your next eternal touchdown going to be?

Fourth Quarter
TOUCHDOWNS IN ETERNITY

I give you the end of the golden
string,
Only wind it into a ball,
It will lead you in at Heaven's Gate
Built into Jerusalem's wall.

WILLIAM BLAKE, "JERUSALEM"[1]

There is a golden thread that runs through all things, Blake tells us, a divine cord that, when followed, leads us to Jerusalem's gates. But perhaps this thread, when wound, forms something more than just a ball of string. It becomes the very ball we're meant to carry, to pass, to guide into the eternal end zone.

In the physical game, as Coach Bob Knight reminded us, it's not the player who scores, but the ball. One of the most successful and controversial college basketball coaches in USAmerican history, Knight drilled into his players: "People don't score, the ball does. Don't defend players: don't take your eye off the ball." How profound this "don't-take-your-eye-off-the-ball" wisdom becomes when we consider our gospeller calling. We are not the saviors. We are merely the carriers, the passers, the hosts of something far more precious than ourselves. The ball of divine love, wound from that golden string of grace, moves through us but is not us.

A skilled player can pass without looking, sensing rather than seeing. Is this not the essence of faith itself? To move in concert with something we feel more than we see, to trust in a divine momentum that flows through our hands but originates far beyond them? We are asked to keep our senses attuned to this holy sphere, this orb of possibility that contains within it all the potential of wholeness and wellness.

The ball that scores in eternity isn't carried by strength alone, but by paying attention—a deep, abiding consciousness of something precious in our care.[2] Like Blake's golden string, it leads us forward, but also asks us to give each other a "lead." Each pass is an act of trust, each reception an act of grace. We become part of a divine play, a sacred game where the goal isn't personal glory but communal redemption.

FOURTH QUARTER

When we "don't take our eye off the ball," we're maintaining focus on what truly matters—not our own achievements, but the movement of divine love through the field of human experience. Sometimes we carry it, sometimes we pass it, sometimes we simply guard it. But always, always, we remember that we serve the ball; the ball doesn't serve us.

In this eternal game, every person brought into relationship with the divine is a touchdown scored not by us, but through us. We are merely the field players in a cosmic game where the real star is that sphere of incarnate love, wound from Blake's golden string, passed from heart to heart, crossing again and again into the end zone of grace.

I want to Love like Jesus!
FIRST WORDS OF RUSSELL WILSON'S PROFILE ON "X"[3]

The ball, in the end, is love itself—passed, carried, protected, but never possessed. And in this game, there is no final whistle, only the ongoing play of humans in joyful motion, guided by that golden sphere toward heaven's gate, built into Jerusalem's wall.

GAME XIV

WHEN TAILGATES BECOME TALEGATE TESTAMENTS
FELLOWSHIP IN THE PARKING LOT

> We should never allow the passing of a loved one to be the drawing card to keep our family together.
>
> TERRY BRADSHAW, 2014 PRO FOOTBALL HALL OF FAME INDUCTION SPEECH FOR HIS FORMER PITTSBURGH STEELERS COACH, CHUCK NOLL

Every culture that has ever kindled flame has known this truth: stories flow where smoke rises. From the ancestral fires of aboriginal dreamtime to the sanctuary candles of Catholic cathedrals, humans have always understood that sacred stories require sacred smoke.

The NFL, perhaps unwittingly, has tapped into this primordial connection by creating what they call "the last great campfire"—their Sunday games. But the real magic isn't in the stadium lights; it's in the thousands of small fires that burn in parking lots across USAmerica, each one a beacon drawing people into story.

SMOKE AND FIRE

The smoke that rises from tailgate grills echoes the same holy vapor that has marked sacred spaces since the dawn of time. Just as incense in church sanctuaries creates a visible reminder of prayers rising to heaven, the mingled smoke of thousands of grills creates a canopy of communion under which stories naturally flow. It's no coincidence that the Jerusalem Temple, the epicenter of God's story with Israel, was essentially a divine barbecue, its smoke visible for miles—a signal fire announcing "Here, God meets with His people."

Hear the sensory symphony of the tailgate: the snap and pop of burning charcoal, the blue-gray wisps of hickory smoke, the sizzle of meat meeting flame. These aren't just cooking sounds; they're the percussion section of an ancient orchestra that has always accompanied storytelling. When the NFL reports that fifty million USAmericans participate in tailgating culture, they're unknowingly documenting something deeper—our hardwired need to gather around flame to share our stories.

The famous Belichick family anecdote about their European vacation—where young Brian didn't recognize images of Jesus[1]—takes on new significance in this light. Perhaps the failure wasn't just in not sharing the story, but in trying to share it without the elements that make stories stick: the smoke of shared meals, the fire of genuine fellowship. Those European churches Brian visited were full of candles and incense holders, sacred smoke-makers designed to create the very atmosphere where stories become memory becomes faith.

Look at Jesus' own ministry: He didn't just tell stories; He created smoking, sizzling environments for them. The fish breakfast on the shore with Peter wasn't just about food—it was about creating a sacred space with smoke and flame where restoration could happen through story. The road to Emmaus story hinges on a meal, likely cooked over fire, where eyes were opened and the Greatest Story was finally understood when two disciples saw through the smoke to the wounds in his hands. If you want to see Jesus, look for the wounds of our world.[2]

TAILGATING TO TALE-GATING

Today's tailgating phenomenon reveals this primal connection. When 35 percent of tailgaters never even enter the stadium, they're telling us something profound: they're coming for the smoke and the stories. The charcoal grill has become our tribal fire, the smoke creating a temporary sanctuary where stories flow as naturally as breath. Each parking lot becomes a sacred grove, marked out by columns of smoke rising like prayer.

One of your author's (Chris) experience at MetLife Stadium becomes more than just a pleasant memory when viewed through this lens. Those grills weren't just cooking stations; they were story stations. The smoke created a visible boundary of sacred space where Steelers fans and Jets fans could share not just food but their stories, their lives, their very selves. The "terrible towels" became props in a larger narrative of belonging, all under the canopy of holy smoke.

Homegating

The NFL's move toward "homegating"—bringing tailgating inside to climate-controlled homes rather than gathering outdoors with the wider community—points to this truth, though it misses something vital in trying to sanitize the experience. The early church met in homes, yes, but they would have had cooking fires, oil lamps, perhaps even incense—all creating that atmosphere where stories naturally flow. Our sterilized attempts to create fellowship without flame often fall flat precisely because they lack these primal elements that speak to our souls.

The church's challenge today isn't just to share the Greatest Story Ever Told. It's to create the sacred spaces where

WHEN TAILGATES BECOME TALEGATE TESTAMENTS

that story can truly be experienced. When we understand why churches have always used candles and incense, we begin to understand why men gather around smoky grills. It's the same impulse: to create a thin space where heaven and earth meet, where stories can be shared and absorbed into the very fiber of our being.

This is why Jesus so often taught around fires and meals. It's why the early church centered around the table.[3] It's why the smell of incense still triggers something deep in our spiritual memory. And it's why fifty million USAmericans stand in parking lots around smoking grills, sharing their stories. The smoke rising from each of those grills isn't just cooking smoke—it's a signal fire, calling us back to our most basic need: to gather around flame and share the stories that make us who we are.

Perhaps the solution to Brian Belichick's question—"Who is that guy we keep seeing everywhere?"[4]—isn't just to tell the story better, but to create the sacred smoke-filled spaces where stories naturally flow from heart to heart. After all, God's first appearance to Moses was in fire, and His guidance of Israel was in a pillar of smoke. Perhaps God was telling us something not just about the divine nature, but about how God's story best spreads: through the sacred smoke of fellowship and the holy fires of communion.

> The wood does not change the fire
> into itself, but the fire changes the
> wood into itself. So are we changed
> into the likeness of God, that we
> shall know him as he is.
>
> MEISTER ECKHART (1260-1328)[5]

THEOLOGY MEETS TURF: GAME UP

There are two Pentecost moments in the Bible. Both theophanies.

One is at Mt. Sinai, where God gave the Torah.

One is at Mt. Zion, where God gave the Spirit.

One took place on the fiftieth day after a major event: the Exodus (fifty days after Passover and the Exodus from Egypt).

One took place on the fiftieth day after a major event: Jesus' resurrection.

One is where God wrote on tablets of stone.

One is where God wrote on hearts of flesh.

One is where loud sounds from heaven came in thunder and lightning.

One is where loud sounds from heaven came in a rushing mighty wind.

One led to a covenant between God and his people Israel.

One led to a new covenant in Jesus' blood between God and all people.

At the first Pentecost, there was a birthday—the nation of Israel was born.

At the second Pentecost, there was a birthday—the bride of Christ, the church, was born.

At the first Pentecost, there was the thunder of tongues ("kolot" which we translate as "thunder" literally means voices or languages).

At the second Pentecost, there was the thunder of tongues.

At the first Pentecost, about 3,000 Israelites were smitten in sin when Moses found the people worshiping the golden calf (Exodus 32:26–38).

At the second Pentecost, about 3,000 converts were smitten by the Spirit, baptized, and added to the early church as a result of Peter's preaching (Acts 2:41).

At the first Pentecost, God sent the Teaching (Torah means Teaching).

At the second Pentecost, God sent the Teacher: "But the Advocate, the Holy Spirit, whom the Father will send in my name, will teach you all things and will remind you of everything I have said to you."[6]

At the first Pentecost, God spoke to and through his people the Ten Commandments in seventy languages.

At the second Pentecost, God spoke to and through his people speaking in languages and tongues.

At the first Pentecost, a new order and community structure was established in the Levitical priesthood.

At the second Pentecost, a new order and community structure was established in the apostles leading the Jerusalem church.

The same day Jews celebrated God's gift of Living Torah, the Holy Spirit came to raise to life God's gift of the Live Torah, Jesus the Christ, who is both Embodied Torah and Embedded Temple.

At the first Pentecost, God gave guidance for living through the Ten Commandments.

At the second Pentecost, God gave guidance for living through the Holy Spirit.

At the first Pentecost, God gave God's people a person and a law to follow—Moses and the Ten Commandments.

At the second Pentecost, God gave God's people a person who fulfilled the law to follow—Jesus the Christ, who is brought back to live his resurrection in us by the power of the Holy Spirit.

Moses recounted the first Pentecost experience for the

WHEN TAILGATES BECOME TALEGATE TESTAMENTS

people in this way:

> You came near and stood at the foot of the mountain, while flames from the mountain shot into the sky. The mountain was shrouded in black clouds and deep darkness. And the Lord spoke to you from the heart of the fire.[7]

At the Exodus 19 Pentecost, God's presence was manifested in fire with the flames shooting into the sky.

At the Acts 2 Pentecost, God's presence was manifested in fire with the flames landing on the disciples.

THE SACRED FIRE STILL BURNS

Perhaps now we can see why the NFL's "last great campfire" resonates so deeply in our collective soul. The smoke that rises from countless tailgate fires echoes the smoke that rose from Sinai, the flames that danced on disciples' heads, the holy fire that has marked God's presence from the beginning.

At Sinai, God's presence descended in fire and smoke, His voice thundering in seventy languages as He gave the Torah. Today, in parking lots across USAmerica, different tongues and tribes gather around smoking grills, sharing their stories in a contemporary Pentecost of fellowship.

At Zion, tongues of fire rested on each disciple as God wrote His law on hearts of flesh. Today, the smoke of our communal grills creates sacred spaces where hearts are softened and stories shared.

The NFL unknowingly taps into this primal truth: that where fire burns and smoke rises, people gather and stories flow. Just as God used fire to mark sacred space—from the burning bush to the pillar of fire to the tongues of Pentecost—we still instinctively create sacred space with our flames. Every tailgate grill becomes a tiny altar, every curl of smoke a thread in the tapestry of communion.

This is why the Belichick story should both trouble and challenge us. In a world where young eyes can't recognize Jesus in cathedral art, perhaps we need to return to the fire. After all, didn't Jesus often appear most clearly in the breaking of bread, in the cooking of fish over morning flames, in the shared meals where stories could be told and retold?

The pattern is clear:

- At the first Pentecost, God descended in fire to create community through Law.
- At the second Pentecost, God descended in fire to create community through Spirit.

Today, we gather around our own small fires, creating spaces where community can form and reform.

What if we reclaimed this ancient practice? Light a fire pit in your backyard. Invite neighbors over for s'mores and

WHEN TAILGATES BECOME TALEGATE TESTAMENTS

stories. Let your grill become more than just a cooking surface—make it an altar of gathering, where the smoke of fellowship rises like incense. In these flame-lit spaces, we often find what the earliest Christians knew: that holy community forms best around holy fires.

Maybe the NFL's "last great campfire" isn't really the last at all. Perhaps it's just one more echo of those first holy fires—a reminder that we still hunger for the sacred smoke of fellowship, for the flame-lit spaces where stories can be shared and souls can be fed. Whether it's the incense of ancient temples, the candles of church sanctuaries, or the smoke of tailgate grills, we're still drawn to fire because that's where God has always chosen to meet us.

The challenge isn't to compete with football's communal fire, but to recognize and reclaim the sacred power of smoke and story in our own gatherings. When we understand that God has always used fire to mark holy ground—from Sinai to Pentecost to today—we begin to see every shared meal, every lit candle, every smoking grill as an opportunity for divine encounter and holy community.

Let the smoke rise from our tailgates and our tables, our sanctuaries and our celebrations. Let it remind us that the God who spoke through fire at Sinai and sent flames at Pentecost still meets us in these smoke-blessed spaces where stories are shared and community is forged. For wherever people gather around flame and food to share their stories, there echoes the ancient promise:

> "Mount Sinai was covered in smoke because the Lord descended on it in fire" (Exodus 19:18 NIV).

> "Then the Lord spoke to you from the fire" (Deuteronomy 4:12 NIV).

> "The Lord spoke to you face to face out of the fire on the mountain" (Deuteronomy 5:4 NIV).

God speaks still.

Game XV

More Than Games
From Arena to Altar

What we do in life echoes in eternity.

GENERAL MAXIMUS DECIMUS MERIDIUS
(RUSSELL CROWE)
IN *GLADIATOR* (2000)

When Games Become Gospel—The Echo of Ancient Roars

I. The Price of Glory

When we think of sports wealth, our minds drift to familiar icons: Michael Jordan's Nike empire, Tiger Woods' billion-dollar brand, Tom Brady's Super Bowl fortunes. But history holds a secret that puts our sports economy to shame—a tale that begins not in the gleaming stadiums of today, but in the dust and thunder of ancient Rome.

His name was Gaius Appuleius Diocles, and in the sweltering years between AD 122–146, he amassed a fortune that would make today's athletes look like street performers.[1] Here are his stats: 1,462 victories in 4,257 races, 861 second-place finishes, and career earnings of 35,863,120 sesterces—roughly $15 billion in today's currency. When *Forbes* Magazine crowned Michael Jordan the highest-paid athlete of all time at $1.85 billion,[2] they missed the ancient giant whose wealth still casts a shadow over sports history.

But why? Why would Rome pour such astronomical wealth into the hands of a charioteer?

The answer lies in the flame-lit heart of Roman society itself. These weren't just games—they were the heartbeat of an empire, the pulse that kept the masses alive and the powerful in power. So vital were these spectacles that they could spark revolution: witness the Spartacus rebellion, birthed in a gladiator school, that grew from a handful of escaped fighters into an army that shook Rome to its foundations.

The fate of Spartacus and his followers—crucified along the Appian Way like grotesque mile markers—tells us something about the deadly seriousness of Roman sports. Even the generals who crushed the rebellion met grim ends: Crassus, whose wealth came from extorting burning homeowners through his corrupt fire brigade, lost his head to the Parthians, his skull repurposed as a prop in Greek tragedies. Pompey, who shared the victory over Spartacus, would later lose his own head to Egyptian opportunists seeking to curry favor with Julius Caesar.

This wasn't just sport—this was religion, politics, and survival all rolled into one bloody spectacle. The Romans understood something we're still grappling with: when you control the games, you control the story. Through the arena's spectacles, they shaped what their citizens valued, feared, and believed about power, justice, and society itself. The games weren't just entertainment; they were a powerful tool for crafting the empire's narrative. And when you control the story, you control everything.

The Romans didn't just pay their athletes; they worshiped them. Every race, every contest, every victory carried the weight of divine significance. When Diocles raced his chariot, he wasn't just competing. He was performing a secular liturgy, creating a moment where heaven and earth seemed to touch in the dust of the arena.

WHEN ATHLETES BECOME GODS

The Romans didn't just love their sports; they lived them. The Hippodrome wasn't just a stadium. It was a temple where the sacred and secular merged until you couldn't tell them apart. Moments when games became more than games?

- The Spartacus rebellion: What began with a handful of gladiators nearly brought Rome to its knees.
- The Nika riots: When sports fans nearly toppled an empire over team colors.
- Justinian's near-fall: How the greatest Roman emperor of late antiquity almost lost everything to sports politics.

Our stadiums have become our modern coliseums. When NFL games draw larger crowds than any church service, when Super Bowl Sunday becomes an unofficial national holiday, when team loyalties divide cities and unite strangers—we're not so different from those ancient Romans. The smoke of our tailgate grills rises like ancient incense, and our cheers echo those that once filled the Hippodrome. This is what happens when bread and circuses replace bread and wine—entertainment becomes worship, and worship becomes entertainment.

2. The Contemporary Arena

The ancient stones of Rome's Coliseum still whisper tales of spectacle and glory, but their echoes now resound in our modern cathedrals of sport. From the Roman Coliseum to today's gleaming Superdome, we haven't abandoned our hunger for arena drama. We've simply transformed it. The NFL has become our contemporary Coliseum, where the raw elements of that ancient spec-

MORE THAN GAMES

tacle live on in modern dress.

Where once gladiators clashed with swords and shields, today's warriors clash in carefully choreographed violence. The brutal tackle has replaced the sword thrust, while quarterbacks command the field with the same dramatic flair as chariot drivers of old. Though actual death no longer stalks the arena, our language still drips with its imagery—the blitz, the bomb, the sudden death overtime. We've softened the stakes but maintained the theater of mortality.

The political machinery spins on as well. Just as Roman patricians once held court in the Coliseum's luxury boxes, today's team owners preside over their domains from glass-enclosed suites. Players become political symbols in our cultural wars, while the very stadiums themselves become battlegrounds for civic debate and public spending.

Our tribal instincts remain unchanged. The ancient Romans pledged fierce loyalty to their chariot racing factions—the Blues, the Greens, the Reds, and the Whites. Today, we paint our faces in team colors, drape ourselves in jerseys, and stake our civic pride on Sunday's outcome. Cities rise and fall with their teams' fortunes, and fans forge tribal bonds that transcend class and background.

Even our yearning for the divine persists. Where Romans seated their gods in the Coliseum's upper reaches, we build our own Halls of Fame, enshrining our heroes in marble and bronze. We don't call them gods anymore. We call them legends. But through our statistics and stories, through our highlight reels and heated debates about "greatest of all time," we still seek to create immortals. We still need our giants to walk among us, even if they now wear cleats instead of sandals.

The franchise quarterback is the Holy Grail of the football business.

FORMER BALTIMORE RAVENS COACH
BRIAN BILLICK[3]

3. THE SIGNS AND THE STORIES

Malcolm Butler's Super Bowl XLIX interception, which one of your authors (Len) uses in his semiotics courses, teaches us to read the signs in our games. Butler's interception is also regarded as one of the greatest plays in NFL history, and in relation to Super Bowl win probability, it is analytically the most important single play in NFL history.[4] Here is the clip Len requires every student to study: https://www.youtube.com/watch?v=U7rPIg7ZNQ8

Like the ancient augurs who read divine will in the flight of birds, we read meaning in:

- The undrafted rookie who becomes a hero.

- The moment of recognition that changes everything.
- The split-second decision that echoes through history.
- The pride that comes before the fall.

Twenty-six seconds. One yard. That's all that stood between the Seattle Seahawks and NFL immortality. The air in Phoenix's University of Phoenix Stadium crackled with possibility, heavy with the weight of history about to be made. Marshawn Lynch, the running back they called "Beast Mode," had just powered through the Patriots' defense for four and a half yards, leaving cleat marks and broken tackles in his wake. The Seahawks were one yard away from becoming back-to-back Super Bowl champions, a feat as rare as desert rain.

In the stands, a hundred thousand hearts pounded in syncopated rhythm. On the sidelines, Bill Belichick, the Patriots' sphinxlike coach, did something unexpected. Nothing. The clock kept ticking. Pete Carroll, the Seahawks' ever-optimistic leader, faced a decision that would echo through football eternity.

What happened next became more than a play call—it became a parable.

The formation told the story before the ball was snapped. Russell Wilson in shotgun, Lynch offset—a passing formation when the whole world expected a run. This was the moment when cleverness whispered louder than wisdom, when the desire to be brilliant overcame the simple path to victory. How often do we fall into this same trap in our spiritual lives, choosing complexity over clarity, seeking to impress rather than to be faithful?

The Patriots' undrafted rookie cornerback, Malcolm Butler, saw what generations of spiritual teachers have always known: sometimes the biggest moments arrive disguised as ordinary ones. While everyone else saw chaos, Butler saw signs. He'd seen this formation in practice, had been beaten by it earlier. But this time, he was ready.

The pass was thrown. Butler crossed in front of the receiver like destiny itself, and the ball—along with Seattle's dreams of dynasty—ended up in his hands. But what happened after the interception reveals an even deeper truth about pride and its consequences.

In the post-game interviews, Pete Carroll, respected for his player-first approach and positive energy, found himself unable to say the simplest of phrases: "I made a mistake." Instead, he offered a labyrinth of explanations, each more complex than the last. The clock management, the defensive personnel, the statistical improbability of interceptions from that spot on the field—all of it true, none of it honest.

MORE THAN GAMES

"Football is a game of seconds and inches," Carroll explained to the press, his usually bright eyes clouded with justification. But what he couldn't say was what everyone knew: sometimes the hardest distance to travel is the space between our slips and the truth.

The days that followed revealed how denial acts like rust on the bonds of community. Players who had bought into Carroll's culture of transparency now faced a cognitive dissonance: their leader, who had preached authenticity, couldn't model it when it mattered most. Marshawn Lynch, the player who should have gotten the ball, maintained a dignified silence that spoke volumes. The team's unity, once their hallmark, showed hairline fractures that would widen in the seasons to come.

Meanwhile, Malcolm Butler's story took its own twist toward paradox. From undrafted rookie to Super Bowl hero, his trajectory seemed aimed at the stars. But three years later, in another Super Bowl, Butler would find himself benched for reasons never fully explained, watching from the sideline as his team's defense crumbled without him. Glory, it seemed, was as temporary as morning dew.

The same NFL that had lifted Butler to its heights now showed its colder face. His story reminds us that every victory contains within it the seeds of future challenge, every triumph the possibility of trial. The young man who had read the signs so perfectly in one moment would have to learn to read different signs in another: signs of grace in disappointment, purpose in pain.

In this drama, we see echoes of an older story. Like Adam in the garden, faced with a simple choice complicated by pride, Pete Carroll reached for cleverness when simplicity would have served. Like Cain after the rejection of his offering, Butler would have to learn that identity runs deeper than performance.

The story becomes a parable that we take into ourselves. The whole tableau—the pride, the fall, the consequences, the redemption still waiting in the wings—plays out like a modern morality play in shoulder pads and cleats. It reminds us that our greatest opponent is often ourselves, and our most crucial plays aren't made on any field, but in those moments when we choose between pride and truth, between justification and confession, between the narrative we wish were true and the one that actually is.

One yard. Twenty-six seconds. An infinite distance between what could have been and what was. But in that space, we find our own stories, our own battles with pride, our own need for the grace that catches us when we fall, that lifts us when we fail, that loves us through both victory and defeat.

> [Faith is] the No. 1 thing in my life. You can ask anyone who knows me, that's the first thing they should tell you, and if they don't, then I'm not doing the right thing ... that is what's the most important thing to me, to be noticed as a Christian first and a quarterback second.
>
> NEW ORLEANS SAINTS QUARTERBACK DEREK CARR[5]

4. Beyond Bread and Circuses

The smoke rises from a hundred grills in the MetLife Stadium parking lot, carrying with it the aroma of belonging. It's three hours before kickoff, and already the faithful have gathered. They come not just for the game, but for something older, something deeper—the ancient human need to gather around fire and food, to share stories and break bread.

This is where Rome got it half-right. They understood hunger—both physical and spiritual. But they tried to fill it with spectacle rather than substance. Their bread and circuses were meant to sedate; they offered escape rather than encounter, distraction rather than direction.

Watch the scene unfold in this modern coliseum's shadow:

A Jets fan offers his bratwurst to a visiting Steelers family, their Terrible Towels draped like tribal colors across their shoulders. They've never met before, but here, in this makeshift sanctuary of smoke and story, they're breaking bread together. This isn't Rome's bread of distraction. It's something closer to communion.

Three spaces over, a group of strangers has become family for the day, their chairs arranged in an impromptu sanctuary around a smoker that looks like an altar. They're sharing stories of games past, of victories and defeats, of fathers who taught them to love this sport and children they're teaching now. This isn't circus entertainment. It's oral tradition, the passing down of a story larger than scores and statistics.

Behind them, an elderly man wearing a vintage Joe Namath jersey is explaining to his grandson about Super Bowl III, his eyes bright with memory. The boy may not understand everything, but he understands this: he's part of a story that started before him and will continue after him. This isn't mindless spectacle. It's membership in something eternal.

Jesus understood this hunger for belonging. But where Rome offered bread and circuses, Jesus offered bread and wine. Where they built coliseums, Jesus built community. Where they sought to distract from life's emptiness, Jesus filled it with presence.

Jesus fed thousands, not to quiet them but to qualify them for deeper hunger.

Jesus told stories, not to entertain but to entrain.

Jesus gathered people, not into crowds but into community.

Jesus offered His body, not as spectacle but as sacrifice.

Even now, in these concrete corridors of our contemporary arenas, you can see glimpses of what Jesus meant. When the stranger becomes neighbor over shared food, when the story becomes saga in the telling, when the game becomes merely the excuse for gathering—these are echoes of the Messiah's table, the Messiah's teaching, the Messiah's way of making family out of foreigners.

GAME XVI

BEYOND THE GOALPOSTS

FROM KICKOFF TO KINGDOM COME

*I don't mind parties.
Jesus went to plenty of parties.*

TONY DUNGY

There's an irony that would make John Wesley weep. In sanctuaries across USAmerica, the spiritual descendants of "shouting Methodists"[1] (the tribe of your authors) now sit in pristine silence, their hands folded neatly in their laps, while across town, Pentecostal congregations rock with the very spirit-filled enthusiasm that once marked Methodist revival meetings. The same denomination that once had to defend itself against charges of "excessive enthusiasm" now seems to need defending against charges of no enthusiasm at all.

Yet on Sunday afternoons, these same silent saints leap to their feet in sports stadiums, high-fiving strangers when their team scores. The contradiction would be comical if it weren't so telling: we've learned to celebrate touchdowns on earth while sitting quietly for touchdowns in eternity. The church has become the morning quiet before the afternoon storm.

Jesus tells us something startling about heaven's response to spiritual victories: "There will be more rejoicing in heaven over one sinner who repents than over ninety-nine righteous persons who do not need to repent."[2] Can't you see it now? Angels leaping to their feet, heaven's bleachers shaking with joy, a celestial celebration that makes the Super Bowl look tame.

Sixty inches of rain fell for days from Hurricane Harvey (2017), turning Houston's streets into rivers and its highways into lakes. In these moments of crisis, character reveals itself not in what we say but in what we do first. Two stories emerged from the deluge, each telling a different tale about how we respond when God's moment finds us.

J. J. Watt, the Texans' defensive end, watched the same rain everyone else did. But where others saw disaster, he saw opportunity—not for glory, but for service. With the same intensity he brought to pursuing quarterbacks, Watt chased down donations through a crowdfunding campaign on YouCaring. His initial goal was modest: $200,000 for relief efforts. But something extraordinary happened. Like loaves and fishes in contemporary form, that goal multiplied exponentially until it surpassed $40 million and created the Justin J. Watt Foundation. Here was a football player reading the signs of his time, understanding that sometimes God puts us in positions of influence for moments precisely like this. Watt's humanitarian efforts earned him the NFL's Walter Payton Man of the Year Award in 2017.

Meanwhile, across town, Joel Osteen's Lakewood Church—the former home of the Houston Rockets, a structure built for moments of community gathering—sat silent behind closed doors. The church's initial refusal to grant shelter to the displaced came through carefully worded statements about inaccessibility and logistics, about insurance and liability, about being a distribution center rather than a shelter. It was all perfectly reasonable, perfectly logical, and perfectly wrong for the moment.

When the church finally opened its doors, after staying in the huddle for forty-eight hours, it apologized for its delay. But the image of the shut doors of the United Center as the storm raged could not be erased from the hearts of Houstonians who needed to see the church be the church. The massive arena, which had housed so many celebrations of God's abundance, had missed its moment to demonstrate what that abundance was for.³ If people were let inside and the worst case happened—the place was trashed—it still could have had the ultimate restorative effect of fire in the forest. It would have showcased a church, not wanting to serve only in the sense of handing something out, but in the sense of being in true relationship with a zip code community, which requires risk and adventure.

> One thing as I grow into a husband is being a spiritual leader of my family, my wife and the people I surround myself with…. That's what I'm striving for, and that's where I hope to continue to go and grow.
>
> TONY ROMO, DALLAS COWBOYS QUARTERBACK (2006–2016)⁴

A Tale of Three Popes

This pattern of crisis revealing character echoes through history, perhaps most clearly in the stories of three popes who faced their own defining moments:

1) The year is AD 452. The place is Rome. Attila the Hun's armies have carved a path of destruction across Europe. The Western Roman Empire, already rotting from within, offers no resistance. The emperor cowers, the legions are

absent, and into this vacuum steps an unlikely hero—Pope Leo I. Armed with nothing but faith and holy courage, Leo rides out to meet the man everyone else fears to face.

What passed between them, history doesn't fully record. But we know the result: Attila, the man who had terrorized empires, turned back. One man's courage, driven by faith, had accomplished what armies could not. Leo read the signs of his moment and acted with holy boldness.

2) Fast forward to World War II, where Pope Pius XII faced his own moment of truth. The smoke rising from death camps carried with it the stench of evil that could not be mistaken. But where Leo had found courage, Pius found caution. A skilled diplomat in normal times, he chose diplomatic silence in history's darkest hour. While the Italian people, moved by basic human decency, worked to save their Jewish neighbors, their spiritual leader spoke in whispers and diplomatic nuances.

It wasn't that Pius was evil. He was simply small in a moment that demanded greatness. Like the servant who buried his talent for safekeeping, he chose to preserve the church's institutions rather than risk them for the kingdom's cause.

3) Then came John Paul II, a pope who understood both evil and courage from his youth in Nazi-occupied Poland. When communism tried to silence the church, he amplified its voice. When an assassin's bullet tried to stop him,

he became even bolder. Like Leo before him, he faced down an empire—not with armies, but with the unshakeable conviction that truth speaks louder than power.

> I am a Christian that loves the Lord that just happens to play football.... I'm a Godly man first. I chase after God. I play football for the sole reason to give God Glory.
>
> SHAUN ALEXANDER SEATTLE SEAHAWKS RUNNING BACK (2000–2007),[5] HOLDER OF TWENTY CAREER/SEASON/SINGLE-GAME FRANCHISE RECORDS

READING THE SIGNS

The quarterback who can't read the defense won't last long in the NFL. Similarly, Christians who can't read the signs of their moment will miss their opportunities to impact eternity. Jesus criticized the religious leaders of His day who could predict the weather but couldn't discern the spiritual climate of their moment.[6]

Reading these signs requires more than Bible knowledge. It demands spiritual alertness, what the old Methodists called "watching and praying." It means seeing Hurricane Harvey not just as a weather event but as a moment for kingdom action. It means recognizing that sometimes God positions us, like Esther, "for such a time as this."

When J. J. Watt read the signs correctly, he didn't just raise money. He raised hope. When John Paul II read his moment clearly, he didn't just speak against communism. He spoke hope into a nation's soul. When Leo I read his situation rightly, he didn't just turn back an army. He demonstrated that spiritual authority trumps physical might.

Running the Right Routes

Every football play has a design, but great players know when to improvise within the system. Similarly, scoring touchdowns in eternity requires both preparation and spontaneity. We train ourselves in righteousness, study the playbook of Scripture, and practice the fundamentals of faith. But just as a quarterback must read the defense and adjust, Christians must read their cultural moment and respond with Spirit-led wisdom.

When Hurricane Harvey hit Houston, churches didn't just pray. They launched boats. When refugees flee war, faithful communities don't just quote scripture. They open homes. When injustice demands action, believers don't just stick to the old plays. They innovate new ways to serve while staying true to the fundamentals.

> I'm just a vessel for what God's trying to accomplish here in this city.
>
> PHILADELPHIA EAGLES TIGHT END TREY BURTON[7]
> FAMOUS FOR THE "PHILLY SPECIAL" TRICK PLAY
> WHICH WON SUPER BOWL LII

This is what it means to be "the salt of the earth"—not just preserving ancient traditions, but bringing out the God-flavors of the moment and opening to God's transfigurative presence in each new challenge. Like a veteran player who knows when to break from the designed route, mature faith knows when to move beyond comfortable patterns while maintaining its essential character.

When the early Methodists were kicked out of their pulpits, they didn't quit preaching—they took to the fields. When traditional churches wouldn't receive their message, they created a new delivery system through class meetings and band meetings and quarterly conferences and, later on, camp-meetings. They read their moment and adjusted their routes without losing sight of their goal.

Celebration as Strategic Warfare

The old revival tents of Methodism knew something we've forgotten—celebration isn't just joy overflowing; it's a weapon of spiritual warfare. When the early Methodists let loose their "shouting," they weren't just making a joyful noise; they were declaring victory in territories the enemy thought he owned. Every hymn sung with abandoned enthusiasm, every "amen" that rattled the rafters, every "hallelujah" that hailed the Spirit, every testimony that brought the congregation to its feet—these were advance notices to the powers of darkness that God's kingdom was on the move.

Today, we've surrendered this weapon to others. We've traded our birthright of holy enthusiasm for a mess of dignified pottage. While sports stadiums erupt in collective joy, while concert venues pulse with raised hands and swaying bodies, while political rallies thunder with passionate chants—our sanctuaries often sit in polite and soporific silence. The same Christians who scream themselves hoarse at a touchdown stand stiffly during worship. The disciples of Jesus who dance at weddings sit motionless during praise. We've ceded the territory of public celebration to extra-church spaces, forgetting that enthusiasm itself—being filled with God—and ecstasy itself—to stand outside of oneself—was once our native language.

A Celebration of Faith: The Bound Brook Six

On 10 November 1990, something extraordinary happened on the Bound Brook High School football field in New Jersey. Six high school students, all members of the InterVarsity Christian Fellowship, took a bold stand that would challenge the notion of Christianity as a joyless religion of mere rules and regulations.

In a culture often pulling young people away from faith, these students chose to make their commitment to Christ public and unmistakable. They gathered on their school's football field—a place usually reserved for athletic victories—to reaffirm their baptismal vows before their entire community. This wasn't a quiet, private ceremony tucked away in a church sanctuary. Instead, these young disciples chose to declare their faith in the open, transforming their school's football field into holy ground.

The impact was electric. Their courage created a ripple effect that extended far beyond that afternoon in Bound Brook. Here were six young people who, despite the conflicting messages of popular culture, despite the potential for ridicule or misunderstanding, stood firm in their faith. Their celebration of faith was authentic and unashamed—a pure expression of joy that seemed to bridge the gap between heaven and earth. Any public profession of faith is a joyful expression.

One could almost picture heaven's response: the celestial bleachers erupting in cheers, angels leaping to their feet, as these young disciples displayed what genuine, joyful faith looks like. Their action demonstrated that when a congregation—or in this case, a group of young believers—rediscovers the lost art of celebration, something profound happens. Faith becomes visible. Joy becomes contagious. Courage becomes inspirational.

Their testament serves as a powerful reminder that Christianity isn't meant to be hidden or subdued. When Jesus humans celebrate their faith with authentic, unbridled joy, they don't just honor God—they inspire others to consider what could inspire such bold, public declaration of faith. The Bound Brook Six, as they might be called, showed us that true faith isn't about quiet submission to rules and regulations—it's about joyful, courageous celebration of a life-changing relationship with Jesus Christ.

Think of celebration as a form of spiritual reconnaissance. Every genuine expression of joy in God's presence sends a message to watching not-yets: there's something real here, something worth investigating. When J. J. Watt raised those millions for hurricane relief, his celebration wasn't just in the total raised—it was in the thousands of people who discovered they could be part of something bigger than themselves. That's what true celebration does—it invites others into the story.

THE FINAL QUARTER: OUR CHOICE TO CELEBRATE

The game clock is running down, and we face a choice that would have been unthinkable to our forebears. Will we continue to outsource our celebration to others? Will we let the Pentecostals do our shouting for us while we perfect the art of holy restraint?

Imagine walking into a Methodist church where the spirit of John Wesley still burns bright. The air crackles with expectancy. When someone stands to testify (story-time) about God's grace, hands lift spontaneously in praise. When a prodigal finds their way home, the congregation erupts with the same enthusiasm they'd show at a game-winning touchdown—no, with more, because they know this score counts forever.

This isn't about manufacturing emotion or copying other traditions. It's about reclaiming what was always ours. We haven't lost the ability to celebrate; we've just forgotten we have permission to bring that same passion into God's house.

In the prodigal son story, the father didn't maintain his dignity when his son appeared on the horizon. He didn't form a committee to discuss appropriate ways to welcome him home. He ran—ran!—and threw a celebration so loud the older brother could hear it from the fields. That's our model. That's our heritage. That's what we've traded for something safer, more predictable, more respectable.

But here's the good news: it's not too late to reclaim our voice. Every time a soul turns to Christ, heaven throws a party. The question isn't whether there will be celebration.

It's whether we'll join in or just watch from the sidelines. Every Sunday, every altar call, every baptism, every healing gives us a new opportunity to choose: Will we sit on our hands, or will we raise them in praise? Will we maintain our dignity, or will we risk holy abandonment? Will we let others do our celebrating for us, or will we reclaim our heritage as people who know how to make a joyful noise unto the Lord?

In sanctuaries (church and home) across the land, the spirit of celebration that once marked the Methodist movement is stirring again. The question isn't whether God is doing something worth celebrating. It's whether we'll have the courage to join the party.

Game XVII

Laterals of Love

Passing Faith Through Life's Chaos

*My way of joking is to tell the truth.
Truth is the funniest joke of all.*

MUHAMMAD ALI

In the grand stadium of life, we don't "work" football—we "play" it. This distinction speaks volumes about the nature of both sport and faith, where the highest forms of beauty emerge not from laborious effort, but from the joy of play.[1] Perhaps no moment better illustrates this divine intersection of play and providence than a remarkable college football game from 1982, known simply as "The Play."

Since that first historic match between Rutgers and Princeton in 1869, countless football games have unfolded on

USAmerican soil. Yet none captures the essence of faith, persistence, and divine possibility quite like the spectacular finish between the California Golden Bears and the Stanford Cardinals on 20 November 1982.

"THE PLAY:" WHEN GLORY BREAKS THROUGH

In our minds, there are three ultimate sporting moments in the twentieth century. 1) Muhammad Ali's defeat of George Foreman; 2) John McEnroe's beating of Bjorn Borg; 3) the November 1982 "Rivalry Game" between Stanford, led by John Elway, and California. This latter nicknamed "The Play" is one of the most epic moments in the history of college football and one of the greatest plays in the history of sports.

In the waning seconds of that November afternoon in 1982, as Stanford's band prematurely stormed the field celebrating what they thought was certain victory, God was about to teach us something profound about the divine kingdom. The California Golden Bears were about to show us what faith looks like when it refuses to surrender to apparent defeat.

We've all lived that moment—four seconds on the clock, your team down by six, eighty yards from the end zone. The math says it's over. Statistics say you've lost. But then comes the impossible catch, the missed tackle, the lateral that somehow finds hands instead of turf. They call these "miracle finishes" in football. In God's kingdom, we call them "daily bread."

This pattern shows up everywhere: Moses at the Red Sea, David facing Goliath, Jesus in the tomb. The world's scoreboard always flashes "GAME OVER" too soon, forgetting that in God's playbook, the final whistle never blows until God says so.

You can watch The Play on YouTube.[2] Or you can let us tell you about it. Watch closely as the ball changes hands five times in that legendary play. Each lateral pass represents a moment of trust, a willing surrender of control. The players couldn't see the ultimate outcome; they simply knew they had to keep the play alive. Isn't this how God's kingdom advances? We pass along our faith, not knowing how far it will travel or whose hands it will touch next. "The Play" serves as more than just a sporting spectacle. It's a powerful teleological metaphor for God's kingdom at work.[3]

The opposition was fierce that day. Each time a Cal player advanced, Stanford defenders converged to stop them. Yet somehow, through a series of seemingly impossible movements, the ball kept moving forward. So it is with God's kingdom—though we face the tackles of doubt, the crushing weight of circumstances, the opposition of a world that thinks victory belongs to the strongest, not to mention trombonist resistance—God's purposes prevail.

When Cal's Kevin Moen crossed that final goal line, he had to navigate past one last obstacle—a bewildered Stanford trombonist who became an unwitting defender in God's unfolding drama. Sometimes, the final barrier between us and God's purpose comes wearing the most unexpected uniform. The world will always place its instruments of resistance in our path—sometimes literally!—but even a trombone can't stop God's appointed touchdown. In fact, that trombonist, Gary Tyrrell, became part of the miracle story itself, a reminder that what appears to be our last obstacle might just become part of our testimony. In those chaotic, beautiful moments, we glimpse the truth that the kingdom of God advances not through raw power, but through surrender, trust, and the willingness to keep believing when all seems lost.

After all, we don't build the kingdom of God; the kingdom of God builds us. We don't construct this divine reality; rather, this divine reality constructs us, transfiguring our very essence from within. The kingdom is not our achievement of striving, but a Presence to receive—not our power to wield, but a power that reshapes us into what we were designed to become. "Be all you can be" is too low an ambition for a gospeller. Be all Christ designed you to be.

LATERALS OF LOVE

This is how we're called to carry the gospel. Like that football changed hands that day, each person receiving it must be ready to turn and pass it on. The gospel isn't meant to be cradled safely in our arms; it's meant to be lateraled to others in need of hope. And yes, this passing on will change us. We cannot remain the same when we truly participate in this divine play.

> I think football is a great way to demonstrate the power of teamwork and unity, and that's something that's really important to me as a Christian.
>
> DETROIT LIONS PLACEKICKER JASON HANSON[4]

Just as each Cal player had to adjust their position, their grip, their whole body to keep the play alive, so we too must be transfigured by the gospel we carry. We must turn, pivot, and reorient our lives to effectively pass on the love of Christ. The good news doesn't travel in straight lines but moves in mysterious ways through a world that thinks it knows how the story ends.

Remember: when the world's band is on the field, when defeat seems certain, when only seconds remain—that's often when God does God's most spectacular work. "Thy kingdom come[s]" not through dominating power but through faithful persistence, through believing that the play isn't over until the Creator says it's over.

So take up your position in this grand play. Receive the gospel with open hands, but don't hold it too tightly. Be ready to turn and pass it on, knowing that in the passing, both you and the message will be transformed. For in God's kingdom, every moment holds the potential for miracle, every seeming end can become a beginning, and victory often comes through the most unexpected means.

What does this look like in practice?

It means the businesswoman who mentors young professionals, passing on not just career advice but testimony of God's faithfulness in her own journey.

It's the recovering addict who, instead of hiding his past, shares his story of redemption with others still struggling.

It's the elderly church member who, despite physical limitations, makes daily phone calls to check on shut-ins, lateraling Christ's love through simple conversation.

Each person must adjust their 'grip' on the gospel—finding their unique way to pass it on through their particular circumstances and gifts.

LATERALS OF LOVE

I believe God is in all of us, and He's given us all certain talents, and I think it's our obligation to use those talents to the best of our ability.

BART STARR, METHODIST-RAISED LEGENDARY GREEN BAY PACKERS QB, TWO-TIME SUPER BOWL CHAMPION (1967-1968)[5]

"The Play" happens in unexpected places: in hospital waiting rooms where strangers comfort each other, in coffee shop conversations where friends wrestle with doubt together, in food pantry lines where volunteers see Christ in those they serve.

Sometimes it's as simple as the parent who, instead of rushing through bedtime, takes time to pray with their child, passing on faith through small, daily moments of presence.

"The Play" reminds us: God's kingdom advances not through our strength, but through our willingness to keep the faith alive, to receive it and regift it, to pass it on, to trust in God's ultimate victory even when the opposing band is on the field. For the divine kingdom comes not with obvious power, but like a football finding its way through a matrix of impossibility to ultimate victory.

Christ offers us a different playbook. He doesn't permit us

the luxury of non-engagement or the comfort of ideological isolation. Just as football demands active participation and face-to-face encounter, Jesus commands us to engage with the world and love our neighbors—regardless of their political jersey colors. Staying in our ideological huddle is equivalent to forfeiting the game of life itself.

When we gather in worship, we glimpse the transfiguring power of unity in Christ. In these sacred moments, political affiliations fade into meaninglessness, much like team rivalries dissolve when players kneel together in prayer after a hard-fought game. Whether we're breaking bread in fellowship or cheering together in stadiums, we participate in something greater than ourselves—a community bound by shared purpose and divine love.

The gridiron reminds us that victory often comes through unexpected channels and requires trust in something bigger than ourselves. Just as those California players trusted each other in that chaotic final play, we must trust in God's providence, even when the field seems crowded with obstacles. Football, like faith, demands we keep moving forward, keep trusting, keep playing until the final whistle and wrap up.

As we leave the field of this earthly game, let us remember that Christ's power renders our temporal divisions meaningless. In eternity's end zone, no one will ask about our political playbook or our team affiliations. Instead, what matters is how we played the game—how we loved, how we served, how we contributed to God's kingdom.

Let us go forth with the spirit of those Golden Bears, never giving up, always ready for one more lateral, one more chance to advance the ball. For in God's kingdom, the game is never truly over, and the possibility of victory exists in every moment. Through Christ, we are all players in the greatest game ever played—a game where love conquers division, faith overcomes doubt, and grace scores the ultimate touchdown.

To God be the glory, now and forever. Amen.

THE FINAL DRIVE
FOURTH DOWN FAITH AND HAIL MARY LIVING

In life, as in football, you won't go far unless you know where the goalposts are.

HUMORIST ARNOLD H. GLASGOW, MOST OFTEN MISATTRIBUTED TO "PAPA BEAR" COACH AND OWNER GEORGE HALAS

The game of football reminds us that it's all about the wood—acceptance or denial. Every stadium bears its crosses, thirty feet high. Like the chains that measure our forward progress in life, we move toward these crosses seeking breakthrough, carrying the gospel-leather in our hands. This sacred ball, shaped like the seed of faith itself, sometimes meets the wood in moments of denial—a small echo of that cosmic collision at Calvary.

And beneath these crosses, like disciples at Golgotha, we witness moments of triumph and defeat, believing always in resurrection—the next attempt, the next game. In football's sacred geometry, every shot that greets the crossbar is a meditation on the cross, every chain measurement a test of how far we've come in our journey.

Just as Christ's arms stretched east to west, the crossbar spans the width of human hope. And like the vertical post climbing skyward, our prayers rise, seeking grace. The chains remind us: we move the ball forward by faith, ten yards at a time, toward that ultimate goal line.

Hail Mary Living

The Hail Mary pass in football is often seen as a desperate final attempt—a prayer thrown skyward when all other options have been exhausted. But what if we've misunderstood its spiritual significance entirely? What if the Hail Mary isn't meant to represent desperation, but rather divine abundance?

The typical mindset around the Hail Mary is this: Teams save it for last, holding it in reserve like a final card to play. This approach stems from a scarcity mentality—the belief that our best efforts must be rationed, preserved, and protected. It's the same mindset that leads us to save our "good china" for special occasions that never come, or to

THE FINAL DRIVE

hold back our most profound insights for some hypothetical future moment, or to wrap our living room furniture in plastic, saving the upholstery for whenever guests show up and celebrations take place.

But gridiron gospel calls gospellers to a radically different way of living. When Jesus fed the five thousand, he didn't portion out the loaves and fishes sparingly—he broke them freely, trusting in divine multiplication. When the widow of Zarephath gave her last meal to Elijah, she wasn't operating from scarcity but from holy abundance, and her jar of flour never ran empty.

Every pastor faces this choice every Sunday. Do they save their most powerful insights for a special occasion? Do they hold back their most profound revelations for a larger audience? Or do they, like the widow, pour out their last measure of flour, trusting that God will provide fresh manna for the next week?

The Hail Mary play, properly understood, isn't an act of desperation—it's an act of faith. It's the quarterback releasing the ball with everything they have, trusting in possibilities they cannot yet see. It's receivers sprinting full-speed toward the end zone, believing in completion before the ball ever leaves the quarterback's hand. This is how gospellers are called to live: not cautiously hoarding our gifts, but boldly throwing them skyward.

Think of the preacher who approaches each sermon like

a Hail Mary pass—not in desperation, but in faithful abundance. They pour out their best insights, their deepest studies, their most profound revelations, knowing that God's wisdom, like the manna in the desert, is renewed every morning. They understand that biblical insights, like the loaves and fishes, multiply in the breaking and sharing.

This abundance mindset transforms how we view our resources, our gifts, and our calling. The scarcity mindset whispers, "Save something for later." The abundance mindset declares, "Give your best now, trusting God for tomorrow's provision." The scarcity mindset sees the Hail Mary as a last resort; the abundance mindset sees it as a first fruit—an offering thrown heavenward in faith.

Just as the quarterback must release the ball to achieve any possibility of completion, we must release our gifts, our insights, our resources into the world for them to bear fruit. The ball that never leaves the quarterback's hand cannot score. The sermon that never leaves the preacher's study cannot bless. The gift that's forever held in reserve cannot multiply.

In this light, every new day becomes a Hail Mary—not in desperation, but in celebration. Every sermon, every lecture, every lesson plan becomes an act of faith—not in our own reserves, but in God's endless supply. Every offering becomes a declaration: we serve a God of abundance, not scarcity; a God who multiplies loaves and fishes; a God who makes manna fall fresh every morning.

The Hail Mary play thus becomes more than a desperate final attempt—it becomes a model for faithful living. It teaches us to release our best efforts with full force, to sprint toward divine possibilities we cannot yet see, and to trust that when we empty ourselves in faith, God fills us anew with resources for tomorrow's game.

"HAIL FLUTIE"

On 23 November 1984, the impossible became possible on a rain-soaked field and mist-fogged goal-post in Miami.[1] Boston College, led by an undersized quarterback named Doug Flutie, stood against the mighty Miami Hurricanes—defending national champions and goliaths of college football. What transpired in those final seconds would become more than a game-winning play; it would become a testament to the divine partnership between faith and action.

With six seconds remaining and trailing 45–41, Flutie stood at his own 48-yard line. The odds weren't just against him—they were mathematically improbable. Yet in that moment, as the rain fell and 30,000 hearts held their collective breath, Flutie demonstrated what theologians have preached for millennia: faith is the evidence of things not seen.

The play called was the "Hail Mary"—a name that itself

bridges the sacred and secular. As Flutie rolled right and launched the ball into the darkening Miami sky, he wasn't just throwing a football; he was offering a prayer in spiral form. The ball traveled 63 yards through sheets of rain, beyond the reach of Miami's defenders, and into the waiting arms of Gerard Phelan. In that suspended moment, as the ball descended through the Miami air, physics met faith, and probability bowed to possibility.

This wasn't just a victory for Boston College; it was a victory for every human who has ever faced impossible odds. The play embodied the very essence of Boston College's Jesuit tradition—the pursuit of "magis," the more, the greater glory. It wasn't merely about winning a football game; it was about transcending human limitations through a combination of preparation, courage, and divine grace.

In the Jesuit tradition, education forms not just the mind, but the whole person—body, spirit, and soul. Flutie's pass represented this holistic formation in dramatic fashion. The countless hours of practice met the moment of grace; human effort aligned with divine possibility. The play demanded everything Flutie had learned: the physical skill to throw, the mental strength to believe, and the spiritual courage to attempt what others deemed impossible.

Today, the "Hail Flutie" stands as more than a highlight in sports history. It serves as a parable for our times, and the reason for writing *Gridiron Gospel: A Faith that Moves Chains* isn't passive waiting but active believing. Sometimes, God's greatest miracles come not through the suspension of natural laws, but through the elevation of human potential to heights we never imagined possible.

We conclude our theological exploration of football with "Hail Flutie" as our final sermon. In those six seconds, we witness the convergence of preparation and providence, of human effort and divine grace. "Hail Mail" stands as an eternal reminder that in both football and faith, the size of the challenger matters less than the size of their faith, and that sometimes, when we dare to throw our hopes heavenward, God reaches down and makes the impossible possible.

For every reader who has faced their own fourth-quarter challenges, for every human who has stood against overwhelming odds, let Flutie's spiral serve as a reminder: faith isn't just about believing in unseen outcomes. It's about acting on that faith with everything we have.

> It was a Hail Mary pass. I just threw it up there as far as I could.
>
> DALLAS QB ROGER STAUBACH,
> A SELF-DESCRIBED "CATHOLIC KID FROM CINCINNATI"
> DESCRIBING HIS 50-YARD TOUCHDOWN PASS AGAINST
> THE MINNESOTA VIKINGS IN A 1975 PLAYOFF GAME
> AFTER SAYING A QUICK PRAYER TO THE VIRGIN MARY[2]

Faith is what turns knowledge into knowing, information into illumination, what we know into being known. In the end, that's what makes both football and faith transfigurative: the courage to attempt the impossible, trusting that where human capacity ends, divine possibility begins.

PRAYER:

Lord of Impossible Victories,
You who turned shepherd boys into kings
And fishermen into fishers of men and women,
We come before You in humble recognition
That our greatest limits often lie
Not in our circumstances, but in our belief.

Grant us, O God, the courage of Doug Flutie—
Not just to see the distant goal,
But to throw our whole selves toward it,
Even when the odds tower against us
Like defenders in the end zone.
Give us the wisdom to prepare as if everything depends on us,
And the faith to trust as if everything depends on You.

In our fourth-quarter moments,
When the clock runs down
And hope seems beyond our reach,
Remind us that Your power perfects our weakness.
Teach us, Father, that faith is more than a Hail Mary—
It is the daily practice of believing
Beyond what our eyes can see

THE FINAL DRIVE

And our minds can measure.

Let us be bold in attempt and humble in victory,
Knowing that every achievement
Is a partnership between human effort and divine grace.
For those who stand where Flutie stood,
Facing their own impossible distances,
Grant them the strength to take the snap,
The courage to release their fears,
And the faith to launch their hopes heavenward.

May we remember that in Your kingdom,
The size of the challenger matters less
Than the size of their faith,
And that through You, all things are possible.

Lord of every field and every faith journey,
help us carry your gospel forward.
When we meet the wood of denial,
give us strength for the next play.

Let us measure our progress
not just in yards gained,
but in faith deepened.
And may every game remind us
of the greatest game ever played—
where death met defeat on a cross,
and victory was won for all.

Amen.

VICTORY CELEBRATION
THE CHAMPIONSHIP MINDSET

One of the most stirring and timeless motifs woven through religious and literary traditions is that of a divine liberator—a figure who shatters chains, topples walls, and flings wide the gates of freedom. In Micah 2:13, we glimpse this power unleashed:

> The breaker (*ha-poretz*) goes up before them; they break through and pass the gate, going out by it. Their king passes on before them, the Lord at their head.[1]

The Hebrew word *poretz* pulses with raw energy, rooted in *parats* (פרץ)—to burst forth, to breach, to shatter. It invites the picture of a force unstoppable, splintering barriers, leading captives out from the shadows of confinement. This isn't just a moment—it's a movement, echoing the Exodus, where God Himself strides ahead, a king who doesn't merely rule but redeems. The parallel of "their king" and "the Lord" fuses into a single, breathtaking truth: this is no ordinary liberator, but the Divine in motion.

Forget Daenerys from *Game of Thrones* with her dragons and bravado. The true Breaker, the ultimate Chain Mover and Chain Breaker, is Jesus. He doesn't just crack shackles—He forges freedom from the cross. Where Micah's breaker storms the gate, Jesus kicks down the doors of death itself and harrows hell. He's the one who strides before us, not with a sword, but with scars and wounds—leading us out of sin's prison into a wide-open promise. Every chain of guilt, despair, or fear trembles at His step. He doesn't just move the chains; He melts them down and makes us new.

The following prayer serves as the final huddle of our journey through faith and football, bringing together the metaphors, meanings, and divine movements we've explored throughout *Gridiron Gospel*. Like a game-winning drive that draws from every lesson learned during the season, this prayer weaves together the sacred language of sport with the eternal truths of faith, reminding us that in God's kingdom, every play has purpose and no clock ever runs out on grace. As we break this final huddle, may these words carry us from the gridiron of game day to the greater field of God's eternal purpose.

THE GRIDIRON GOSPELLER'S PRAYER

Almighty God, Creator, Redeemer, and Great LifeCoach,
You who designed the perfect playbook in Your Word
And sent Your Son as the ultimate quarterback of our
  salvation,
We come before Your throne of grace with hearts full of
  gratitude.
Lord of every field and every contest,
You who turn our fumbles into opportunities,
Our defeats into wisdom,
And our victories into humble praise—
We thank You for the game of life You've given us to play.

Just as Jesus broke through the defensive line of death
And scored the winning touchdown of resurrection,
Help us run our race with perseverance,
Following the chalk lines of Your commandments,
And keeping our eyes fixed on the goal posts of Your
  Kingdom.

When we are tackled by doubt,
Grant us the strength to lateral the ball of faith to our
  brothers and sisters.
When we face fourth and long in life's toughest
  moments,
Give us courage to trust Your game plan.
When we're tempted to retreat to our own end zone of
  comfort,

SWEET AND ERIKSEN

Push us forward into the open field of Your mission.

Unite us as one team under Your banner,
Breaking down the divisions of jersey colors and team loyalties,
Until we see that in Your stadium, we all play for Your glory.

Make us both good winners and gracious losers,
Knowing that every game is but practice for eternity.

Coach our hearts to love like special teams—
Sacrificing our position so others might advance.

Train our minds like quarterbacks—
Reading the defense of deception and choosing truth.

Strengthen our spirits like offensive lines—
Standing firm against the blitz of temptation.

In the fourth quarter of our lives,
When the clock of mortality winds down,
Help us remember that through Christ's victory,
We play in a game that never truly ends,
Where every touchdown scored in love
Echoes in the hallways of heaven.

And when the final whistle blows on our earthly game,
May we cross the goal line of faith
Into Your eternal end zone of glory,
Where we'll join the greatest cloud of witnesses
In the forever celebration of Your championship love.

VICTORY CELEBRATION

We pray this in the name of Jesus Christ,
The MVP of all creation,
Who took the field of humanity,
Ran the play of perfect obedience,
And won the Super Bowl of salvation
For all who put their trust in Him.
To You be the victory,
The trophy,
And the glory,
Forever and ever.

Amen.[2]

> I have fought the good fight, I have finished the race, I have kept the faith. Now there is in store for me the crown of righteousness, which the Lord, the righteous Judge, will award to me on that day—and not only to me, but also to all who have longed for his appearing.
>
> APOSTLE PAUL[3]

Acknowledgments

Some say books are born. Others say they're built. This one? It was drawn up like a game-winning play over steaming cups of Starbucks coffee (Len adds two shots of espresso to his Grande bold, Chris adds six shots to his Venti bold), where two football zealots couldn't stop connecting the spiritual dots in USAmerica's favorite collision sport.

"I'll do the theology," Len declared with the confidence of a coach calling an all-out blitz.

"I'll do the research," Chris countered, as if reading the defense perfectly. Our tribal chief John Wesley's famous saying "The world is my parish" became "The world is my gridiron."

What followed was a years-long drive down field, with timeouts for life's big moments and audibles called when needed. Like any good football game, you can practically timestamp each chapter to when it was written—a reflection of how the sport, and we ourselves, have evolved through the seasons.

Neither of us has mastered the art of sitting still (perhaps why we're so drawn to a sport that's always in motion). This book came together in the margins of legal briefs and sermon notes, between courtroom appearances and Sunday services. Some might call us "deserters" from the ivory towers of pure academe and jurisprudence. We prefer to think of ourselves as running a new kind of option play—one that embraces pop culture as the perfect field for faith to play out.

Our study walls have proven as permeable as offensive lines, with our kids breaking through regularly to add their own special brand of color commentary. My nine-year-old son Luke (Len here) has taught me that sometimes the pure joy of the game transcends understanding all its rules. Our wives, Tia and Jean, have been our faithful offensive coordinators in different but equally helpful and supportive ways. Raised in the aura of the Auburn battle cry "War Eagle," Tia occasionally shocks me with her superior knowledge of the game: "You mean I know more about this than you boys?"

Jean, on the other hand, is not a football fan. The only football game that Jean enjoys watching each and every year is the secular sacrament of the Super Bowl. On that de facto national holiday, Jean enjoys sharing the joy, fellowship, food, and communion that is traditionally part of that special day. Jean is most interested from a viewership perspective in the high-priced and entertaining commercials and the A-List star-studded halftime show. Jean otherwise lovingly abides Chris's great interest and his related level of intense distraction on Sunday afternoons throughout the football season.

ACKNOWLEDGMENTS

An all-star coaching staff has helped us perfect this playbook. Landrum Leavell III, our "Comma King," has been our special-teams coordinator, ensuring our punctuation hits its marks with the precision of a field goal kicker. Pastor Jason Bollinger gifted us with our perfect subtitle, "The Faith That Moves Chains"—a touchdown pass we'll always celebrate and appreciate. "Spotter" Guy Taylor, who jokes that the best time to go shopping in Alabama is when families gather at the altar of a University of Alabama or Auburn game, sent valuable insights from his "birds-eye" view in the press box.

Will Clegg, who coached us in using the Old English word "gospeller," also played the crucial role of opposing coach, challenging our premise by reminding us that football's physicality would be considered violence anywhere else—a sobering thought that's haunted every page. David McGrew was the book's objective viewer.

No championship team is complete without its support staff. Content editor Erin Healy has been our strategic coordinator, with an unmatched gift for improving the architectural grandeur in our game plan. Carmen Barber, our trusted copy editor and interior formatter, has become part of the Sweet family roster. Kris White is a master interior book designer and did a fantastic job with formatting the study guide.

In football, as in life, we players long to be seen as

rounded, not just specialists in one position. This book has allowed us both to step out of our "professional" end zones and play the full field of who we are. Or to put it in current lingo, here you get a whole vibe of who we are.

Writers love their projects into existence. And like a perfectly executed two-minute drill that ends in victory, this labor of love has scored something far greater than points on a board. It's drafted a playbook for finding faith in life's most unexpected fields.

ABOUT THE AUTHORS
FROM SIDELINE TO SCRIMMAGE

In the arena of human experience, your authors bring a unique blend of outsider insight and insider knowledge to the theological gridiron of football (the non-soccer variety). We may not have NFL rings, but our gospelling journeys have given us a field-level view of football's power. We confess: Each of us has our share of AMJ-Accumulated Male Junk—time capsules of games, which become religious relics almost.

LEN SWEET: THE TALL TALE OF THE RELUCTANT QUARTERBACK

At 6'4", Len Sweet stood poised for gridiron greatness—sharing the stature of legends like Tom Brady and Randy Moss. Yet, fate, weight (a human exclamation point at 144 pounds)[1], and parental intervention benched his football aspirations before they could take flight.[2] Instead, Len did make a brief foray onto the college basketball court, perfecting the art of bench-warming with dubious dedication.

While Len's personal playbook might be as thin as a kicker's body-fat percentage, his family tree is rooted deep in the rich soil of football lore. Enter Tia Teague, Len's better half and a gridiron goddess in her own right. Once upon a time, her pom poms whipped football and basketball teams into a frenzy of fandom.

But Tia's cheerleading days were mere warm-ups for the main event: surviving the blood-soaked battlefields of the Iron Bowl. Alabama is a state divided, not by Mason and Dixon, but by "Roll Tide" and "War Eagle." Front yards became demilitarized zones, sprouting "House Divided" signs. In this gridiron Cold War, even the trees weren't safe. One rabid, vengeful Alabama "fan" took rivalry to new depths of depravity. The target? Auburn's majestic oaks of Toomer's Corner, living landmarks that had seen more touchdown celebrations than Bear Bryant had houndstooth hats. This arborcidal maniac poisoned these leafy legends, as if murdering joy itself.

Tia emerged from this pigskin pandemonium not just unscathed, but armed with a playbook of tales about "The Greatest Show on Earth" that would make John Madden's eyebrows dance the Charleston. Her stories don't just add color to our theological tailgate; they're like dumping a vat of day-glo paint into a monotone mural. And speaking of tailgates, we hope we've inspired you to serve a heaping helping of "tale-gate" that'll make your grandmother's secret sauce and your grandfather's apple butter taste like bland tofu by comparison.

ABOUT THE AUTHORS

CHRIS ERIKSEN: FROM BENCHWARMER TO BLIND-SIDE GUARDIAN

Chris Eriksen's football journey reads like a classic underdog story—a tale of perseverance that would make even Rudy proud. It's 1980, and freshman Chris is a walking question mark on the Chatham Borough High School field. Coach Joseph Milde, with a twinkle in his eye and hope in his heart, gives young Chris a mission: "Kill the kicker!" on kickoff returns. Spoiler alert: The kickers survived, and Chris mostly kept the bench warm that season.

But like any good comeback story, Chris didn't throw in the towel. Through sheer grit and a hefty helping of protein shakes, he transformed himself into a formidable force. By his senior year in 1983, Chris had claimed the coveted left tackle position—the quarterback's blind side bodyguard. This Cinderella story of sweat and determination earned him the "Most Improved" player award, proving that even in football, slow and steady can win the race.

Chris's time on the gridiron wasn't just about personal glory. It was a crucible that forged lifelong friendships with teammates like David Jones and Joe Schuchard. These bonds, tempered in the heat of competition, have stood the test of time—a testament to football's power to unite.

Sure, Chris's knee eventually met the business end of a surgeon's scalpel, but ask him if it was worth it, and you'll get an emphatic "yes!" faster than a quarterback's snap count. The lessons learned on that field—accountability, discipline, and the art of gracefully facing both triumph and defeat—proved invaluable in the game of life.

Years later, life threw Chris a beautiful curveball. At the seasoned age of fifty, he and his beloved wife, Reverend Jean Arlea Eriksen, welcomed their daughter Thea Jennifer into the world. At Thea's baptism, her godfathers, Charles Tamasaukas and Dwayne Davis, stood proud—both former college football stars whose gridiron prowess opened doors to higher education and brighter futures.

Sports scholar Robert J. Higgs offers a useful framework by categorizing four distinct types of activities often labeled as "sports."[3] These range from traditional outdoor pursuits like hunting and fishing to competitive physical games that pit athletes against one another. His third category encompasses physical education and fitness activities, whether competitive or not, such as jogging and weightlifting. The fourth and broadest category views sport as a subset of play, including numerous recreational activities like card games, dance, choral singing, and bowling. For the purposes of this book, we have concentrated specifically on the second category: competitive physical games, particularly football.

ABOUT THE AUTHORS

We do so following in the footsteps of the Apostle Paul, who routinely used athletic images for the life of faith,[4] as well as early church writers like St. John Chrysostom, who frequently employed athletic metaphors, such as referring to Christians as "athletes of Christ" engaged in a "spiritual arena," to illustrate the rigors and discipline of the Christian life.[5]

PERSONAL NOTES

PERSONAL NOTES

GAMEDAY HUDDLE GUIDE
FOR
GRIDIRON GOSPEL
FAITH THAT MOVES CHAINS

LEONARD SWEET

The Salish Sea Press
Orcas Island
Washington

Gameday Huddle Guide
Contents

Pregame Warmup
  How to Use This Playbook 387

Game I
  First Down, First Love
  Touchdowns in the Kingdom 391

Game II
  The Divine Handoff
  When God Calls the Play 397

Game III
  From the Sidelines to the Stars:
  Rediscovering Faith in a Faithless Game 403

Game IV
  Two-Minute Warning
  Divine Timing 409

Game V
  Breaking Huddle
  Steps of Faith 415

Game VI
  Resilient Roots
  The Enduring Triumph of Faith and Football 421

Game VII
  Heaven's Scoreboard
  Measuring What Matters 427

Game VIII
  The Lombardi Legacy
  Discipline as Devotion 433

GAME IX
THE BELICHICK BLUEPRINT
STRATEGY AND SPIRIT.. 439

GAME X
CROSSING THE GOAL LINE
WHERE HEAVEN MEETS EARTH 443

GAME XI
RED ZONE REDEMPTION
FROM FUMBLES TO FAITH.. 447

GAME XII
PLAYING INJURED
GRACE UNDER PRESSURE.. 451

GAME XIII
THE ULTIMATE CHAMPIONSHIP
BUILDING GOD'S TEAM... 455

GAME XIV
WHEN TAILGATES BECOME TALEGATE TESTAMENTS
FELLOWSHIP IN THE PARKING LOT...................................... 461

GAME XV
MORE THAN GAMES
FROM ARENA TO ALTAR 465

GAME XVI
BEYOND THE GOALPOSTS
FROM KICKOFF TO KINGDOM COME 469

GAME XVII
LATERALS OF LOVE
PASSING FAITH THROUGH LIFE'S CHAOS........................... 473

Pregame Warmup
HOW TO USE THIS PLAYBOOK

This *Gameday Huddle Guide* which accompanies *Gridiron Gospel*, is designed to turn game day into growth day.* Like an NFL season, it spans seventeen chapters, each structured for maximum impact during your football gatherings.

*Note: A more extensive devotional and discussion Playbook is available for purchase under separate cover. It is entitled *Playbook for Gridiron Gospel: Faith that Moves Chains* (The Salish Sea Press, 2025).

Game Plan

Head Coach: Designate a host/facilitator

Home Field: Rotate meeting locations

Game Clock:

- ⏱ Pregame (30–60 minutes before kickoff): Fellowship and opening prayers
- ⏱ Halftime: "Throw a SPIRAL" discussion

HUDDLE GUIDE

⏱ Post-Game: Wrap-up reflections and closing prayers

FORMATION

Your group will move through four quarters each session:

- First Quarter: Pregame prayers and fellowship
- Second Quarter: Game viewing
- Third Quarter: Halftime SPIRAL discussion
- Fourth Quarter: Postgame reflection and prayers

SPECIAL TEAMS

The SPIRAL format (Spirit-led, Prayer, Imagination, Redemptive Relationships, Authentic Action, Life Story) provides structure while allowing flexibility based on your group's dynamics and desires.

PREGAME WARMUP

Moving the Chains: Why This Playbook Matters

Like the eighty strangers who formed a human chain on Panama City Beach in 2017 to save nine lives from a riptide, faith moves forward when we link together. Some chain members couldn't even swim, but they held firm, allowing stronger swimmers to reach those in need. Similarly, this playbook helps us form spiritual chains—connecting, supporting, and pulling each other toward growth through football gatherings.

Each chapter provides links in this chain:

- Pregame prayers connect us to God
- Halftime discussions strengthen our bonds
- Postgame reflections pull us toward action

Just as that beach rescue showed how ordinary people can achieve extraordinary things together, these gatherings can transform game day into an opportunity for meaningful connection and spiritual growth.

Final Whistle

May God bless your gatherings, turning each game day into an opportunity for Christ formation. Like that human chain on Panama City Beach, may we link arms in fellowship, pull each other toward deeper faith, and advance the ball for God's kingdom. Let every first down become a chance for victory in Christ, every touchdown an occasion for eternal celebration.

Now, it's game time. The whistle has blown. Let's take the field together.

Kickoff!

GAME I

FIRST DOWN, FIRST LOVE
TOUCHDOWNS IN THE KINGDOM

PREGAME PRAYER

Divine Coach, guide us through Your playbook of life,
Help us move from spectators to players on Your field,
Let every down advance Your kingdom.

Amen.

COACH'S CORNER

 In football, as in life, your first step is the most important. ~Coach Bruce Mayer

HIGHLIGHT REEL

This chapter explores the powerful intersection of faith and football in American culture. Through the story of Richard and Jane Jameson—a couple divided by Tennessee-Alabama loyalty but united in faith—we examine how football shapes communities much like religious observances. The rise of "Global Fandom" presents both challenges and opportunities for faith communities, as sports culture increasingly provides ready-made communities and instant belonging. The chapter positions Christians as "gospellers on kingdom's gridiron," active players rather than passive spectators in God's game plan, where each down carries eternal significance.

Challenge Flag

⚠ Just as Jesus used agricultural metaphors for his agricultural society, we use sports metaphors that resonate with our sports-saturated culture.

Throw a SPIRAL

 S: Spirit-led Steadfastness

- How does the Jamesons' commitment to their teams mirror steadfast faith in challenging times?
- What can football players' dedication to practice teach us about spiritual discipline?

 P: Prayer

- How might we approach studying scripture with the same intensity that football players study their playbooks?
- In what ways could we transform our "spectator" prayer life into an active conversation with God?

I: Imagination

- How can we reimagine church community in an age where stadium worship often draws bigger crowds than sanctuaries?
- What creative ways can we use sports analogies to share the gospel with others?

 R: Redemptive Relationships

- How do rivalries like Tennessee-Alabama challenge and strengthen our ability to love others despite differences?
- Where have you seen faith transcend deeply held rivalries in your own life?

 A: Authentic Action

- What would it look like to approach our faith with the same intensity as a football player preparing for the Super Bowl?
- How can we move from being spiritual spectators to active participants in God's kingdom work?

 L: Life Story for a Living Legacy

- How are you contributing to God's "highlight reel" through your daily choices?
- What would it look like for you to move from the grandstand to the playing field in your spiritual life?

HUDDLE GUIDE

Coach's Corner

 The cathedral of Global Christendom is being rapidly outpaced by the coliseum of Global Fandom.

Overtime Exercises

Field Assessment: Map out your "fan zones" vs. your "playing fields" in life. Where are you just watching from the sidelines?

Training Regimen: Choose one area where you'll move from spectator to participant this week. Create a specific game plan for engagement.

Chain-Moving Challenge: Identify someone with opposing "team loyalties" in your life. Take a concrete step to build a bridge of understanding, following the Jamesons' example.

Chain-Moving Challenge

 Remember, in God's stadium, there are no nosebleed seats—only field positions waiting to be filled.

Postgame Prayer

Lord of every touchdown and fumble,
Transform us from fans to faithful players on Your field,
For Your glory and in Your name.

Amen.

GAME II

THE DIVINE HANDOFF
WHEN GOD CALLS THE PLAY

PREGAME PRAYER

Divine Coach,
as our culture shifts between sanctuary and stadium,
Guide us to see Your presence in all spaces and faces.

Help us transform every gathering into holy ground.

Amen.

COACH'S CORNER

 You don't lose ground in a single play. You lose it in a series of uncontested drives.

HIGHLIGHT REEL

This chapter explores the transformative moment when football began reshaping America's Sunday traditions, marked by the 1958 NFL Championship game between the Baltimore Colts and New York Giants—"The Greatest

HUDDLE GUIDE

Game Ever Played." Through strategic vision and cultural evolution, football gradually assumed Sunday's central role in American life. Tailgating replaced church potlucks, fantasy leagues superseded Bible study groups, and "What's the score?" became more common than "What was the sermon about?" This "divine handoff" represents more than just a scheduling conflict—it reflects a profound shift in how Americans experience community, ritual, and sacred time.

CHALLENGE FLAG

 The NFL didn't just win Sunday—it rewrote the playbook on cultural influence by understanding that people don't just need something to watch, they need something to belong to.

THROW A SPIRAL

 S: SPIRIT-LED STEADFASTNESS

- How has football's rise to "religion" status challenged or strengthened your own spiritual steadfastness?
- What can we learn from maintaining faith in pressure-filled moments, like a rookie crossing himself before a big play?

P: Prayer

- How might viewing prayer as a "holy huddle" change our approach to communication with God?
- What can we learn from finding "pockets of silence" amid life's roaring crowds?

 I: Imagination

- How does seeing football as "sacramental" help us recognize God's presence in unexpected places?
- In what ways might viewing our church as a "team" rather than an audience change our participation?

 R: Redemptive Relationships

- What can the post-game prayer of winners and losers teach us about unity in Christ?
- How might viewing competition through a lens of communion change our relationships?

 A: Authentic Action

- How can we move from being "mere fans" to "fellow pilgrims" in our faith journey?
- What would it look like to approach our faith with the same dedication as a professional athlete?

HUDDLE GUIDE

 L: Life Story for a Living Legacy

- How are we contributing to God's story in our community beyond Sunday mornings?
- What legacy are we leaving as we navigate the balance between faith and cultural influences?

Coach's Corner

 The church's challenge isn't just about keeping people in the pews. It's about remembering that faith, like football, thrives when it creates not just converts, but community.

Overtime Exercises

Sunday Audit: Track how you spend your Sundays for one month. Note the balance between spiritual nourishment and other activities.

Cultural Commentary: Visit both a local church service and a sports bar during a big game. Compare the rituals, community dynamics, and ways people find meaning in each space.

Bridge Building: Organize an event that brings together your faith community and sports community. Consider a service project that unites both groups.

CHAIN-MOVING CHALLENGE

When two teams kneel together after a game, they remind us that some things matter more than the scoreboard.

POSTGAME PRAYER

Lord of every stadium and sanctuary,
Help us find You in both the roar and the silence,
Making every gathering a chance for grace.

Amen.

Game III

From the Sidelines to the Stars
Rediscovering Faith in a Faithless Game

Pregame Prayer

Divine Coach,
In a world where faith seems to be playing defense,
Grant us courage to run bold new plays
Without compromising truth.

Let us see beyond limitations to Your possibilities.

Amen.

Coach's Corner

 We're not playing defense. We're on an eternal offensive drive. The culture's scoreboard isn't the final word.

HUDDLE GUIDE

Highlight Reel

This chapter examines Christianity's current position in modern culture through the lens of football strategy. While faith faces cultural marginalization in many spheres, the NFL remains a unique sanctuary where religious expression flourishes openly. Players like C. J. Stroud, Russell Wilson, Patrick Mahomes, and Jalen Hurts demonstrate how authentic faith can thrive in the public square. Through stories ranging from Tom Dempsey's record-breaking field goal to Buzz Aldrin's lunar communion, the chapter illustrates how faith can transcend cultural limitations when expressed boldly and authentically. The underlying message is clear: Christianity isn't called to play prevent defense, but to advance with purpose in an increasingly post-Christian world.

Challenge Flag

 Culture follows courage. Wonder precedes witness. Mystery ministers to materialism.

Throw a SPIRAL

 S: Spirit-led Steadfastness
- How can we maintain spiritual steadfastness in what the authors call "the ruins of our own creation"?

- What can Tom Dempsey's story teach us about persevering in faith despite apparent limitations?

🏈 **P: Prayer**

- How might we approach prayer differently if we viewed it as preparation for spiritual "game time"?
- What can we learn from NFL players who openly pray on the field about authentic spiritual expression?

🏈 **I: Imagination**

- How can we creatively express our faith in a culture that increasingly views Christianity with skepticism?
- What new "playbooks" might we need to develop for sharing faith authentically in today's world?

🏈 **R: Redemptive Relationships**

- How can we build authentic koinonia (spiritual team spirit) in our church community?
- What can Tom Osborne's "Move the Line Forward, Not the Ball" philosophy teach us about Christian unity?

🏈 **A: Authentic Action**

- In what ways can we move from being spiritual "fans" to active "players" in God's kingdom?
- How can we demonstrate authentic faith in public

Huddle Guide

spaces without retreating or becoming combative?

 L: Life Story for a Living Legacy

- How can our personal faith stories contribute to a larger narrative of hope in a skeptical world?
- What legacy are we building in terms of authentic Christian witness for future generations?

Coach's Corner

 Like those Apollo astronauts, we don't leave our faith behind when we enter new frontiers—we carry it forward.

Overtime Exercises

Cultural Audit: List three spaces where you've felt hesitant to express your faith. Create a game plan for authentic witness in each setting.

Wonder Watch: Document moments of awe and wonder in unexpected places this week, following Buzz Aldrin's example of seeing God's glory in new frontiers.

Team Building: Identify your unique "position" on God's team. How can your specific gifts contribute to the larger mission?

Chain-Moving Challenge

You're not just playing another down—you're advancing an eternal victory.

Postgame Prayer

Lord of limitless possibilities,
Make us bold like Dempsey,
Help us carry faith into every frontier like Aldrin
For Your glory and the advancement of Your kingdom.

Amen.

Game IV

Two-Minute Warning
Divine Timing

Pregame Prayer

Lord of Every Moment, help us see beyond spectacle to sacred participation.

Transform our time into opportunities for Your purpose.

Make us ready to move from observers to active players in Your story.

Amen.

Coach's Corner

 This isn't about competition between church and football, but about understanding deeper human needs for community, meaning, and participation.

HUDDLE GUIDE

HIGHLIGHT REEL

On 28 December 1958—"The Greatest Game Ever Played" between the Baltimore Colts and New York Giants—marked a cultural watershed moment. This chapter explores how this game helped transform football from a minor sport into a dominant cultural force that reshaped American Sundays. The NFL mastered what scholar Edwin Schlossberg calls "interactive excellence" through EPIC experiences: Experiential, Participatory, Image-rich, and Connective. From Texas A&M's "12th Man" tradition to modern sports bars serving as contemporary fellowship halls, football has created new sacred spaces and rituals that satisfy deep human longings for community and transcendence.

CHALLENGE FLAG

 When Johnny Unitas engineered that final drive in 1958, he wasn't just winning a game—he was helping redirect the future of American Sundays.

THROW A SPIRAL

 S: SPIRIT-LED STEADFASTNESS

- How can we maintain spiritual steadfastness in a culture that increasingly views Sunday as game day?

- What can the "12ᵗʰ Man" tradition teach us about faithful readiness to serve?

P: PRAYER

- How can our prayer life become more participatory and less spectator-oriented?
- How might viewing ourselves as part of the "great cloud of witnesses" change our approach to prayer?

I: IMAGINATION

- How can we reimagine church spaces to foster more active participation?
- How can we make faith more "EPIC" without compromising its essence?

R: REDEMPTIVE RELATIONSHIPS

- What can we learn from how football creates "tribal identity" about building authentic Christian community?
- How might we transform our church fellowship to be as engaging as a sports gathering?

A: AUTHENTIC ACTION

- In what ways can we move from being passive receivers to active participants in our faith?
- What would it look like to be as ready to serve as E. King Gill was in the original "12ᵗʰ Man" story?

HUDDLE GUIDE

 L: Life Story for a Living Legacy
- How can our faith communities create lasting impact like legendary football moments?
- What role do we play in writing the next chapter of Christian community in our culture?

Coach's Corner

 Remember EPIC: Experiential not theoretical, Participatory not passive, Image-rich not abstract, Connective not isolated.

Overtime Exercises

Sacred Time Survey: Track how you spend your Sundays for a month. Note moments of passive observation vs. active participation in both spiritual and social activities.

Community Mapping: List the places where you experience genuine community. What makes these gatherings meaningful? How could these insights enhance church fellowship?

EPIC Challenge: Design one way to make your faith community more Experiential, Participatory, Image-rich, or Connective this week.

TWO-MINUTE WARNING

CHAIN-MOVING CHALLENGE

Your presence isn't just about attendance—it's about engagement. The scoreboard of faith measures participation, not just observation.

POSTGAME PRAYER

Divine Coach,
Help us recognize the tipping points
in our culture and lives.

Make us ready like E. King Gill
to step from the stands into service
For Your glory in every season of change.

Amen.

Game V

Breaking Huddle
Steps of Faith

Pregame Prayer

Divine Coach,
Help us move from comfortable circles
To kingdom advances.

Give us courage to break formation and
Trust Your future plays.

Save us from becoming spiritual wildebeests
Frozen in fear.

Amen.

Coach's Corner

 The huddle is for direction, not destination. Don't confuse preparation with procrastination.

HIGHLIGHT REEL

Using Bill Walsh's warning that "quarterbacks cannot be wildebeests," this chapter examines how churches often remain in "eternal huddles" rather than advancing God's mission. While the NFL creates dynamic, forward-moving communities, many churches run outdated plays and form ever-tighter, inward-facing circles. With 4,000 churches closing annually and Christian identification dropping significantly, the chapter challenges believers to break huddle and move into active formation. Like the early church in Acts 8:1, which needed persecution to scatter from Jerusalem, today's churches must choose between comfortable circles and kingdom advances.

CHALLENGE FLAG

 No team ever scored from inside a huddle, and no church ever changed the world from inside its comfort zone.

THROW A SPIRAL

 S: SPIRIT-LED STEADFASTNESS

- How can we avoid becoming "wildebeests" in our faith—frozen by fear rather than moving forward?
- What makes us hesitate to break huddle in our spiritual lives?

P: Prayer

- How might our prayer life change if we viewed it as preparation for action rather than just communion?
- What can we learn from NFL quarterbacks about anticipating where God is leading?

 I: Imagination

- How can we reimagine church gatherings to be more "EPIC" (Experiential, Participatory, Image-rich, Connective)?
- What would it look like to be "mobile, agile, and hospitable" rather than "sterile, puerile, and senile"?

 R: Redemptive Relationships

- How can we ensure our church circles face both inward and outward, like wheel spokes?
- What can we learn from football teams about balancing preparation with action?

 A: Authentic Action

- What "plays" have we been preparing for but never running in our faith life?
- How can we move from "eternal huddle" to active engagement in our mission field?

HUDDLE GUIDE

 L: Life Story for a Living Legacy
- How can we ensure we're not just running "plays from 1985" in today's spiritual landscape?
- What legacy are we creating through our willingness or unwillingness to break huddle?

Coach's Corner

 Like a quarterback reading the defense, we must throw not to where people are, but to where they're going to be.

Overtime Exercises

Circle Check: Draw your church's "formation." Does it face inward or outward? Create a plan to transform your circle into spokes of impact.

Play Analysis: List three "outdated plays" your faith community keeps running. Brainstorm fresh approaches that maintain the truth while updating the delivery.

Forward Motion: Identify one area where you're stuck in an "eternal huddle." Take one concrete step toward breaking formation this week.

Chain-Moving Challenge

Your comfort zone might be God's "delay-of-game" penalty.

Postgame Prayer

Lord,
Transform our huddles from bunkers to launching pads.

Make us bold as lions in sharing Your love
For Your kingdom's advance and glory.

Amen.

GAME VI

RESILIENT ROOTS

THE ENDURING TRIUMPH OF FAITH AND FOOTBALL

PREGAME PRAYER

Eternal Coach,
Help us see beyond temporary scorecards
To Your eternal game.

Grant us wisdom to navigate complex truths with grace.

Give us courage to embrace both
Victory and vulnerability.

Amen.

COACH'S CORNER

 The eternal scoreboard counts different points than the temporal one.

HUDDLE GUIDE

Highlight Reel

This chapter explores the remarkable resilience of both Christianity and the NFL in the face of predictions of their demise. From Notre Dame's conversion to a "Temple of Reason" in 1793 to modern-day prophecies of football's downfall due to CTE concerns, both institutions face existential challenges yet endure. Through stories like Dave Duerson's tragic sacrifice for brain research and Colin Kaepernick's controversial kneeling protest, the chapter examines how both faith and football transform endings into beginnings. Their endurance stems not from perfection but from their ability to provide authentic community, purpose, and moments of transcendence in an increasingly virtual world.

Challenge Flag

 Like the ancient paradox of the cross, what threatens to destroy these institutions may ultimately be what preserves them.

Throw a SPIRAL

 S: Spirit-led Steadfastness

- How can we maintain spiritual resilience in the face of predictions of Christianity's decline?
- What distinguishes between death throes and birth pangs in beloved institutions?

P: PRAYER

- How can prayer help us move from defensive to offensive positions in our faith?
- How might we pray differently if we truly believed in "victory beyond the scoreboard"?

I: IMAGINATION

- How can we reimagine the church's role in society beyond just surviving cultural shifts?
- What creative ways might we engage with controversial issues while maintaining gospel integrity?

R: REDEMPTIVE RELATIONSHIPS

- How can we build bridges across cultural divides without compromising truth?
- How might we better support those paying a high price for their convictions?

A: AUTHENTIC ACTION

- How can we move from "playing not to lose" to "playing to win" in our faith journey?
- What would it look like to demonstrate moral courage rather than just physical courage?

L: LIFE STORY FOR A LIVING LEGACY

- What story will future generations tell about how we navigated these challenging times?

HUDDLE GUIDE

- How can our faith communities become known more for what we're for than what we're against?

Coach's Corner

> Whether in cathedrals or stadiums, we create spaces where strangers become family and individual stories connect to larger narratives.

Overtime Exercises

Ethics Audit: Examine where you might be choosing entertainment over ethics in your life. Create a plan to better align your actions with your values.

Prophetic Voice: Identify one issue where God might be calling you to speak uncomfortable truth to comfortable power. What's your next step?

Legacy Planning: List three ways your faith community could better serve future generations. Choose one to implement this month.

Challenge-Moving Challenge

Like Dave Duerson's final sacrifice, sometimes our greatest impact comes through our willingness to face hard truths.

POSTGAME PRAYER

Lord of Resurrection
Who turns crosses into victory signs,
Help us discern when to stand,
When to kneel, and when to speak
For Your eternal glory beyond earthly scoreboards.

Amen.

GAME VII

HEAVEN'S SCOREBOARD
MEASURING WHAT MATTERS

PREGAME PRAYER

Divine Referee,
Help us measure what truly matters in Your eyes.

Give us courage to challenge our assumptions like Raymond Berry.

Let us see beyond narrow fields to Your grand and glorious game.

Amen.

COACH'S CORNER

 You're playing on a field measured by eternity, not just your next first down.

HIGHLIGHT REEL

This chapter explores the complex intersection of faith, football, and measuring true success. Through Raymond

Berry's discovery of a too-narrow football field, we examine how accepted boundaries often limit our spiritual vision. Like the space race vs. poverty debate raised by Martin Luther King Jr., the chapter challenges us to navigate competing "goods" and recognize that evil often operates within legal boundaries. While Christ has secured the ultimate victory, we live in the tension of the "already but not yet," where earthly scoreboards may not reflect heaven's measure of success. The challenge isn't just to win, but to question whether we're playing on God's full field.

CHALLENGE FLAG

⚠ Satan may claim quarters, but God owns eternity.

THROW A SPIRAL

 S: SPIRIT-LED STEADFASTNESS

- How can we maintain spiritual authenticity while engaging with morally complex cultural phenomena?

- What boundaries in our faith life need to be questioned or expanded?

 P: PRAYER

- How might our prayers change if we truly believed in God's "full-sized field"?

- What keeps us praying "safe" prayers instead of

kingdom-advancing ones?

I: IMAGINATION

- How can we reimagine faith beyond our self-imposed limitations?
- What might our churches look like if we measured success by God's standards?

R: REDEMPTIVE RELATIONSHIPS

- How can we build bridges with those who see the "field" differently than we do?
- How might we better balance celebration with service in our relationships?

A: AUTHENTIC ACTION

- What steps can we take to expand our "field of faith"?
- How can we move beyond comfortable church roles to kingdom-advancing action?

L: LIFE STORY FOR A LIVING LEGACY

- What legacy are we creating through our current measurements of success?
- How can we contribute to a broader narrative of faith that transcends cultural boundaries?

HUDDLE GUIDE

Coach's Corner

 Sometimes your greatest limitation isn't the defense—it's the artificial boundaries you've accepted without measuring.

Overtime Exercises

Field Measurement: Like Raymond Berry, measure the "field" of your ministry. Where have you accepted artificial boundaries? Draft a plan to expand your territory.

Competing Goods Analysis: List situations where you're choosing between competing "goods" (like the space program vs. poverty). How do you discern God's priorities?

Scoreboard Check: Create two columns: "Earthly Success" and "Kingdom Impact." Evaluate your current activities against both metrics.

Chain-Moving Challenge

 Don't confuse winning the game with winning the season—God's scoreboard operates on eternal time.

Postgame Prayer

Lord of every field and measure, expand our vision
Beyond comfortable boundaries.

Help us see victory through Your eternal lens
Not just temporal success
For the advancement of Your kingdom
without end.

Amen.

Game VIII

The Lombardi Legacy
Discipline as Devotion

Pregame Prayer

Divine Coach,
Help us see discipline as a path to devotion.

Teach us that excellence flows from
Character and preparation.

Let every moment carry eternal significance.

Amen.

Coach's Corner

> If you're not fifteen minutes early for heaven's appointments, you're already late for God's best.

Highlight Reel

This chapter examines Vince Lombardi's transformative legacy beyond mere football success. Through his famous

"Lombardi Time"—where being fifteen minutes early was considered merely on time—we explore how disciplined preparation becomes spiritual formation. Lombardi embodied powerful paradoxes: a tough taskmaster who fought fiercely for players' dignity, a demanding coach who attended pre-dawn Mass daily. The chapter uses the striking statistic that an NFL game contains only eleven minutes of actual play within three hours to illustrate how brief moments, properly prepared for, can have eternal significance. Through stories like Drew Pearson choosing team success over personal records, we see how excellence combined with ethics creates lasting impact.

Challenge Flag

 Excellence isn't about perfection; it's about persistence and participation. Character isn't formed in comfort but in challenge.

Throw a SPIRAL

 S: Spirit-led Steadfastness

- What can Lombardi's "fifteen minutes early" philosophy teach us about spiritual discipline?
- How might viewing discipline as devotion change our approach to faith?

 P: Prayer

- How can we approach prayer with the same dedi-

cation Lombardi brought to daily Mass?
- How might we prepare for those brief but crucial moments of spiritual action?

I: Imagination

- How can we reimagine discipline as a path to freedom rather than restriction?
- What would our churches look like if we applied Lombardi's standards of excellence?

R: Redemptive Relationships

- How can we balance high standards with grace in our relationships?
- What can we learn from Lombardi's zero-tolerance policy toward discrimination?

A: Authentic Action

- What does it mean to give our spiritual gifts "to the fullest"?
- How can we move from good intentions to consistent spiritual practice?

L: Life Story for a Living Legacy

- What kind of legacy are we creating through our daily spiritual disciplines?
- How can our brief moments of faithfulness impact future generations?

HUDDLE GUIDE

Coach's Corner

 Like those crucial eleven minutes in a three-hour game, your brief moments of faithful action flow from hours of preparation in God's presence.

Overtime Exercises

Time Audit: Track how early you arrive for appointments this week. Then commit to being fifteen minutes early ("Lombardi Time") for everything next week. Note the impact on your spiritual preparation.

Excellence Inventory: List three areas where you're "cheating the Lord" by not using your gifts to their fullest. Create a practice plan for improvement.

Character Challenge: Identify one situation where you need to balance high standards with grace, like Lombardi did. How can you demand excellence while showing compassion?

Chain-Moving Challenge

 Your life contains precious moments of ecstatic play—make sure your preparation honors their eternal significance.

Postgame Prayer

Lord of sacred moments and eternal significance,
Help us find strength in quiet preparation
Like Lombardi at pre-dawn Mass
For Your glory in every practice and play.

Amen.

Game IX

The Belichick Blueprint
Strategy and Spirit

Pregame Prayer

Divine Strategist,
Help us see beyond surface victories.

Grant us wisdom to adapt like Belichick
While standing firm in truth.

Let us seek Your approval above the world's scoreboard.

Amen.

Coach's Corner

> Like Timothy learning from Paul, greatness often begins in quiet rooms, studying at a mentor's feet.

Highlight Reel

This chapter examines Bill Belichick's journey from football apprentice to controversial legend, paralleling biblical narratives of mentorship and leadership. From his early film study under his father's guidance to the miraculous 28–3 Super Bowl comeback against Atlanta, Belichick's story illustrates both the triumphs and temptations of excellence. Through moments like the Brady dynasty and controversies like Spygate, we explore how success can breed both glory and compromise. His story becomes a lens for examining larger truths about leadership, innovation, and the complex relationship between winning and virtue.

Challenge Flag

 Success without integrity is just achievement; integrity without excellence is just intention.

Throw a SPIRAL

 S: Spirit-led Steadfastness

- How can we maintain spiritual integrity while pursuing excellence?
- How do we balance flexibility in methods with firmness in principles?

 P: Prayer

- How might viewing God as our "Head Coach" change our prayer life?
- What can we learn from Belichick's preparation habits about spiritual readiness?

 I: Imagination

- How can we reimagine our spiritual "positions"

to serve in unexpected ways?

- How might we adapt our ministry approaches while maintaining core truth?

🏈 R: Redemptive Relationships

- How do we maintain team (community) focus over individual success?
- What can we learn from Belichick's "Do Your Job" philosophy about serving others?

🏈 A: Authentic Action

- How can we pursue excellence without compromising integrity?
- Is excellence more about quality of performance or quality of participation?
- How do we respond when facing our own "28–3 moments" of seeming defeat?

🏈 L: Life Story for a Living Legacy

- What kind of legacy are we creating through our daily choices?
- How can our response to criticism shape our witness?

Coach's Corner

> Don't judge the game at halftime. Heaven's clock runs differently than ours.

HUDDLE GUIDE

OVERTIME EXERCISES

Innovation Audit: List three areas where your ministry needs fresh approaches. How can you honor tradition while embracing necessary change?

Preparation Study: Document your spiritual preparation habits for one week. What can you learn from Belichick's meticulous film study approach?

Comeback Plan: Identify your current "28–3 moment." Create a strategy for victory that maintains both excellence and integrity.

CHAIN-MOVING CHALLENGE

🏈 Your current wilderness season might be God's preparation for your greatest win.

POSTGAME PRAYER

Lord of impossible comebacks and quiet preparation,
Help us pursue victory in ways that honor
Both the game and its Maker
For Your glory and Your kingdom's advance.

Amen.

GAME X

CROSSING THE GOAL LINE
WHERE HEAVEN MEETS EARTH

PREGAME PRAYER

Eternal Coach,
Help us see the sacred in each transition.

Transform our shattered dreams into unexpected grace.

Guide us to recognize Your redirecting hand.

Amen.

COACH'S CORNER

> Sometimes God gives us one perfect season to show us what's possible, not what's sustainable.

HIGHLIGHT REEL

This chapter traces John Madden's journey from catastrophe to legacy, beginning with a career-ending knee injury in 1958 that led to his extraordinary impact on football. Through Madden's story—from injured player to legend-

HUDDLE GUIDE

ary coach to broadcasting pioneer to video game innovator—we explore how God often works through apparent setbacks to achieve greater purposes. His evolution demonstrates how traditional truth can speak through new methods to reach new generations, illustrated by his three simple commandments: be on time, pay attention, and play like hell when called upon. His story becomes a masterclass in how divine purpose often works through apparent defeats, turning obstacles into opportunities.

CHALLENGE FLAG

⚠ Every setback contains a seed of comeback. The question isn't whether you can recreate yesterday's miracle, but whether you're ready for tomorrow's.

THROW A *SPIRAL*

 S: SPIRIT-LED STEADFASTNESS
- How do we maintain faith when apparent endings become divine beginnings?
- What can we learn from Madden's journey about adapting to God's unexpected plans?

 P: PRAYER
- How might viewing setbacks as divine classrooms change our prayer life?
- How can we pray through seasons of apparent defeat or redirection?

I: Imagination
- How can we reimagine apparent failures as opportunities for divine adaptation?
- What new "languages" might God be calling us to learn to reach others?

 R: Redemptive Relationships
- Who has been your "Norm Van Brocklin," teaching you during injury time?
- Where are you called to be a mentor to others in transition?

 A: Authentic Action
- How can we create more EPIC (Experiential, Participatory, Image-rich, Connective) faith communities?
- What practical steps can we take to translate eternal truth into contemporary contexts?

 L: Life Story for a Living Legacy
- What symphony are we contributing to in God's greater narrative?
- How can our response to setbacks shape our witness to others?

Coach's Corner

> Like Madden crashing the Hogs' party, true fellowship can transcend rivalry and variance.

Overtime Exercises

Door Check: List three closed doors in your life. For each, identify one unexpected opening that resulted. What might God be teaching you through these transitions?

EPIC Audit: Evaluate your faith community through the EPIC framework (Experiential, Participatory, Image-rich, Connective). Create an action plan to strengthen one component.

Innovation Inventory: Identify three new methods or technologies you could use to share timeless truth with your community. Choose one to implement this month.

Chain-Moving Challenge

   Your current crisis is God's classroom for your next calling.

Postgame Prayer

Lord of new beginnings and divine detours,
Help us stop asking, "Why me?"
And start asking, "What next?"
For Your transfiguring mission in every setback.

Amen.

Game XI

Red Zone Redemption
From Fumbles to Faith

Pregame Prayer

Divine Coach,
Help us see victories beyond the scoreboard.

Show us touchdowns that matter in eternity.

Transform our fumbles into opportunities for grace.

Amen.

Coach's Corner

> In God's playbook, the greatest plays often come from our deepest pain.

Highlight Reel

This chapter examines powerful stories of redemption through football, centered on the 1970s Pittsburgh Steelers, where Bible study replaced trash talk and prayer warriors wore Super Bowl rings. Through Tony Dungy's

HUDDLE GUIDE

Christ-centered "Dungy Way," we learn about winning without yelling and leading through quiet strength. The narrative deepens through three transformative stories: Ernie Holmes' journey from highway breakdown to Baptist minister, Fran Tarkenton's "Broken Pattern" principle of divine creativity, and Warrick Dunn's path from tragedy to ministry through his Homes for the Holidays program. These stories reveal how heaven celebrates transformed lives more than touchdowns, and how grace outscores justice in God's eternal playbook.

CHALLENGE FLAG

 You can't out love the Lord. No one is beyond grace's reach.

THROW A SPIRAL

 S: SPIRIT-LED STEADFASTNESS

- What can we learn from Tony Dungy about staying faithful in both victory and loss?
- How do we maintain spiritual steadiness in our own "red zone" moments?

 P: PRAYER

- How might viewing prayer as heaven's celebration change our approach to intercession?
- What can we learn from Warrick Dunn about praying through pain toward purpose?

I: Imagination

- How can we reimagine our failures as opportunities for God's grace?
- What would our churches look like if we celebrated spiritual victories like touchdown moments?

 R: Redemptive Relationships

- How can we better support those going through their own "broken patterns"?
- What can we learn from the Steelers about creating communities of grace?

 A: Authentic Action

- What does it mean to choose forgiveness over revenge in practical terms?
- How can we create "Homes for the Holidays" moments in our own spheres?

 L: Life Story for a Living Legacy

- What kind of spiritual touchdowns are we scoring that will echo in eternity?
- How can our own stories of redemption inspire hope in others?

Coach's Corner

> When you can't outrun your pain, let it fuel your purpose.

Overtime Exercises

Grace Audit: List three "Ernie Holmes moments" in your life where grace outscored justice. How can these experiences fuel your ministry to others?

Broken Pattern Study: Identify a "broken play" in your life. Using Tarkenton's principle, map out how God might transform it into an opportunity.

Kingdom Scoreboard: Create two columns: "Earthly Victories" and "Eternal Touchdowns." List your recent wins in each category. Which matter more?

Chain-Moving Challenge

 Heaven's highlight reel features different victories—each time forgiveness defeats bitterness, every moment grace transfigures a life.

Postgame Prayer

Lord of every redemption story and transformed life,
Help us choose forgiveness over revenge
And grace over grievance
For Your eternal victory through love.

Amen.

Game XII

Playing Injured
Grace Under Pressure

Pregame Prayer

Divine Strengthener,
Help us choose conviction over convenience.

Show us the power of Your grace in our weakness.

Let us embrace the cross over shortcuts.

Amen.

Coach's Corner

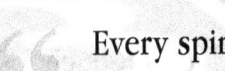

> Every spiritual shortcut promises paradise but delivers prison.

Highlight Reel

Through three powerful narratives—the empty chairs at Cooperstown from baseball's steroid era, Arnold Schwarzenegger's transparent embrace of enhancement at Gold's

HUDDLE GUIDE

Gym, and Churchill's rationalized dependencies—this chapter explores humanity's quest for shortcuts to glory. At its heart lies Dietrich Bonhoeffer's distinction between "cheap grace" and "costly grace," illustrated perfectly by Eric Liddell's choice of conviction over convenience at the 1924 Olympics. Like Christ choosing the cross over calling twelve legions of angels, true champions embrace weakness as the vessel of divine strength, understanding that authentic transformation never bypasses the cross.

CHALLENGE FLAG

⚠ Heaven's record books will show different measures than Cooperstown's—not our shortcuts but our scars.

THROW A SPIRAL

 S: SPIRIT-LED STEADFASTNESS

- How do we maintain authenticity in a culture that values quick results?
- What can we learn from Eric Liddell about choosing conviction over convenience?

 P: PRAYER

- How might our prayer life change if we truly embraced weakness as strength?
- How can we pray through plateaus rather than seeking shortcuts?

I: IMAGINATION

- How can we reimagine weakness as a vessel for God's strength?
- What might our faith look like without "spiritual steroids"?

 R: REDEMPTIVE RELATIONSHIPS

- How do we support others choosing the harder right over the easier wrong?
- What can we learn from Bonhoeffer about costly vs. cheap grace?

 A: AUTHENTIC ACTION

- What "spiritual shortcuts" do we need to surrender?
- How can we embrace the "sacred slowness" of genuine growth?

 L: LIFE STORY FOR A LIVING LEGACY

- What story will our lives tell about choosing the cross over shortcuts?
- How can our struggles become testimonies of God's sufficient grace?

COACH'S CORNER

> True transfiguration always involves death before resurrection, cross before crown, and surrender before strength.

HUDDLE GUIDE

OVERTIME EXERCISES

Dependency Check: Like Churchill's bottle, what dependencies do you rationalize? Create an honest inventory of your spiritual "performance enhancers."

Cross or Chemical: List three areas where you're tempted to take shortcuts in your spiritual life. Develop a plan to embrace authentic growth instead.

Legacy Audit: Write your spiritual "record book" entry. What achievements would have asterisks? Which ones showcase authentic grace?

CHAIN-MOVING CHALLENGE

Christ didn't take a shortcut to save the world. Neither should we.

POSTGAME PRAYER

Lord of authentic victory and sufficient grace,
Help us choose the cross over convenience
For Your glory through our weakness.

Amen.

GAME XIII

THE ULTIMATE CHAMPIONSHIP
BUILDING GOD'S TEAM

PREGAME PRAYER

Divine Coach,
Help us see beyond earthly championships.

Give us eyes to recognize divine opportunities
In daily moments.

Make us players, not spectators, in
Your kingdom's greatest game.

Amen.

COACH'S CORNER

> While Super Bowl victories fade, kingdom touchdowns last forever.

HUDDLE GUIDE

Highlight Reel

From Lamar Hunt finding Super Bowl inspiration in his daughter's toy to modern stadium cathedrals, this chapter explores how America's biggest game mirrors our hunger for transcendence. Through stories of everyday disciples—from Sarah the barista to Linda the praying widow—we see how ordinary moments become opportunities for eternal impact. The Super Bowl's evolution from humble origins to sacred ritual provides a lens for understanding how daily life offers countless "end zones" for kingdom advancement. Like players studying their playbooks, we're called to prepare intensely for these divine opportunities, transforming from spectators to active participants in God's ultimate championship team.

Challenge Flag

 In God's game plan, every down is a chance for redemption, every timeout is an opportunity for transfiguration.

Throw a SPIRAL

 S: Spirit-led Steadfastness
- How can we maintain kingdom focus in a culture obsessed with temporal victories?
- What can we learn from the everyday "touchdown makers" in our lives?

THE ULTIMATE CHAMPIONSHIP

🏈 **P: Prayer**
- How might viewing prayer as a "play call from heaven" change our approach to intercession?
- What can we learn from Linda's phone ministry about faithful prayer?

🏈 **I: Imagination**
- How can we reimagine our daily interactions as potential eternal end zones?
- What might our churches look like if we celebrated spiritual victories like Super Bowl moments?

🏈 **R: Redemptive Relationships**
- How can we move from spectating to participating in others' spiritual journeys?
- What can we learn from Sarah the barista about divine interruptions?

🏈 **A: Authentic Action**
- What "plays" are God calling us to make in our daily lives?
- How can we move from huddle to action in sharing our faith?

🏈 **L: Life Story for a Living Legacy**
- What kind of eternal impact are we creating through our daily choices?

Huddle Guide

- How can our current struggles become tomorrow's ministry opportunities?

Coach's Corner

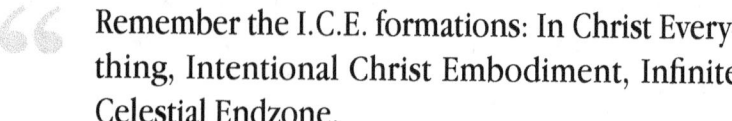

Remember the I.C.E. formations: In Christ Everything, Intentional Christ Embodiment, Infinite Celestial Endzone.

Overtime Exercises

Divine Audibles: Keep a weekly log of unexpected opportunities for kingdom impact. How did you respond? What could you do differently?

Playbook Study: Compare your Bible study habits with how NFL players prepare for games. Create a spiritual training regimen that matches this intensity.

End Zone Analysis: List your daily "fields of play" (i.e., work, home, social media). For each, identify three ways to score "touchdowns for eternity."

Chain-Moving Challenge

You're playing for the greatest Coach of all time. The whistle has blown. The game is on.

THE ULTIMATE CHAMPIONSHIP

POSTGAME PRAYER

Lord of every field and play, help us run with purpose.

When we fumble remind us of Your grace
For Your glory and eternal victory.

Amen.

Game XIV

When Tailgates Become Talegate Testaments

Fellowship in the Parking Lot

Pregame Prayer

Sacred Fire-Starter,
Help us see beyond the smoke of our grills.

Show us the holy ground You create in our gatherings.

Let every shared meal become a sacred story.

Amen.

Coach's Corner

> Stories flow where smoke rises.

Highlight Reel

This chapter weaves together humanity's ancient practice of gathering around fire with modern tailgating culture, revealing profound connections between sacred smoke

Huddle Guide

and storytelling. From aboriginal dreamtime through biblical history to NFL parking lots, we explore how smoke creates "thin spaces" where heaven and earth meet. Drawing parallels between God's use of fire at Sinai and Pentecost with today's grill-side gatherings, we discover how every shared meal can become an opportunity for divine encounter. The smoke from our grills, like the incense of ancient temples, marks spaces where stories naturally flow and community forms.

Challenge Flag

⚠ Don't rush to sanitize gathering spaces of their "smoke and fire" elements in the pursuit of relevance.

Throw a SPIRAL

 S: Spirit-led Steadfastness

- How do we recognize and create sacred spaces in everyday gatherings?
- What can we learn from the biblical pattern of God speaking through fire?

 P: Prayer

- How can we make our communal gatherings more intentionally spiritual?
- What role does shared food and fellowship play in our spiritual formation?

WHEN TAILGATES BECOME TALEGATE TESTAMENTS

 I: Imagination

- How can we reimagine our parking lots and back yards as sacred spaces?
- How can we better create "thin spaces" where heaven and earth meet?

 R: Redemptive Relationships

- How do shared meals and stories create deeper community?
- What stories from your faith journey might be at risk of being lost?

 A: Authentic Action

- What practical steps can we take to make our gatherings more intentionally sacred?
- How can we better use our homes and grills as gathering spaces for God's stories?

 L: Life Story for a Living Legacy

- What stories are we creating around our own sacred fires?
- How can we better pass on faith through fellowship and food?

Coach's Corner

 Just as God marked His most significant moments with fire and smoke—from Sinai to Pentecost—may we learn to mark our moments of ministry with the sacred smoke of hospitality.

Overtime Exercises

Sacred Space Survey: Host a "Sacred Smoke Sunday" where your small group meets around a grill or fire pit. Document how the setting affects story sharing.

Story Collection: Interview three older members of your community about their memories of gathering around fire and food. Record these stories for future generations.

Sensory Worship: Create a plan to incorporate more elements of fire, feast, and fellowship into your worship gatherings.

Chain-Moving Challenge

Smoke without story, or story without sacred space, loses much of its power.

Postgame Prayer

Divine Host of every sacred gathering,
Help us create spaces where Your stories can be shared
For Your glory around every table and flame.
Amen.

Game XV

More Than Games
From Arena to Altar

Pregame Prayer

Eternal Storyteller,
Help us see beyond spectacle to significance.

Transform our gatherings from entertainment
To eternal truth.

Make us readers of Your signs in every game.

Amen.

Coach's Corner

" Control the games, and you control the narrative.

Highlight Reel

From Roman charioteer Gaius Appuleius Diocles's $15 billion earnings to Malcolm Butler's Super Bowl interception, this chapter explores how sports transcend entertainment to shape society and spirituality. Modern stadiums echo Rome's coliseums, with players becoming gladiators in cleats and owners watching from luxury boxes like ancient patricians. Yet where Rome used "bread and circuses" to distract, we find opportunities for genuine community through shared meals, stories, and traditions. Pete Carroll's pride and Butler's later benching illustrate larger spiritual truths about human nature, while parking lot gatherings become sacred spaces where strangers become family.

Challenge Flag

⚠ Don't substitute programs for praise or mistake quietness for reverence.

Throw a SPIRAL

 S: Spirit-led Steadfastness

- How do we maintain spiritual authenticity in a culture of spectacle?
- How do we balance appreciation for sports with proper spiritual perspective?

 P: Prayer

- How might viewing our gatherings as sacred spaces change our approach to community?
- What can we learn from Jesus's approach to feeding and gathering people?

 I: Imagination

MORE THAN GAMES

- How can we reimagine our stadiums as opportunities for genuine community?
- What might our churches learn from sports culture's community-building power?

🏈 **R: REDEMPTIVE RELATIONSHIPS**

- How do we build authentic community beyond mere entertainment?
- What's the difference between a fan base and a faith community?

🏈 **A: AUTHENTIC ACTION**

- What practical steps can we take to move from spectacle to substance?
- How can we create more opportunities for genuine connection?

🏈 **L: LIFE STORY FOR A LIVING LEGACY**

- What kind of stories are we creating in our communities?
- How can we better pass on faith through shared experiences?

COACH'S CORNER

> Sports can be sacred if we see them rightly: community matters more than competition, grace covers both victory and defeat.

HUDDLE GUIDE

Overtime Exercises

Sacred Story Search: Document three sports moments that taught you about grace, redemption, or community. How might these stories serve in ministry?

Community Comparison: Create a chart comparing your church's welcome with a tailgate party's hospitality. What can you learn and implement?

Spectacle Survey: Identify places where your faith community might be choosing entertainment over engagement. Develop a plan to deepen connection.

Chain-Moving Challenge

The real victory isn't on the scoreboard but in the story we're telling with our lives.

Postgame Prayer

Divine Host of every gathering and game,
Help us create communities that offer more
Than bread and circuses
For Your eternal feast and glory.

Amen.

Game XVI

Beyond the Goalposts
From Kickoff to Kingdom Come

Pregame Prayer

Divine Celebration Starter,
Awaken in us holy enthusiasm.

Help us shed our dignity for Your glory
Like the prodigal's father.

Let us rediscover the joy that made angels leap.

Amen.

Coach's Corner

> Every moment of spiritual victory deserves at least as much celebration as a touchdown. Heaven is shouting. Why aren't we?

HUDDLE GUIDE

HIGHLIGHT REEL

This chapter explores the irony of how Methodist churches, once mocked as "Enthusiasts" for their shouting spirituality, have become bastions of quiet restraint while saving enthusiasm for stadiums. Through contrasting narratives—J. J. Watt vs. Joel Osteen during Hurricane Harvey, three popes facing historical moments, and the Bound Brook Six's bold faith declaration—we examine how character reveals itself in crucial moments. The chapter challenges Christians to reclaim their heritage of holy celebration, arguing that authentic spiritual warfare requires the same passion we bring to sporting events—and more, because these celebrations count for eternity.

CHALLENGE FLAG

⚠ Don't let false dignity replace holy abandonment.

THROW A SPIRAL

 S: SPIRIT-LED STEADFASTNESS

- How do we maintain authentic enthusiasm in our faith expression?
- What keeps us from celebrating spiritual victories as passionately as sports victories?

 P: PRAYER

- How might viewing heaven as a celebrating community change our approach to prayer?

- What role does spiritual celebration play in warfare against darkness?

I: IMAGINATION

- How can we reimagine our churches as centers of authentic celebration?
- What might our worship look like with stadium-level enthusiasm?

R: REDEMPTIVE RELATIONSHIPS

- How do we build communities that celebrate spiritual victories authentically?
- What can we learn from the early Methodists about combining passion and purpose?

A: AUTHENTIC ACTION

- In crisis moments, are you more like J. J. Watt or Joel Osteen?
- How can we better respond to God's moments with bold action?

L: LIFE STORY FOR A LIVING LEGACY

- What kind of celebratory heritage are we creating?
- How has your spiritual tradition changed from its origins?

COACH'S CORNER

> Like David dancing before the ark, sometimes the most spiritual act is letting go of our dignity.

HUDDLE GUIDE

OVERTIME EXERCISES

Joy Audit: Track one week of your celebrations. Compare your enthusiasm for sports vs. spiritual victories. If needed, create a plan to balance them.

Heritage Research: Study your denomination's historic expressions of joy. How can you help reclaim this legacy of holy celebration?

Victory Journal: Start recording spiritual victories daily, creating specific celebration rituals for each type of victory.

CHAIN-MOVING CHALLENGE

 Make spiritual touchdowns as exciting as sports victories—they matter infinitely more.

POSTGAME PRAYER

Lord of the Dance who taught David to leap,
Free us from false dignity and spiritless religion
Until heaven's bleachers ring with our praise.

Amen.

Game XVII

Laterals of Love
Passing Faith Through Life's Chaos

Pregame Prayer

Divine Playmaker,
Help us see beyond apparent defeat to eternal possibility.

Give us courage to keep lateraling Your truth
Like those California players.

Let us presence Your kingdom through
Unexpected channels.

Amen.

Coach's Corner

 In God's kingdom, like in that memorable game, the final whistle never sounds until God calls it.

HUDDLE GUIDE

Highlight Reel

The book's final chapter uses "The Play"—the legendary 1982 California-Stanford game with five laterals and a bewildered trombonist—to illuminate how God's kingdom advances. Each element carries spiritual significance: the laterals represent moments of trust and surrender, the Stanford defenders symbolize life's obstacles, and even the trombonist becomes an unwitting participant in God's unfolding drama. This iconic moment teaches us that kingdom advancement comes not through raw power but through surrender, trust, and persistent belief when all seems lost. Like those Cal players adjusting their grip and position, we must constantly reorient our lives to effectively pass on Christ's love, understanding that in God's kingdom, apparent endings often become divine beginnings.

Challenge Flag

 The highest forms of both athletic and aesthetic beauty emerge not from laborious effort but from the joy of play.

Throw a SPIRAL

 S: Spirit-led Steadfastness

- How do we maintain faith when the scoreboard says "game over"?

- What can we learn from "The Play" about trusting God's process?

🏈 **P: PRAYER**
- How might viewing faith as "play" rather than "work" change our prayer life?
- How can we pray with more expectancy for divine possibilities?

🏈 **I: IMAGINATION**
- Where might God be asking you to "keep the play alive" despite apparent defeat?
- How can we reimagine obstacles as opportunities in God's kingdom?

🏈 **R: REDEMPTIVE RELATIONSHIPS**
- How do we effectively "lateral" our faith to others?
- How might our obstacles become part of others' testimonies?

🏈 **A: AUTHENTIC ACTION**
- What practical steps can we take to keep God's play alive in our sphere?
- How can we maintain strong convictions while building bridges?

🏈 **L: LIFE STORY FOR A LIVING LEGACY**
- What stories of God's impossible victories are we creating?

HUDDLE GUIDE

- How can our persistence inspire future generations?

Coach's Corner

> The gospel isn't meant to be cradled safely—it's meant to be passed on, transforming both carrier and message.

Overtime Exercises

Play Analysis: List three "lateral passes" you could make to keep moving forward in areas where you feel stuck. Create an action plan for each.

Team Formation: Identify your spiritual teammates—those ready to receive your "lateral pass" when life tackles you. How can you strengthen these connections?

Victory Vision: Document a seemingly impossible situation you're facing. Using "The Play" as inspiration, map out unexpected ways God might bring victory.

Chain-Moving Challenge

In God's playbook, persistence trumps power, and what appears to be the end can become a divine beginning.

Postgame Prayer

Lord of divine possibilities and unexpected victories,
Help us keep Your play alive through every obstacle
Until every knee bows to Your eternal championship.

Amen.

Bibliography

Books:

Steve Almond, *Against Football: One Fan's Reluctant Manifesto* (2015).

Lars Anderson, *The Mannings: The Fall and Rise of a Football Family* (2016).

Lars Anderson, *Chasing the Bear: How Bear Bryant and Nick Saban Made Alabama the Greatest College Football Program of All Time* (2019).

Gretchen Atwood, *Lost Champions: Four Men, Two Teams, and the Breaking of Pro Football's Color Line* (2016).

Ben Austro, *So You Think You Know Football? The Armchair Ref's Guide to the Official Rules* (2015).

Steve Belichick, *Football Scouting Methods* (2008).

Jeff Benedict & Don Yaeger, *Pros and Cons: The Criminals Who Play in the NFL* (1998).

Matthew Berry, *Fantasy Life: The Outrageous, Uplifting, and Heartbreaking World of Fantasy Sports from the Guy Who's Lived It* (2013).

Brian Billick with Michael MacCambridge, *More Than a Game: The Glorious Present—and Uncertain Future—of the NFL* (2009).

Terry Bradshaw with David Fisher, *It's Only a Game* (2001).

Jerry Brewer, *Pass Judgment: Inside the Seattle Seahawks' Super Bowl XLIX Season and the Play That Dashed a Dream* (Kindle Single 2015).

Bryan Burwell, *Madden: A Biography* (2011).

Rich Cohen, *Monsters: The 1985 Chicago Bears and the Wild Heart of Football* (2013).

Derrick Coleman and Marcus Brotherton, *No Excuses: Growing Up Deaf and Achieving My Super Bowl Dreams* (2015).

George Howe Colt, *The Game: Harvard, Yale, and America in 1968* (2018).

Kevin Cook, *The Last Headbangers: NFL Football in the Rowdy, Reckless '70s* (2012).

Jeff Davis, *Papa Bear: The Life and Legacy of George Halas* (2005).

Tony Dungy with Nathan Whittaker, *Quiet Strength: The Principles, Practices, and Priorities of a Winning Life* (2007).

Tony Dungy with Nathan Whittaker, *Uncommon: Finding Your Path to Significance* (2009).

Warrick Dunn and Don Yaeger, *Running for My Life: My Journey in the Game of Football and Beyond* (2008).

Gregg Easterbrook, *The King of Sports: Why Football Must Be Reformed* (2013).

John Eisenberg, *That First Season: How Vince Lombardi Took the Worst Team in the NFL and Set It on the Path to Glory* (2009).

Bruce Feldman, *The QB: The Making of Modern Quarterbacks* (2014).

Eric Frenz, *Bill Belichick vs. The NFL: The Case for the NFL's Greatest Coach* (2016).

David Halberstam, *The Education of a Coach* (2005).

David Harris, *The Genius: How Bill Walsh Reinvented Football and Created an NFL Dynasty* (2008).

Joe Humphreys, *Foul Play: What's Wrong with Sport* (2008).

Michael Holley, *Patriot Reign: Bill Belichick, the Coaches, and the Players Who Built a Champion* (2004).

Michael Holley, *War Room: The Legacy of Bill Belichick and the Art of Building the Perfect Team* (2011).

Paul Hornung, *Golden Boy: Girls, Games, and Gambling at Green Bay (and Notre Dame, Too)* (2004).

Rob Huizenga, *You're Okay, It's Just A Bruise: A Doctor's Sideline Secrets*

BIBLIOGRAPHY

About Pro Football's Most Outrageous Team (1994).

Ron Jaworski with Greg Cosell and David Plaut, *The Games That Changed the Game* (2010).

Pat Kirwin, *Take Your Eye Off the Ball 2.0: How to Watch Football by Knowing Where to Look* (2015).

Jerry Kramer with Dick Schaap, *Distant Replay* (1985).

Jerry Kramer, edited by Dick Schaap, *Instant Replay: The Green Bay Diary of Jerry Kramer* (1968).

Jerry Kramer, edited by Dick Schaap, *Jerry Kramer's Farewell to Football* (1969).

Jerry Kramer, *Lombardi: Winning Is the Only Thing* (1970).

Tim Layden, *Blood, Sweat and Chalk* (2010).

Adam Lazarus, *Hail to the Redskins: Gibbs, the Diesel, the Hogs, and the Glory Days of D.C.'s Football Dynasty* (2015).

C. S. Lewis, *Mere Christianity* (1952).

C. S. Lewis, *The Screwtape Letters* (1942).

Michael Lombardi, *Gridiron Genius: A Master Class in Building Teams and Winning at the Highest Level* (2018).

Vince Lombardi with W. C. Heinz, *Run to Daylight: Vince Lombardi's Diary of One Week with the Green Bay Packers* (1963).

Vince Lombardi, Jr., *The Lombardi Rules: 26 Lessons from Vince Lombardi—The World's Greatest Coach* (2005).

Vince Lombardi, Jr., *What It Takes to Be #1: Vince Lombardi on Leadership* (2001).

Michael MacCambridge, *America's Game: The Epic Story of How Pro Football Captured a Nation* (2005).

Norman Mailer, *The Fight* (2013).

Norman Mailer with Michael Lennon, *On God: An Uncommon Conversation* (2007).

David Maraniss, *When Pride Still Mattered: A Life of Vince Lombardi* (1999).

Jim McMahon with Bob Verdi, *McMahon!: The Bare Truth About Chicago's Brashest Bear* (1986).

Steve McMichael with Phil Arvia, *Steve McMichael's Tales from the Chicago Bears Sideline* (2004).

Chad Millman and Shawn Coyne, *The Ones Who Hit the Hardest: The Steelers, The Cowboys, The 70s, and the Fight for America's Soul* (2010).

John Mullen, *The Rise and Self-Destruction of the Greatest Football Team In History: The Chicago Bears and Super Bowl XX* (2005).

Gary Myers, *Brady vs. Manning: The Untold Story of the Rivalry That Transformed the NFL* (2015).

Michael O'Brien, *Vince: A Personal Biography of Vince Lombardi* (1987).

Ian O'Connor, *Belichick: The Making of the Greatest Football Coach of All Time* (2018).

Murray Olderman, *Just Win Baby: The Al Davis Story* (2012).

Ernie Palladino, *Lombardi and Landry: How Two of Pro Football's Greatest Coaches Launched Their Legends and Changed the Game Forever* (2011).

Bill Parcells and Nunyo DeMasio, *Parcells: A Football Life* (2014).

Bill Parcells with Mike Lupica, *Parcells: Autobiography of the Biggest Giant of Them All* (1987).

Walter Payton with Don Yaeger, *Never Die Easy: The Autobiography of Walter Payton* (2000).

Jeff Pearlman, *Boys Will Be Boys: The Glory Days and Party Nights of the Dallas Cowboys Dynasty* (2009).

Jeff Pearlman, *Gunslinger: The Remarkable, Improbable, Iconic Life of Brett Favre* (2016).

Jeff Pearlman, *Sweetness: The Enigmatic Life of Walter Payton* (2011).

BIBLIOGRAPHY

Donald T. Phillips, *Run to Win: Vince Lombardi on Coaching and Leadership* (2001).

Gary M. Pomerantz, *Their Life's Work: The Brotherhood of the 1970s Pittsburgh Steelers, Then and Now* (2013).

Joe Posnanski, *Why We Love Football: A History in 100 Moments* (2024).

Peter Richmond, *Badasses: The Legend of Snake, Foo, Dr. Death, and John Madden's Oakland Raiders* (2010).

Allen St. John and Ainissa Ramirez, *Newton's Football: The Science Behind America's Game* (2013).

Leonard Sweet, *The Gospel According to Starbucks: Living with a Grande Passion* (2007).

Leonard Sweet, *Nudge: Awakening Each Other to the God Who's Already There* (2010).

Leonard Sweet, Len Wilson, *Telos: The Hope of Heaven Today* (2022).

Leonard Sweet, *Carpe Mañana* (2001).

Leonard Sweet, *Rings of Fire: Walking in Faith through a Volcanic Future* (2019).

Leonard Sweet, *Post-Modern Pilgrims: First Century Passion for the 21st Century World* (2000).

Leonard Sweet, *The Greatest Story Never Told: Revive Us Again* (2012).

Leonard Sweet, Jay Richard Akkerman, et. al., *Postmodern and Wesleyan? Exploring the Boundaries and Possibilities* (2009).

Lawrence Taylor with David Faulkner, *LT: Living on the Edge* (1988).

Lawrence Taylor with Steve Serby, *LT: Over the Edge: Tackling Quarterbacks, Drugs, and a World Beyond Football* (2003).

John Urschel, *Mind and Matter: A Life in Math and Football* (2019).

Kurt Vonnegut, *Timequake* (1998).

Don Yaeger, *Greatness: The 16 Characteristics of True Champions* (2011).

Academic Articles:

Keith Hopkins, "Murderous Games: Gladiatorial Contests in Ancient Rome," *History Today*, 06 June 1983.

Newspaper and Periodical Articles:

Steve Almond, "Why We Cheer: The Triumph of the 'Us vs. Them' fan mindset," *The Rotarian*, February 2017, 24–25.

Jonathan Clegg, "NFL Rookie Chris Borland is Quitting 49ers, Pro Football, Over Brain Injury Fears," *The Wall Street Journal*, 17 March 2015.

Mac Engle, "Both Trump and Jerry were right about the NFL," *Fort Worth Star Telegram*, 18 January 2018.

Mark Maske, "Tom Brady suspended four games, Patriots fined $1 million and docked two draft choices as 'DeflateGate' punishment," *Washington Post*, 11 May 2015.

Phil Mushnick, "Gets Old Fast, Ripping Scully For His Anthem Stance Nothing But A Low Blow," *New York Post*, 10 November 2017.

Gary Myers, "If Not For Tom Brady, Bill Belichick Would Not Be In The Same Conversation As Vince Lombardi," *New York Daily News*, 21 December 2016.

Gary Myers, "State of NFL Not So Rosy," *New York Daily News*, 12 November 2017.

Lilly Rockwell, "Don Yaeger: Lightning Rod," *Tallahassee Magazine*, March-April 2010.

Dan Shaugnessy, "Belichick Owes Patriot Nation A Real Explanation On Butler," *The Boston Globe*, 06 February 2018.

Michael Starr, "Super Bowl ratings fourth-highest ever," *New York Post*, 17 February 2017.

Mike Vaccaro, "The Greatest," *New York Post*, 27 January 2017.

Don Walker, "NFL Seeks New Fans In Kids, Latinos, Women," *Milwaukee Wisconsin Journal Sentinel*, 11 February 2011.

BIBLIOGRAPHY

"The Prize In the Parking Lot," *Business Week*, 03 September 2007.

"Pumped: The Patriots Are Four Time Super Bowl Champs," *The Boston Globe*, 2015 Special Commemorative Book.

Internet Sites:

Kristi Dosh, "NFL May Be Hitting Stride With Female Fans," *ESPN*, 13 February 2012, https://www.espn.com/espnw/news-commentary/story/_/id/7536295/.

"Is Homegating the New Tailgating?" *AdAge*, 21 September 2011, https://adage.com/article/news/homegating-tailgating/229926/.

Martin Luther King, Jr., "Beyond Vietnam: A Time to Break Silence," *AmericanRhetoric.com*, https://www.americanrhetoric.com./speeches/mlkatimetobreaksilence.htm

http://brucey.net/nflab/statistics/qb_rating.html

https:/./en.wikipeida.org/wiki/The_Play_(USAmerican_football)

"Wells report: Pats Employees probably deflated balls, Tom Brady likely knew," *ESPN*, 7 May 2015, http://www.espn.com/boston/nfl/story/_/id/12833542/wells-reports-finds-new-eengland-patriots-probably-deflated-balls.

"Belichick draws $500,000 fine, but avoids suspension," *ESPN*, 14 September 2007, https://www.espn.com/nfl/news/story?id=3018338.

Kurt Badenhausen, "The 25 Highest-Paid Athletes Of All Time," *Forbes*, 13 December 2017, https://www.forbes.com/sites/kurtbadenhausen/2017/12/13/the-25-highest-paid-athletes-of-all-time/

David R. Williams, "The Apollo 8 Christmas Eve Broadcast," *NASA*, https://nssdc.gsfc.nasa.gov/planetary/lunar/apollo8_xmas.html

"NFL Scores A Touchdown With Female Fans," 24 August 2014, *ADWEEK*, https://www.adweek.com/performance-marketing/nfl-scores-touchdown-female-fans-159674/.

Ben Baskin, "Jackie Smith Speaks Extensively About the Drop That Almost Ruined His Life," 20 January 2016, http://www.si.com/nfl/2016/01/19/Jackie-smith-super-bowl-drop.

Ira Boudway, "How The NFL Woos Female Fans," www.businessweek.com, 05 September 2013.

Seth Stevenson, "Do You Like My $700 New York Giants Handbag?" *SLATE*, 23 April 2012, https://slate.com/business/2012/04/womens-nfl-jerseys-how-football-is-marketed-to-women.html.

John Ourand, "Women Staying Tuned to NFL: Despite Controversies, Female Viewership Swells to Record Levels," *Sports Business Journal*, 14 November 2014, https://www.sportsbusinessjournal.com/Journal/Issues/2014/11/17/Media/NFL-women/.

SCRIPTURE VERSIONS

Scripture quotations marked NIV are taken from the Holy Bible, New International Version®, NIV®. Copyright © 1973, 1978, 1984, 2011 by Biblica, Inc.™ Used by permission of Zondervan. All rights reserved worldwide. www.zondervan.com. The "NIV" and "New International Version" are trademarks registered in the United States Patent and Trademark Office by Biblica, Inc.™

Scripture quotations marked KJV are taken from the Holy Bible, King James Version.

Scripture quotations marked NASB are taken from the NASB® New American Standard Bible®, Copyright © 1960, 1971, 1977, 1995, 2020 by The Lockman Foundation. Used by permission. All rights reserved. lockman.org

Scripture quotations marked NKJV are from the New King James Version.® Copyright © 1982 by Thomas Nelson, Inc. Used by permission. All rights reserved.

Scripture quotations marked ESV are from The Holy Bible, English Standard Version® ESV®, copyright © 2001 by Crossway, a publishing ministry of Good News Publishers. Used by permission. All rights reserved.

Scripture quotations marked NLT are taken from the Holy Bible, New Living Translation, copyright ©1996, 2004, 2015 by Tyndale House Foundation. Used by permission of Tyndale House Publishers, Carol Stream, Illinois 60188. All rights reserved.

Scripture quotations marked NRSV are from the New Revised Standard Version Bible, copyright © 1989, Division of Christian Education of the National Council of the Churches of Christ in the United States of America. Used by permission. All rights reserved.

Scripture quotations marked RSV Revised Standard Version of the Bible, copyright © 1946, 1952, and 1971 National Council of the Churches of Christ in the United States of America. Used by permission. All rights reserved worldwide.

NOTES

Game II

1. During Marino Casem's tenure (1964 to 1985) at Alcorn State University, a historically black college in Mississippi, he led the Braves to seven Southwestern Atlantic Conference (SWAC) championships. He was inducted into the College Football Hall of Fame in 1999.
2. For more on this see Leonard Sweet, *Jesus Human: Primer for a Common Humanity* (2023).
3. For the NFL as "the sports world's most lucrative competition," see "Ball is Life," *The Economist*, 17 June 2023, 56.

FIRST QUARTER

1. "Singletary's Swan Song," *Chicago Tribune*, 27 December 1992. With thanks to Robert Castro for mentioning this.

GAME III

1. Jared Diamond, *Upheaval: Turning Points for Nations in Crisis* (2019), 415.
2. This analogy was first introduced in Leonard Sweet, *SoulTsunami: Sink or Swim in New Millennium Culture* (1999).
3. For more on this see Tom Holland, *Dominion: How the Christian Revolution Remade the World* (2021).
4. https://sportsforthesoul.com/saquon-barkley-book/. "The Book That Influenced Saquon Barkley" by Darrin Donnelly on 8 August 2024.
5. An exception to this is the chapter on "Sports Evangelism" by Joseph Solc in *Mobilizing a Great Commission Church for Harvest: Voices and Views from the Southern Baptist Professors of Evangelism Fellowship* (2011).
6. Isabel Baldwin, "New Orleans quarterback Derek Carr pledges to keep his faith as 'No. 1' after becoming a 'Saint' but promises he won't 'throw Bibles at everybody,'" 16 March 2023, DailyMail.com. https://www.

dailymail.co.uk/sport/nfl/article-11868441/New-Orleans-quarterback-Derek-Carr-pledges-faith-No-1-Saint.html.

7. Richard Lindsay's research on patheos.com in an article titled "Three-Fourths Of NFL Quarterbacks Are Evangelical Christians" (14 October 2015) found that twenty-four out of thirty-two starting quarterbacks identified as evangelical Christians.

8. Jon Ackerman, "Chiefs claim Super Bowl LIV: Owner Clark Hunt thanks the Lord, MVP Patrick Mahomes aims to glorify Him," *Sports Spectrum*, 03 February 2020.

9. Jon Ackerman, "Bills QB Josh Allen describes his 'spiritual awakening' in events surrounding Damar Hamlin," *Sports Spectrum*, 13 January 2023.

10. Cleveland Browns vs. Pittsburgh Steelers, 21 November 2024, https://clutchpoints.com/browns-news-jameis-winstons-profound-take-before-steelers-game.

11. As quoted in Tim Ellsworth, "God Is Everything," *The Alabama Baptist*, 10 February 2023.

12. Rockne was known for his inspirational quotes and speeches, including: "Win one for the Gipper." His famous phrase was immortalized in the 1940 film *Knute Rockne, All American*.

13. This is the theme of Leonard Sweet, *Nudge: Awakening Each Other to the God Who's Already There* (2010).

14. See Freud's book *The Uncanny* (1919), where he explores the concept of the uncanny and its relation to childhood fears and anxieties. Thanks to Ewald for pointing us to this illustration.

15. See Leonard Sweet, *Decoding the Divine: Unveiling the Sacred Through Semiotics* (2025).

16. Hannah Brockhaus, "Jim Harbaugh: My priorities are 'faith, then family, then football,'" Catholic News Agency, 26 April 2017, https://www.catholicnewsagency.com/news/35901/jim-harbaugh-my-priorities-are-faith-then-family-then-football.

17. *In Memoriam: William Anders* (1933–2023), whose lens captured not just an image, but a perspective that changed humanity's view of itself forever. He lived on Orcas Island, where Len lives, and died in a plane crash in the waters off Len's deck.

18. See Buzz Aldrin's autobiography *Magnificent Desolation* (2008).
19. https://premierchristian.news/us/news/article/the-bible-verse-read-on-the-moon-as-buzz-aldrin-took-communion showing the note he had with him.
20. "Bread and Circuses," *Star Trek*, Season 2, Episode 25.
21. "Data's Day," *Star Trek*, Season 4, Episode 11.
22. "Darmok," *Star Trek*, Season 5, Episode 2.
23. "The Chase," *Star Trek*, Season 6, Episode 20.
24. "Who Watches the Watchers," *Star Trek*, Season 3, Episode 4.
25. The International Judo Federation (IJF) suspended Majdov, a twenty-eight-year-old Serbian athlete, for five months following his actions during the Paris Olympics. The suspension prevented Majdov from participating in "all tournaments, camps and preparations" through February 2025.
26. "#FreeLuigi Trends as Support Surges for CEO Murder Suspect Luigi Mangione," *Newsweek*, 09 December 2024; Peter Suciu, "Luigi Mangione Has Become a Social Media Folk Hero," *Forbes*, 12 December 2024.
27. Tim Layden, *Blood, Sweat and Chalk* (2010), 19.
28. As quoted by John Ed Mathison, *Life Lessons II: Learned from Sports* (2024), 26.
29. *The Economist*, 17 June 2023, 56.
30. Adrian Chiles, "Don't Worry, Be Lucky," *The Tablet*, 23 November 2024, 30.
31. A big factor in the incredible global growth of soccer is that it's artisanal (knowledge gained from a lifetime of immersion in clannish clubs), it's participatory (every kid can kick), and it's random. There is an ineradicable core of the unpredictable and erratic at soccer's heart. Forty-five percent of soccer games are significantly affected by a chance action or mistake, according to a study by Christ Anderson and David Sally, who conclude that, "above all the outcome of individual games is highly dependent on luck, mistakes and unpredictable factors, and this is at the core of its wider appeal." Soccer, "is the least predictable of any team sport; favorites win less often and underdogs more often than in

baseball, basketball, ice hockey or handball." See *The Numbers Game: Why Everything You Know About Football is Wrong* (2013).

32. In 2012, the average NFL team was valued at approximately $1.04 billion. By 2022, this average had risen to around $4.47 billion, marking an increase of approximately 330 percent. Over the same decade, the S&P 500 index, which represents a broad spectrum of the U. S. stock market, grew by about 170 percent. These figures illustrate that, from 2012 to 2022, the average NFL team's value increased at a rate nearly double that of the S&P 500 index.

GAME IV

1. Michael O'Brien, *Vince: A Personal Biography of Vince Lombardi* (1987), 127.

2. The EPIC interface has been introduced and explored in various Len Sweet books: *Post-Modern Pilgrims, The Gospel According to Starbucks, SoulTsunami, AquaChurch 2.0, Carpe Mañana, Viral, Nudge, Rings of Fire,* etc.

3. Mike Krzyzewski (Coach K) led Duke to five NCAA national championships as part of his legendary forty-two-season career as Duke's head coach from 1980–2022, during which he became the winningest coach in NCAA Division I men's basketball history. One of the reasons why he believes his teams appeared in thirteen Final Fours was that he involves the whole Duke community, whom he calls "the sixth man." He also makes few rules on the premise that the fewer the rules, the better he can deal individually with the problems that arise.

4. Edwin Schlossberg, *Interactive Excellence: Defining and Developing New Standards for the 21st Century* (1998).

5. On 08 January 2011, Marshawn Lynch's 67-yard touchdown run in the fourth quarter of the NFC Wild Card playoff game against the New Orleans Saints unleashed the "Beast Quake." Breaking multiple tackles and stiff-arming defenders, Lynch powered the Seattle Seahawks to a 41–36 upset over the defending Super Bowl champions, despite their 7–9 record and underdog status. The Seattle crowd's roar was so intense it triggered seismic activity, registering as a small earthquake on a University of Washington seismograph. This iconic play, cemented as

NOTES

one of the NFL's most memorable playoff moments, earned Lynch his "Beast Mode" nickname and showed how passion can shake the earth.

6. As referenced in John Ed Mathison, *Life Lessons II* (2024), 28.
7. As quoted by Mississippi State University professor Eric A. Moyen and University of Kentucky professor John R. Thelin, *College Sports: A History* (2024).

SECOND QUARTER

1. George Will, "The Sport That Makes Football Look Like Chess," *Newsweek*, 27 January 1993.

GAME V

1. David Halberstam, *The Education of a Coach* (2005), 230.
2. Sarah Norgate, *Beyond 9 to 5: Your Life in Time* (2006).
3. Stroud said this immediately after being selected by the Houston Texans. See his post-draft interview as reported by Kevin Mercer, "C. J. Stroud drafted 2nd overall by Houston Texans: 'I have the armor of God on me,'" *SportsSpectrum*, 28 April 2023.
4. Kurt Vonnegut, *Timequake* (1998).
5. Ryan Morik, "Eagles' Jalen Hurts, Nick Sirianni Praise God after Winning Super Bowl LIX: 'Thanks to Him': It's the Eagles' Second Lombardi Trophy," *Fox News*, 09 February 2025. https://www.foxnews.com/sports/eagles-jalen-hurts-nick-sirianni-praise-god-after-winning-super-bowl-lix-thanks-him.

GAME VI

1. Rob Huizenga, *You're Okay, It's Just a Bruise* (1994), 314.
2. This widely quoted (and misquoted) phrase appears in Marx's work *A Contribution to the Critique of Hegel's Philosophy of Right* (1844). The exact German phrase was "die Religion... ist das Opium des Volkes" (literally "religion is the opium of the people"). The full quote is much more nuanced and subtle than only the famous phrase. "Religion is the sigh of the oppressed creature, the heart of a heartless world, and the soul of soulless conditions. It is the opium of the people. The abolition

of religion as the illusory happiness of the people is the demand for their real happiness. To call on them to give up their illusions about their condition is to call on them to give up a condition that requires illusions."

3. The anti-religion brigade, sometimes called "The New Atheism," made itself visible in 2004 with the publication of a barrage of books attacking Christianity: Sam Harris' *The End of Faith*, Richard Dawkins' *The God Delusion*, Daniel Dennett's *Breaking the Spell*, and Frederick Crews' *Follies of the Wise*. The late British-American literary critic and biographer Christopher Hitchens came out with *God is not Great: How Religion Poisons Everything* (2007). This new movement was picked up on the cover 13 November 2006 issue of *Time* magazine. It was a "God vs. Science" debate between Dawkins and Francis Collins, the Director of National Human Genome Research Institute. See his book *The Language of God: A Scientist Presents Evidence for Belief* (2006). Len once had his students read John Gray's *Seven Types of Atheism* (2018) with *It Keeps Me Seeking: The Invitation from Science, Philosophy and Religion* (2018) by Andrew Briggs, Andrew Steane and Hans Halvorson, opposing The New Atheism vs. The New Theism.

4. Bertrand Russell discussed the idea of the universe's brute existence in works like "Why I Am Not a Christian" (1927) and "The Philosophy of Logical Atomism" (1918–19). The phrase "just thereness" appears in *Human Knowledge: Its Scope and Limits* (1948), and specifically addresses objective reality outside of human perception.

5. Martin E. P. Seligman, "And Then Man Created God," *Science&Spirit*, November/December 2002, 32.

6. These words are a summary of Camus' position, not his exact words in this order. In works like *The Myth of Sisyphus* (1942), Camus shows how he was more interested in how humans could find meaning in what he saw as an absurd universe, whether or not God existed. See his chapter on "Absurd Freedom."

7. Richard Dawkins, "Bible Belter," *Times Literary Supplement*, 07 September 2007, 3. His article is reviewing Christopher Hitchens' *God is Not Great* (2007).

8. See "God vs. Science" article in *Time Magazine*, 13 November 2006.

NOTES

9. This is one of the earliest hymns of the church, originating from the ancient Christian Church's Liturgy of St. James, also known as the "Liturgy of Jerusalem."
10. Friedrich Nietzsche, *On the Genealogy of Morals* (1887), Preface.
11. Dan Brown, *The DaVinci Code* (2003).
12. Gloria and Bill Gaither wrote the song "There's Something About That Name," and published it in 1970. Shea's other two signature songs were "How Great Thou Art" and "I'd Rather Have Jesus" (Len's father's favorite song).
13. As quoted by John Ed Mathison, *Life Lessons II*, 40.
14. Eric A. Moyen and John R. Thelin, *College Sports: A History* (2024), 16.
15. John Ourand, "Women Staying Tuned to NFL: Despite Controversies, Female Viewership Swells to Record Levels," 14 November 2014, https://www.sportsbusinessjournal.com/Journal/Issues/2014/11/17/Media/NFL-women/.
16. Gladwell started his campaign in a slew of articles and interviews around 2012–2013, including his 2012 article in *The New Yorker*, "Does Football Have a Future?" and interviews like his 2012 conversation with NPR's Terry Gross on *Fresh Air* as well as his 2020 podcast episode, "The Standard Case," on his *Revisionist History* podcast.
17. Gary Pomerantz, *Their Life's Work, the Brotherhood of the 1970s Pittsburgh Steelers, Then and Now* (2013), 357.
18. Pat Kirwin, *Take Your Eye Off the Ball* (2010), 260.
19. Brian Billick, *More Than a Game: The Glorious Present and Uncertain Future of the NFL* (2009), 37.
20. Walter Payton with Don Yaeger, *Never Die Easy: The Autobiography of Walter Payton* (2000), 151–52.
21. Rich Cohen, *Monsters: The Chicago Bears and the Wild Heart of Football* (2013), 299.
22. Michael McCambridge, *America's Game, The Epic Story of How Pro Football Captured a Nation* (2005), 52.
23. Murray Olderman, *Just Win Baby: The Al Davis Story* (2012). Without the AFL, NFL Hall of Famer Nick Buoniconti, who got his start with the

Boston Patriots of the AFL, would likely never have led the "no name defense" of the Miami Dolphins dynasty of the early 1970s to multiple titles and the NFL's still only (as of the 2024–2025 season) undefeated season.

24. Billick, *More Than a Game*, 25.

25. *The Economist*, 04 January 2025, 46–47.

26. MacCambridge observes that NFL football was "one of the few solid pieces of common ground left on the increasingly balkanized map of modern American popular culture." Michael MacCambridge, *America's Game* (2008), xix.

27. Michael Starr, "Super Bowl Ratings Fourth-highest Ever," *New York Post* (07 February 2017), 47.

28. Gary Myers, "State of NFL Not So Rosy," *New York Daily News*, 12 November 2017, 68–69.

29. The quote is so good it's worth quoting in full: "Now we see how extraordinarily stupid it is to defend Christianity, how little knowledge of human nature it manifests, how it connives even if unconsciously, with offense by making Christianity out to be some poor, miserable thing that in the end has to be rescued by a champion. Therefore, it is certain and true that the first one to come up with the idea of defending Christianity in Christendom is de facto a Judas No. 2: he too, betrays with a kiss, except that his treason is the treason of stupidity. To defend something is to disparage it. Suppose a person has a warehouse full of gold, and suppose he is willing to give every ducat to the poor—but in addition, suppose he is stupid enough to begin with a defense in which he justifies it on three grounds: people will almost come to doubt that he is doing any good. Well, he who defends it has never believed it. If he believes, then the enthusiasm of faith is not a defense—no, it is attack and victory; a believer is a victor." Søren Kierkegaard, *The Sickness Unto Death*. Translated by Alastair Hannay (2008), Part Two: Despair and Faith.

30. The new edition of Reinhold Niebuhr's *The Irony of American History* (2008) carries an endorsement by Barack Obama, who summarizes Niebuhr's position: "There's serious evil in the world, and hardship

NOTES

and pain. And we should be humble and modest in our belief we can eliminate those things."

31. Gospellers' crazy confidence comes through the resurrection of Jesus: "thanks be to God, who gives us the victory through our Lord Jesus Christ" (1 Corinthians 15:57 NKJV).

GAME VII

1. Matthew 23:27–28. He called them blind guides (Matthew 23:24), a brood of vipers (Matthew 23:33), children of hell (Matthew 23:15) who shut the kingdom of heaven in people's faces (Matthew 23:13), and ended his diatribe with this: "Woe to you, scribes and Pharisees, hypocrites! For you are like whitewashed tombs, which outwardly appear beautiful, but within are full of dead people's bones and all uncleanness. So you also outwardly appear righteous to others, but within you are full of hypocrisy and lawlessness" (Matthew 23:27–28 ESV).

2. C. S. Lewis, *Mere Christianity* (1952), 46.

3. The core of true tragedy isn't simply misfortune or suffering, but the unavoidable collision between competing moral goods or noble values where no perfect solution exists.

   In Antigone, we see this in the central conflict between the good of divine law and family duty (Antigone's obligation to bury her brother), and the good of civil order and state authority (Creon's duty to enforce the law). Both Antigone and Creon pursue what they sincerely believe is right and good, yet their competing "goods" cannot coexist.

   This is why tragic heroes often aren't brought down by their flaws so much as by their virtues—their unwavering commitment to one good forces them to become the destroyer of another good. The evil that results isn't just an external consequence but is woven into the very nature of having to choose between competing goods in an imperfect world. Hence the phrase that Len uses so much—"sublime tragedy."

4. Jeff Benedict and Don Yaeger, *Pros and Cons: The Criminals Who Play in the NFL* (1998).

5. Joe Humphreys, *Foul Play: What's Wrong with Sport* (2008). Just as one of your authors (Len) once had a professor who was philosophically

and theologically opposed to "humor," so Humphreys has no use for sports. He argues that sports (and religion) is harmful to both players and spectators. The various sins of which sports fans and participants are accused include racism, blood lust, promotion of conflict and colossal wastes of time, effort, and energy. Humphreys further decries how sports make its participants and observers "stupid." This is itself utter stupidity, as is Humphreys' summarial statement: "All things considered, perhaps the kindest statement you can make about sport is the following: the more seriously you take sport the more likely you are to do harm to yourself or others." For the opposite position, see Colin McGinn, *Sport (The Art of Living)* (2016).

6. Jeff Pearlman, *Boys Will Be Boys: The Glory Days and Party Nights of the Dallas Cowboys Dynasty* (2009).

7. Zaheer Baber, "Whitey on the Moon," *Times Literary Supplement*, 01 September 2017, 9.

8. The lyrics were written by South African Anglican priest Samuel John Stone, based on the ninth article of the Apostles' Creed.

9. Pat Kirwin, *Take Your Eye Off The Ball 2.0: How to Watch Football By Knowing Where To Look* (2015), 247.

10. Jerry Kramer, *Instant Replay*, xi.

11. Brian Costello, "Jets give Aaron Rodgers another chance with disastrous season's fate nearly sealed," *New York Post*, 07 December 2024, 3

12. Quoted in Walter Kerr, *Tragedy and Comedy* (1967), 105.

13. Isaiah 54:2 NIV

HALFTIME

1. Larry Lage, "NFL players who use platform to share their faith say it's their duty to spread their love of Jesus," *The Independent*, 24 December 2024.

GAME VIII

1. Lombardi left no room for debate regarding the question of racial equality and his disdain for those who engaged in discriminatory practices: "If I ever hear a man on this squad use … [a] derogatory

NOTES

racial slur, you're through with this team. If you're black or white, you're part of the family. We make no issue over a man's color. I just won't tolerate anyone in this organization making it an issue. We respect every man's dignity, black or white." See Donald T. Phillips, *Run to Win: Vince Lombardi on Coaching and Leadership* (2001), 63.

2. Bob Brunet, one of the Washington Redskins' running backs who left the team because of Lombardi, observed that "Things that are said stay with me all day and all night.... He says he forgets what he says right away. But I will remember exactly things that were said to me twenty years from now."

3. David Maraniss, *When Pride Still Mattered: A Life of Vince Lombardi* (1999), 374.

4. Michael O'Brien, *Vince: A Personal Biography of Vince Lombardi* (1987), 367.

5. Paul Hornung, *Golden Boy: Girls, Games and Gambling at Green Bay* (2004).

6. Michael O'Brien, *Vince: A Personal Biography of Vince Lombardi* (1987), 181.

7. David Maraniss, *When Pride Still Mattered*, 374.

8. Michael O'Brien, *Vince: A Personal Biography of Vince Lombardi* (1987), 262.

9. #88 became a legacy number for the Cowboys, later worn by Michael Irvin and Dez Bryant.

10. This is the theme of Roger Staubach's book *Time Enough to Win* (1980).

GAME IX

1. *Star Wars: Episode V—The Empire Strikes Back* (1980).

2. Mark 8:36 KJV.

3. 1 Corinthians 9:19–23 NIV.

4. 2 Corinthians 12:9.

5. Ron Jaworski with Greg Cosell and David Plaut, *The Games That Changed the Game* (2010), 233.

6. Jaworski, *The Games That Changed the Game*, (2010), 232.
7. David Halberstam, *The Education of a Coach* (2005), 50.
8. 1 Corinthians 15:54 KJV.
9. See Chapter 1, titled "The Human Drive," in Eric Butterworth's *In the Flow of Life* (1975), where he discusses how a small difference in performance can lead to significant distinctions in success.
10. Matthew 13:55 NIV.
11. Psalm 34:19 KJV.
12. John 15:18 NIV.
13. Matthew 5:11 NIV.
14. 2 Corinthians 4:7 KJV.

GAME X

1. Phil Jackson, *Eleven Rings: The Soul of Success* (2013).
2. Bryan Burgess, *Madden: A Biography* (2011), 32,
3. Burgess, *Madden*, 33–35.
4. Peter Richmond, *Badasses: The Legend of the Snake, Foo, Dr. Death and John Madden's Oakland Raiders* (2010), 74.
5. Bill Parcells and Nunyo DeMasio, *Parcells: A Football Life* (2014), 164.
6. David Halberstam, *The Education of a Coach* (2005), 195.
7. Bill Parcells and Mike Lupica, *Parcells: Autobiography of the Biggest Giant of Them All* (1987), 248.
8. With thanks to Guy Scholz for this insight.
9. Lawrence Taylor with David Faulkner, *LT Living on the Edge* (1989), 219.
10. Lawrence Taylor with Steve Serby, *LT: Over the Edge: Tackling Quarterbacks, Drugs, and a World Beyond Football* (2003), 85; David Halberstam, *The Education of a Coach*, 87.
11. John Mullen, *The Chicago Bears and Super Bowl XX: The Rise and Self-Destruction of the Greatest Football Team in History* (2005), ix.
12. Richard Cohen, *Monsters: The 1985 Bears and the Wild Heart of Football* (2013), 163.

13. Jeff Pearlman, *Sweetness: The Enigmatic Life of Walter Payton* (2011), 321.
14. Billick and McCambridge, *More Than a Game*, 213.
15. A 2020 survey by the Pew Research Center found: 27 percent of Christians pray for less than 5 minutes daily; 23 percent pray for 5–10 minutes.
16. John Wesley encouraged Christians to "plunder the Egyptians" in a sermon titled "On Dissipation" (Sermon 89), preached on 25 June 1786, and published in 1787. Wesley referenced Exodus 3:22 and 12:36, where the Israelites, before leaving Egypt, took riches and valuables from the Egyptians. He applied this biblical principle to spiritual growth. For Wesley, "Plundering the Egyptians" means: 1) Learning from non-Christian sources (e.g., philosophy, science); 2) Appropriating valuable insights and knowledge; 3) Using worldly resources for spiritual purposes.
17. For the EPIC interface of digital culture where E is Experiential, P is Participatory, I is Image-rich, and C is Connective, see Leonard Sweet, *Post-Modern Pilgrims: First Century Passion for the 21st Century World* (2000), *SoulTsunami: Sink or Swim in New Millennium Culture* (1999), *The Gospel According to Starbucks: Living with a Grande Passion* (2007), and *Carpe Mañana* (2001).
18. For the Operating System (OS) of the church as MRI where M is Missional, R is Relational, and I as Incarnational, see Leonard Sweet, *So Beautiful: Divine Design for Life and the Church* (2009).
19. 2 Corinthians 12:9 NIV.
20. Jeff Davis, *Papa Bear: The Life and Legacy of George Halas* (2005), 48.
21. Ibid.
22. John Hanretty, "Morning Air," *Relevant Radio*, 11 February 2023.

GAME XI

1. "A Time To Break the Silence Speech," 04 April 1967.
2. Len has written extensively on the collapse of the middle and the new Well Curve world.

3. Don Yaeger, *Greatness, The 16 Characteristics of True Champions* (2011), 41.

4. Tony Dungy with Nathan Whittaker, *Quiet Strength: The Principles, Practices and Priorities of a Winning Life* (2007), 201.

5. Ibid.

6. Pomerantz, *Their Life's Work*, 292.

7. Ibid.

8. Pomerantz, *Their Life's Work*, 139.

9. Chad Millman and Shawn Coyne, *The Ones Who Hit the Hardest: The Steelers, the Cowboys, the 70s and the Fight for America's Soul* (2010), 218, 149.

10. Ibid., 150.

11. Ibid.

12. Matthew 6:12. NIV

13. Warrick Dunn and Don Yaeger, *Running for My Life* (2008), 140.

14. Cole Claybourn, "QB Derek Carr preaches at church, endures struggles with 'absolute peace' in God," *SportsSpectrum*, 16 January 2023.

15. Dunn and Yaeger, *Running for My Life*, 8.

16. Ibid., 11.

17. Ibid., 151.

GAME XII

1. 1 Corinthians 2:2 NASB.

2. Alex Duff, *Le Fric: Family, Power and Money: The Business of the Tour de France* (2022).

3. See the interview for *The Times* on the world's greatest sports stars, as quoted in *Times Literary Supplement*, 04 November 2016, 27.

4. Dietrich Bonhoeffer, *The Cost of Discipleship* (1937). *Nachfolge* was the original German title.

5. Elizabeth Jennings, translator, *The Sonnets of Michelangelo* (1970), Sonnet LIX, 95.

NOTES

6. As referenced in John Ed Mathison, *Life Lessons II*, 56.
7. Liddell's best biographer, Duncan Hamilton, interviewed his surviving fellow inmates about what happened in this Weihsien camp, "a kind of cramped and squalid hell on earth," he called it. See his *For the Glory: The Life of Eric Liddell from Olympic Champion to Modern Martyr* (2016).
8. 2 Corinthians 12:9 NIV.

GAME XIII

1. Gary M. Pomerantz, *Their Life's Work: The Brotherhood of the 1970s Pittsburgh Steelers, Then and Now* (2013), 174.
2. Despite his excommunication from the Cubs' family after the infamous foul ball incident, Bartman remains a devout Cubs fan and had been "overjoyed" when the team won the World Series in 2016.
3. For the power of nudging, see Leonard Sweet, *Nudge: Awakening Each Other to the God Who's Already There* (2010).

FOURTH QUARTER

1. Preface to *Milton, a Poem* (1803-1810).
2. For more on the deeper meaning of "Pay Attention," see Sweet, *Nudge* (2010).
3. https://x.com/DangeRussWilson.

GAME XIV

1. Michael Holley, *Patriot Reign: Bill Belichick, The Coaches and The Players Who Built a Champion* (2004), 4.
2. For this interpretation of the Emmaus Road story, see Leonard Sweet and Frank Viola, *Jesus Speaks: Learning to Recognize and Respond to the Lord's Voice* (2021),
3. See Leonard Sweet's *From Tablet to Table* (2015) and *The Bad Habits of Jesus* (2016).
4. Holley, *Patriot Reign*, 4.
5. From Meister Eckhart's Sermon 58, "Of the Eternal Birth of the Word

in the Soul" as found in *Eckhart's Sermons and Treatises*, translated by Maurice O'Connell (1982), 284.

6. John 14:26 NIV.
7. Deuteronomy 4:11–12 NLT.

GAME XV

1. Rosella Lorenzi, "Highest Paid Athlete in Ancient Rome," 02 September 2010, https://www.nbcnews.com/id/wbna38957186.
2. Kurt Badenhausen, "The 25 Highest Paid Athletes of All Time," *Forbes*, 13 December 2017, https://forbes.com/sites/kurtbadenhausen/2017/12/13/the-25-highest-paid-athletes-of-all-time.
3. Brian Billick candidly admitted that his professional coaching career was shortened by an inability to develop a pro bowl quarterback, and titled a book chapter on this subject: "Nobody Knows Anything."
4. For particularly masochistic Seahawks fans like me (Len), a kindle book authored by Jerry Brewer entitled *Pass Judgment: Inside the Seattle Seahawks Super Bowl XLIX Season and the Play That Crushed A Dream* tries to make sense of all of this. It fails to do so.
5. "Five faith-based quotes from current and former NFL quarterbacks," *Sports Spectrum*, 12 October 2015.

GAME XVI

1. See Winthrop Still Hudson's article "Shouting Methodists," *Encounter*, 29 (Winter 1968), 343–356. Hudson explores the enthusiastic worship practices of early nineteenth-century Methodists, who were often referred to as "shouting Methodists" due to their expressive forms of praise, including shouting, singing, and dancing. The article provides extensive historical context and examines how these practices influenced the development of Methodist worship.
2. Luke 15:7 NIV.
3. Two days after the Hurricane Harvey hit, on 28 August 2017, Lakewood Church announced it would open as a shelter, providing food, water and shelter to victims. Joel Osteen apologized for the delay, stating that the church was committed to helping the community but needed to ensure

NOTES

safety first. In response to criticism, Pastor Victoria Osteen said: "We were here, ready to serve, but the city and the county didn't ask us to become a shelter." (Does the church really need government permission to follow Christ's call?) Lakewood Church ultimately provided significant aid, and played a vital role in supporting Hurricane Harvey victims.

4. "Tony Romo says he's striving to be the spiritual leader in his home," *Sports Spectrum*, October 2013.

5. "Shaun Alexander: Chasing After Christ," *CBN*, 10 December 2022, https://cbn.com/article/not-selected/shaun-alexander-chasing-after-christ.

6. For the importance of "reading the signs," see Leonard Sweet, *Decoding the Divine: Unveiling the Sacred through Semiotics* (Revised edition 2025).

7. @The_Increase, post on X (formerly Twitter), 07 July 2017. https://x.com/The_Increase/status/883310133350105088. Accessed 08 January 2025.

GAME XVII

1. See Leonard Sweet, *The Well-Played Life: Why Pleasing God Doesn't Have to Be Such Hard Work* (2021).

2. https://www.youtube.com/watch?v=jYhn2CGFQ9I.

3. For why we chose the word "teleology" over "eschatology," see Leonard Sweet and Len Wilson, *Telos* (2022).

4. Words spoken at Livonia Community Prayer Breakfast on 05 May 5 2017. David Veselenak, "Former Lions kicker talks about football," *Hometown Life*, 05 May 2017, https://www.hometownlife.com/story/news/local/livonia/2017/05/05/former-lions-kicker-talks-football-faith/101210570/.

5. Bart Starr, "How I Found Strength in Faith," *Guideposts* (January 1967). Here is an interesting tidbit from the legendary Montgomery pastor John Ed Mathison: "When the pro draft came, Bart Starr was one of the last people selected. I have been told that he was selected because an assistant coach at Auburn University had some friends in the front office of the Green Bay Packers. The Packers trusted the judgment of the Auburn coach when he insisted that they take Bart Starr. At the end of the draft, they did. Think about that—an Auburn coach helped an

Alabama player become a star in the pros!" See Mathison's *Life Lessons II: Learned from Sports* (2024), 36–37.

THE FINAL DRIVE

1. With thanks to Jules Glanzer for reminding us of this play.
2. Kate O'Hare, "Here's a look at the NFL's Catholic roots," *Catholic News Service*, 11 February 2022.

VICTORY CELEBRATION

1. With thanks to my brother, Dr. John Sweet of Princeton, New Jersey, for this biblical passage.
2. This prayer was written with the "corporate anthem" of the dystopian sports and society drama "Rollerball" (1975) playing in the background as its anti-type. James Caan magnificently plays superstar "Jonathan E."
3. 2 Timothy 4:7–8 NIV.

ABOUT THE AUTHORS

1. Len confesses that he stopped sneaking to play high school football when he heard the story of the skinny kid who weighed in at 144 pounds and turned out for the first practice of a major football team. His enthusiasm diminished when the coach handed him the football and said, "Let's see what you can do, son." So he tucked the ball under his arm and began to run down the field. One big bruiser grabbed his left leg. A second bruiser grabbed his right leg. Then he heard the first bruiser say to the second bruiser, "Make a wish."
2. Len grew up in a fundamentalist household where sports—but not athletics—was the enemy of faith. He and his brothers were taught to be wary and chary of sports.
3. Robert J. Higgs, *Sports: A Reference Guide* (1982), 6,
4. For metaphors of running and racing, see 1 Corinthians 9:24–27; Galatians 5:7; Philippians 3:13–14. For metaphors of boxing, see 1 Corinthians 9:26; 1 Timothy 5:12. For wresting metaphors, see Ephesians 6:12. For finishing the course, see 2 Timothy 4:7–8. For training and discipline, see 1 Timothy 4:8, 2 Timothy 2:5.

NOTES

5. For one example of the athletic metaphor as a recurring theme in St. John Chrysostom's works, see Homily 6 on 1 Corinthians, where he says: "You have a contest to wage, a crown to win, a course to run. Do not let your exertions be in vain." (Homily 6 on 1 Corinthians, §4, NPNF1, vol. 12, p. 37).

www.ingramcontent.com/pod-product-compliance
Lightning Source LLC
Chambersburg PA
CBHW072142070526
44585CB00015B/988